MODEL WOMAN

"A fascinating look at the woman who, perhaps more than anyone, shaped our ideas of what it means to be a sophisticated American beauty." —*People*

"A treat for biography lovers and those interested in the business side of beauty. Fashion mavens will appreciate Eileen's musings on the rise of supermodels as bona fide celebrities." —*Library Journal*

"Unputdownable . . . left me not only full of admiration for her achievements but also rather liking her. . . . . Lacey weaves riveting narratives into his account of the life of Ford . . . with an eye for detail and juicy anecdotes." —Penelope Tree, *Financial Times*

"Exhaustively and painstakingly researched, yielding a biography that serves as a testament both to this woman's professional prowess as well as her personal life. . . . In the world of fashion-related biographies, this surely ranks up there with some of the best." —*New York Journal of Books*

"Culled from countless hours of interviews with talent scouts, bookers, celebrities, and Ford herself, Lacey diligently maps the agency's explosive success and skillfully intertwines the glitz and cutthroat melodrama of the modeling world with Ford's shrewd, intimidating business strategies, uncanny vision, and ability to merge beauty with fame. . . . A briskly written, unapologetically frank portrait of 'the empress of American modeling'—a mixture of Mary Tyler Moore and Barbara Walters, but tougher." —*Kirkus Reviews*

"Ms. Ford's status as a controversial, demanding figure isn't ignored in Mr. Lacey's portrait of one of the hardest-working women in fashion. The juicy details of a tell-all are met with the nuance of a memoir in this portrait of the woman he recalls as the 'matriarch of modeling.' . . . Heavyweights like Richard Avedon, Diana Vreeland, and Grace Coddington traipse in and out of this book's pages, but Ms. Ford is the biography's headstrong star. . . . Mr. Lacey's vivid interviews include chats with colorful industry insiders."

—*New York Observer*

"In the fascinating *Model Woman*, author Robert Lacey paints Ford as an intriguing paradox. . . . A wholly entertaining, insightful, and slightly bitchy look inside the moneyed world of modeling."

—*BookPage*

"An intensive look at a highly competitive business, with fabulous turf battles and clashing egos among the biggest names in fashion. . . . A compelling portrait of a savvy businesswoman who transformed the modeling business."   —*Booklist*

"One of the ten best fashion reads of 2015."   —*New York Examiner*

"A high-powered page-turner."   —*Daily Beast*

MODEL WOMAN

MODEL WOMAN

EILEEN FORD

AND THE

BUSINESS OF BEAUTY

Robert Lacey

HARPER

NEW YORK · LONDON · TORONTO · SYDNEY

HARPER

"Lucky to Be Me," from *On the Town*, lyrics by Betty Comden and Adolph Green, music by Leonard Bernstein. © 1944 (Renewed) WB Music Corp. All rights reserved. Used by permission of Alfred Music.

Excerpt from "Annus Mirabilis" from *High Windows* by Philip Larkin. Copyright © 1974 by Philip Larkin. Reprinted by permission of Farrar, Straus and Giroux, LLC. and Faber & Faber, London.

A hardcover edition of this book was published in 2015 by HarperCollins Publishers.

HarperCollins books may be purchased for educational, business, or sales promotional use. For information please e-mail the Special Markets Department at SPsales@harpercollins.com.

FIRST HARPER PAPERBACK EDITION PUBLISHED 2016.

Designed by Betty Lew

Library of Congress Cataloging-in-Publication Data has been applied for.

ISBN 978-0-06-210808-1 (pbk.)

16 17 18 19 20   OV/RRD   10 9 8 7 6 5 4 3 2 1

FOR JANE

My own Model Woman

CONTENTS

Contents

Color photograph sections appear after pages 150 and 214.

SUPERMODELS FOR BREAKFAST

model: A person or thing regarded as an excellent example
of a specified quality . . . A person employed to display
clothes by wearing them.

—Oxford English Dictionary

IT WAS STILL BARELY LIGHT ON A CRISP MANHATTAN MORNING, and John Casablancas was dozing contentedly, lying alone in his wide Carlyle hotel bed. Such solitude was not the custom for the dashing thirty-three-year-old. As the owner and very hands-on manager of Paris's hottest fashion sensation, Elite Model Management, Casablancas was directing the destinies of some of the world's most desirable women. Yet on this late-fall morning in 1976, the man known as Paris's Sundance Kid had serious business in his sights.

He had arrived in New York the previous night, purportedly on a "leisure" trip, and had gone straight up to his suite, taking pains to ensure that no one in the fashion world knew he was there. His mission was secret, and he had discussed his ambitions with very few. After the tear-away success of Elite in Paris, Casablancas was plotting to set up his own model management agency in New York, defying the no-poaching protocols that had applied across the Atlantic since modeling began, and challenging the dominance of America's grandest and most established model managers: Zoli, Wilhelmina, Stewart Cowley, and the very grandest and longest-established model agent of them all, Eileen Ford.

Casablancas was still half asleep at 8:30 a.m. when the phone beside his bed rang.

"Good morning, Johnny," growled a female voice dripping with malevolence and delight at its owner's cleverness. "How are you? I just want to be the first to give you the big news. Your business in New York . . . is not going to happen, my friend."

FIERCE, DEMANDING, AND UNASHAMEDLY EAGER TO TRIUMPH IN EVery battle, Eileen Ford was more than the queen; she was the empress of American modeling—a mixture of Mary Tyler Moore and Barbara Walters, but tougher. John Casablancas liked to refer to his bitter rival as Catherine the Great. Love her or loathe her, no one could deny that Eileen Ford had clawed her way to the very top of the rag trade pantheon, and could jostle her padded power shoulders with its most powerful titans. Sarah Doukas, the young British agent who made her name when she discovered Kate Moss in a JFK airport check-in line, recalls the designer Valentino catching the eye of Eileen Ford at a fashion show and nodding to her with wary respect. "The two of them saluted each other like royalty."

Eileen Ford had founded her modeling agency in 1947 with her husband, Jerry, and for more than a quarter century the Fords had been at the top of the heap. If you bought a Ford car, you knew you would get solid, workmanlike performance. If you booked a Ford model, you got Ferrari and Porsche glamour—with Rolls-Royce prestige and prices. Dorian Leigh, Suzy Parker, Jean Patchett, Dovima, Carmen Dell'Orefice, Lauren Hutton—by 1976 the Fords had model-managed America's finest, and Europe's as well. When Jean Shrimpton came to New York for a break from Swinging London, it was always with Ford that she worked.

The queen held court at East Fifty-Ninth Street, in a five-story converted warehouse facing the ramp from the Queensboro Bridge, its reception area decorated with wood panels like a chalet in the Austrian Alps. At first glance, the world's largest modeling agency appeared to be operating out of the log cabin of the Von Trapp Family Singers.

"Why not?" was Eileen's response to being questioned on her choice of décor. "I liked that style since I read *Heidi* as a child."

It was one of Eileen's regal prerogatives to be capricious. Stomping across her reception area one morning in the summer of 1977, she swept past two bright-eyed hopefuls waiting to see her, ignoring their eagerly proffered model books, and walked straight up to her office as if the young women were another set of panels on the wall. Having made them wait an hour or two while she conducted an interview with journalist Anthony Haden-Guest, she then retraced her steps and deigned to stop in front of one of the women, jabbing with a pencil in her direction.

"What are you doing here?"

"Waiting to see you, Miss Ford."

The pencil remained poised as Eileen scanned the woman, before her eyes went totally and rather alarmingly blank. It was as if a torch had been brightly pointed in the candidate's direction, wrote Haden-Guest, to be switched off just as suddenly.

"Come back and see me," she said to the young woman. "Come back and see me when you've lost *twelve pounds*."

Eileen Ford liked to explain how apparent cruelty was kinder to most wannabe beauty icons than thoughtlessly prolonging their hopes. "There is not one girl in two hundred of those who present themselves to me has got a chance of making it as a professional model, and it is wicked to let them think otherwise. It is part of my duty to help the other hundred and ninety-nine to get on with their lives."

The preeminence of the Ford Modeling Agency was based on Eileen Ford's uncanny ability to pick out the success story lurking inside candidate number two hundred, blending her "eye" for talent with some other sixth sense that detected the originality in, say, Lauren Hutton—for whom Jerry Ford, in 1973, had negotiated modeling's largest-ever advertising contract to that date: two hundred thousand dollars with Revlon—when other agents had not been able to see beyond Hutton's quirkily misaligned gaze and the gap in her front teeth. Jerry Ford took care of the business side of things, leaving his wife free to act as the agency's "eye," and four times a year that "eye" headed across the Atlantic with her husband to scout the talent of Europe. London, Paris, and Scandinavia were her happiest hunting grounds, providing regular consignments of comely young women capable of earning a hundred thousand dollars a year, the going rate for a top model in the early 1970s.

Ford's revenue from that was roughly twenty thousand dollars— two-thirds or so from the 15–20 percent commission charged to the model, with a further 10 percent charged to any advertising client. In 1970 the agency raked in some five million dollars' income from its stable of 180 models, and John Casablancas had come to New York in 1976 to start hewing out his own loot from the gold mine that never seemed to stop giving.

In Eileen Ford's mind, however, revenue was not the sole or even the principal reason she could not allow Elite Model Management and its raffish owner to "happen" in New York. In the eyes of the "godmother" of modeling—the title that *Life* magazine bestowed upon Eileen Ford in November 1970—money came second to her particular version of morality. "Johnny's problem was that he didn't just want to steal the talent," she later explained; "he wanted to boff it."

From the start of her career Eileen Ford had prided herself on shielding her "girls" from the predatory males who lurked in every corner of the business, from lascivious photographers to clients looking for extra favors in return for their patronage. "She really could be ferocious," recalls Rusty Donovan Zeddis, a Ford booker for many years. "If a girl came back to the office with a story of suggestiveness or any sort of inappropriate pressure, Eileen would get straight on the phone and bawl the guy out. Then he was blacklisted. He would be lucky to hire a Ford model again."

Even the sainted Richard Avedon, against whom no accusations of impropriety were ever made, lived in fear of "the call" that might come if ever a photo session with a Ford model stretched out longer than intended. "I remember Dick quite losing his cool and going to the phone himself," recalls a Ford model from the late 1940s. "He couldn't concentrate until he'd made certain Eileen would let him have the extra half hour—and, of course, he had to pay extra for it."

All underage models, and many girls needing help to get established in New York, went to stay as nonpaying guests at the Fords' five-story town house at East Seventy-Eighth Street, off Third Avenue. There Eileen presided as an all-seeing über-matron, giving the girls lessons in table manners and the finer points of eating crab or artichokes as they sat down to dinner (at 7:30 prompt) with the entire Ford family (three daughters and a son). If *Swan Lake* was playing at the Met, she would take the girls along as part of their higher education, and she enforced a strict curfew on any of her surrogate daughters who wished to venture out alone at night. Far more than the Fifty-Ninth Street office, the supervised dormitory on East Seventy-Eighth Street summed up the essence of Eileen Ford's style.

For John Casablancas, all this was outdated and puritanical rubbish—he had his models for breakfast in a completely different fashion. "Eileen and I had radically contrasting philosophies, and of the two of us, I think that my approach was the more honest. Fashion is all about sex. Look at the runway shows, all the models with their breasts out. Then they cover it up a little for the high street and sell it in the shops. Why does a woman buy any item of clothing unless it's going to make her look and feel sexier? That's why women buy clothes and makeup: to attract men. Girls are objects of desire and they know it. They are hot. So I would encourage my girls to be relaxed. I preferred them loose."

Casablancas made no secret of the fact that he slept with his models, and he delighted in the fact that the Elite masthead logo, designed with two lowercase *e*'s on either side of three upright letters—elite—was inspired by the image of two testicles nestling on either side of an upright phallus.

"I was the playboy, enjoying everything with one big, tremendous roar of laughter. Modeling is a superficial, phony world, and you make a mistake if you take it too seriously. Eileen was twenty years older than me. She played the mother figure and she wanted to be in control—that was how she got young girls away from their parents. I was much closer to the age of the models. So I played their friend, and sometimes their boyfriend."

The gulf was unbridgeable.

THE SHOWDOWN CAME ON EILEEN'S FAVORED TERRITORY, AT THE restaurant "21" at 21 West Fifty-Second Street, not far from Fifth Avenue and a block away from the Museum of Modern Art. Often known as the "21" Club, on account of its exclusive clientele, whose horse-racing liveries were represented in the gaudy cast-iron jockeys on the balcony over the door, the former speakeasy was the locale of Eileen's ultimate service to many in her own stable. She would invite eligible bachelors to luncheon parties at "21," with a selection of her unattached "girls" whose years had ticked by and whose bookings were easing off. Not a few of them were able to leave her service on the arm of a rich or even titled husband. Eileen was particularly proud of the contribution that Ford girls made over the years to the gene pool of the English upper classes: Jenny Windsor Elliott, who became Jenny Guinness; Janet Stevenson, who became Lady Beamish; Anna Karin Bjorck, Lady Erne; and Baroness Howard of Lympne—though in this last case, as with many others, the 1975 marriage of Ford model turned novelist Sandra Howard to the leader of Britain's Conservative Party owed nothing to Eileen's matchmaking.

Now she booked the private dining room at "21" for another type of party—a hanging party, as John Casablancas later remembered it. Eileen invited the owners of New York's major agencies (Wilhelmina, Stewart Cowley, and Zoli) to join her and Jerry in confronting the young upstart from Paris and issuing him his marching orders.

The gentle and eccentric Zoli—Zoltan Rendessy, an openly gay

Hungarian who had the exotic Veruschka on his books and had made his name with an array of striking, long-haired, hippie-style male models—judiciously chose to miss the confrontation. He sent his apologies. Yet there was no shortage of aggression across the table, with the charge led by Wilhelmina, the Dutch-born ice maiden whose high cheekbones made her look like a third sister to siblings Dorian Leigh and Suzy Parker. Wilhelmina had been Eileen Ford's top model in the early sixties, before she broke away to form her own agency with her husband, Bruce Cooper, in 1967.

"Obviously Jerry and I were not happy when Willy went out on her own," Eileen Ford later recalled. "It was probably her dreadful lowlife of a husband who gave her the idea to set up against us. But she was a great model, and when it came to competition, she was a lady. She followed the rules."

John Casablancas was *not* following the rules. The international etiquette of modeling prescribed that an agent who crossed national boundaries, or even recruited a model from another city in the United States, should negotiate a percentage, and transmit the equivalent of royalties to the model's "mother" agency. By seeking to bring a French agency into New York without paying his dues, Casablancas was trampling on conventions, and it was Wilhelmina who voiced the collective outrage.

"She pointed her long fingernails at me," Casablancas later recalled, "and said, 'We're going to get you. We're going to finish you off!'" Wilhelmina's pugnacious husband, Bruce Cooper, joined in. In his opinion, Casablancas was a "pimp."

"Willy and Bruce were furious," Eileen later remembered. "They both carried on and on about what they would do. Bruce had been drinking—he was always drinking. They were out of control."

"It was a torrent of accusations," recalled Casablancas. "I was going to hold orgies. I was going to pervert all the youth of America. They attacked me with a fury I had never seen before in my life."

Fighting back, Casablancas retorted that American agents—and Eileen, in particular—were stealing his models whenever they came on their scouting trips to Paris, and across Europe as a whole. "We cannot even recruit in Scandinavia, because Eileen went there and closed all the doors," he protested. "You don't understand. I haven't got any interest in doing business here. I'd hate to live in Manhattan. I hate the hypocrisy of the American way of life, and I don't like American food. My personal life and the agency are in Paris, and are doing very well. I haven't got any desire to open an agency in New York."

CASABLANCAS WAS LYING, OF COURSE. DIFFERENT PARTICIPANTS give varying dates for this particular model showdown in the private room at "21," but according to Anthony Haden-Guest, whose article on the conflict ran in *New York* magazine in July 1977, the gathering took place on March 10, 1977. Less than two weeks later, on March 22, legal papers were filed in Albany for the New York incorporation of Elite Model Management Inc.

"So many lies!" Casablancas later wrote apologetically. For, as a matter of fact, by the time of the "21" meeting, he had already secured and paid the deposit on luxurious offices on East Fifty-Eighth Street, next door to Bloomingdale's, and had been discreetly recruiting models for months through his friend, the young photographer Alain Walch, who had been using his fashion contacts to spy inside the agencies. "Alain," Casablancas later wrote, "and his beautiful Swedish girlfriend, Marie Johansson, whom I represented, were the only people in New York who knew all my plans."

Maaret Halinen, the blonde Finnish model who was one of Wilhelmina's stars, was the first to declare openly for Elite. "Wilhelmina had not been doing a great job with her," Casablancas later sneered. "She was becoming a catalogue queen"—meaning that her agency had kept her on the lucrative but nonprestigious mail order treadmill, and had been failing to secure her creative editorial or advertising work. Early in May 1977, Halinen gave two weeks' notice to Bruce Cooper—only to receive a phone call two days later telling her to leave the agency forthwith and send a messenger for her personal effects.

Then came the first defectors from Ford: Barbara Minty, Christie Brinkley, and Janice Dickinson. The twenty-three-year-old Brinkley had been originally discovered as a young art student from California working in Paris and had been launched by Casablancas—an example of his complaint that Ford crudely raided any talent that Europe uncovered—while the abrasive Dickinson, a practiced agency hopper, claimed that although Eileen had put her on the books, Ford was prejudiced against her as "much too ethnic" on account of the size of her lips. "I'm sorry, dear," the model alleged that Eileen had once told her. "You'll never work."

Dickinson delighted in flouting the Eileen Ford moral code. In her post-model existence she wrote an uninhibited kiss-and-tell memoir about her couplings with celebrities from Mick Jagger to Sylvester Stallone, publicizing herself on TV talk shows by discussing such matters as the penis size of her famous lovers. In 1977 she maintained she had signed only briefly for Ford after Jerry Ford promised to get her twenty thousand dollars a day for a JVC advertising campaign for which Wilhelmina, her agency at the time, could not get more than five thousand. She now seized on the arrival of Casablancas in New York as an opportunity "to punish Eileen." "It's me, big-lipped Janice," she later recalled telling her former boss over the phone. "I'm going to Elite. I don't like you. I never liked you."

Eileen Ford denied any recollection of Dickinson's claims. "She was in my life such a short time," Ford later commented. "I'm an Aries. We try not to mention unpleasant things. If something is unpleasant, I usually try to forget about it."

The Aries in Eileen was more sorely tested by a couple of defections from the very heart of her agency—for Alain Walch had not been talking to models alone. He had been tasked by Casablancas with locating New York's very best bookers: the day-to-day, at-the-desk women (and occasionally men) who dealt directly with the top models, cosseting their egos and talking hard down the phones to

secure them the highest-possible fees for their work. Successful bookers were the essence of a successful agency, and Walch's researches
had alighted on one of Eileen Ford's top staff, Monique Pillard.

A hardworking, stocky Frenchwoman with a taste for four-letter
words, Pillard was warm toward her models and fierce toward the
rest of the world. "Sitting beside her in the office," remembered her
fellow booker Tischka Nabi, "was like sitting at the guillotine beside
Madame Defarge. Your ear went dead with the noise of her voice
shouting down the phone."

Like Eileen Ford, Pillard operated professionally with a minimum
of sentiment, so she had no hesitation in accepting the handsome salary raise offered by Casablancas for her to jump ship. "I'll always be
grateful for what Eileen taught me," she later explained. "She met me
when I was running the Revlon Beauty Salon and she invited me to
be a booker. But when I got too good, she tried to beat me down emotionally. She could be so harsh and cruel. She had me in her office every day telling me that no one liked me. I lost all my self-confidence.
I felt that I was just a pencil on her desk."

On April 29, 1977, Monique Pillard handed in her notice to Ford
and walked out of the agency, taking with her Jo Zagami, the Fords'
financial controller, who knew Ford's every balance sheet and the secret of how the world's leading modeling agency was run.

Star Wars was the movie of the moment. It took New York by storm
when it opened on May 25, 1977. So "Model Wars" became the obvious title for the real-life battle being fought in Manhattan's galaxy of
fashion, and if the debonair young Casablancas sought to cast himself as Luke Skywalker, Eileen Ford now thundered into unashamed
Darth Vader mode. She was consumed with fury at the treachery of
those she had nurtured, and she launched a series of multimillion-
dollar lawsuits against Casablancas, Pillard, and Zagami, alleging
commercial wrongdoing and betrayal of fiduciary trust. As her legal enforcer, she hired no less a force of darkness than the predatory
Roy Cohn, who had started his career as counsel to Senator Joseph
McCarthy's House Un-American Activities Committee and went on

to offer advice and, where necessary, legal representation to Richard Nixon, the John Birch Society, and mobsters Tony Salerno, Carmine Galante, and John Gotti.

Eileen had a couple of Bibles brought to her office with a marker pen. Closing the door, she painstakingly went through the New Testament, underlining in red ink every reference to Judas Iscariot: "And as they sat and did eat, Jesus said, 'Verily I say unto you, One of you which eateth with me shall betray me'" (Mark 14:18).

She then had the red-marked Bibles hand-delivered to Zagami and Pillard in their homes—"And I would do it again," she insisted later with pride. "She [Pillard] had said to me, 'I love you. You're like my mother.' Then she left me the next day."

Monique Pillard well remembers receiving the highlighted Bible. "It was only a paperback," she sniffed.

CHAPTER 1

NOTHING TO DO BUT LOOK PRETTY

I'd LOVE to be a model! What an EASY job! Nothing to
do but look PRETTY all day!

—*Millie the Model, Marvel Comics*

IN THE SPRING OF 1704 THE FRENCH AND ENGLISH ARMIES AGREED
to suspend hostilities in northern France to allow the passage
across the battlefield of a carriage bearing the "French fashion doll,"
a life-size wooden figure that had been elaborately clothed to display
the latest Paris fashions. According to Abbé Prévost, the author and
gossipy chronicler of the times, ministers of both courts had granted
the full-size doll a special pass "for the benefit of the ladies."

Fashion dolls had been dispatched to London's drapers since the
Middle Ages so that English dressmakers could study what Europe's
smart set was wearing. The dolls often sported the latest hairstyles
as well. By the eighteenth century the mannequins had made land-
fall in the New World, and in 1733, Miss Hannah Teats, a Boston
dressmaker, proudly announced the arrival of such a doll, charging
two shillings if you wanted to view it in her Summer Street shop—
"if you send for it, seven shillings." As late as 1796, Sally McKean in
Philadelphia was writing to her friend Dolley Madison about the doll,
"which has just come from England to give us some idea of the latest
fashions."

It was Charles Frederick Worth, the Lincolnshire-born Paris couturier, who was credited with setting aside puppets in the late 1850s and displaying his clothes on the bodies of actual, flesh-and-blood women—starting, according to legend, with the elegant and shapely Mrs. Worth, née Marie Vernet, who thus became the world's first-ever formally designated fashion "model." Madame Worth would display her husband's designs not only in his salon, but also at the races, the opera, and anywhere else they might catch the eye of Paris's fashionable elite.

High-society America proved initially resistant to the concept of haute couture. A few top-drawer Bostonians might buy Worth dresses while in Paris in the late nineteenth century, but according to Edith Wharton in *The Age of Innocence*, they would then hide the outfits away for a full two years before letting them be seen at the symphony. Only a middle-class arriviste would force his wife to "clap her new clothes on her back as soon as they arrived."

"In my youth it was considered vulgar to dress in the latest fashions," explains Mrs. Archer in *The Age of Innocence*, recounting how old Mrs. Baxter Pennilow, one of Boston's grandest matrons, would import a dozen or so of the latest Worth dresses every year, then leave them to "mellow under lock and key" before wearing them in public after a season or so.

Ladies in the South were similarly disdainful of the siren call of modishness, though for more austere motives. As the grandes dames of Charleston, Richmond, and Savannah struggled through the stringencies of post–Civil War Reconstruction, it was a badge of honor to wear mended clothes and hand-me-downs—"Quality shone through." To dress fashionably was to break ranks—though, as life returned to normal, a few might quietly ask their seamstress to copy a costume or two from the images in the social pages.

Wealthy female customers regarded live models with suspicion—after all, they came from the very showgirl class from which their husbands might recruit mistresses. In the mid-nineteenth century, Worth's real-life fashion dolls were required to wear a puritanical *fourreau*, a black satin sheath, beneath the garments they were showing, and according to designer Pierre Balmain, French models were still required to wear these high-necked, long-sleeved undergarments in the early twentieth century if they were modeling grand evening gowns: "It was not seemly for them to be gowned like the aristocrats of fashion."

Models were mere menials, paid by the hour. It scarcely seemed likely that, in less than a century, mannequins would outshine marchionesses. When the up-and-coming magazine magnate Condé Montrose Nast staged a charity Fashion Fête at New York's Ritz-Carlton hotel in November 1914 in aid of "the women and children in every nation left destitute by the European War," there was no pool of trained mannequins to be found in Manhattan. A group of shop assistants had to be hastily recruited and coached in the parading of clothes down a runway.

Then, sometime around 1915, a lean and handsome, thin-faced "resting" actor named John Robert Powers found that he could make more money modeling clothes for a few hours—a full thirty dollars per session—than he could earn for a whole week spouting Shakespeare on the theatrical payroll of Sir Herbert Beerbohm Tree. A few years later, Baron Adolph de Meyer, the world's first-ever salaried fashion photographer, asked Powers to recruit seven handsome men for a group pose for *Vogue*, the New York social magazine that Condé Nast was turning into a specialized journal of fashion. When other photographers started calling with similar requests, the light finally "smote me in the face," as Powers later remembered in enduringly Shakespearean terms.

In 1923 the actor turned model turned entrepreneur published his first photo catalogue of some forty male and female "models," with full descriptions and precise body measurements, then set up the offices of the John Robert Powers Agency in an old brownstone over a speakeasy off Broadway. The modern modeling industry had been born.

———

IT WAS NOT BY CHANCE THAT PROFESSIONALLY ORGANIZED MODELING started after World War I in America rather than in France, where fashion and modeling developments had set the pace until that date. In Paris the mannequins were underpaid, subservient employees of the traditional fashion houses—and were to remain so for many years. But in New York the infant profession of modeling had acquired more potent patrons, thanks to the new technology of the "rotogravure" press that made possible the printing of modern halftone photographs in bulk. By 1920 no fewer than forty-seven American newspapers were producing lavish rotogravure sections, where the pictures covered everything from the geographic wonders of the world to the frilly outfits of the Easter Parade—the grandest of which, as Judy Garland sang in her MGM sonnet to the Easter bonnet, would get snapped by the Fifth Avenue photographers to appear in the pages of the "ro-to-gra-vure."

Many of the rotogravure sections of the American press appeared as Sunday supplements, and they depended on graphic consumer advertising to finance their expensively produced pages. If one single factor promoted the creation of the modern modeling agency, it was this vast new visual marketplace, since many of these pictorial advertisements promoted fashion and the increasingly profitable business of beauty. In 1916 the Hollywood makeup artist Maksymilian Faktorowicz enjoyed stunning success when he started to offer his Max Factor eye shadow, eyebrow pencils, colored face powders, and other professional makeup products to the general public. The age of mass-produced beauty lotions and potions had begun. By the end of the 1920s, various manufacturers were producing more than three thousand different face powders and several hundred rouges, not to mention lipsticks, for sale over the new "beauty counters" that had sprung up in stores and shops around America. Looking good was good for you—and, in some respects, was becoming an essential part of *being* good as well.

———

IN 1920 THE PSYCHOLOGIST EDWARD THORNDIKE, A LECTURER AT the Columbia School of Education, staged an experiment in which he asked two U.S. Army Air Service commanders who had recently returned from the Great War to evaluate their platoons of airmen according to the attractiveness of their outward appearance—neatness, voice, physique, bearing, and "energy." Then he asked them to assess the same set of aviators according to their "inner" qualities of personality and character—among which he included intellect, dependability, loyalty, selflessness, and leadership skills.

In his seminal paper "A Constant Error in Psychological Ratings," Thorndike reported that the aviators who were rated highly on their external qualities were 33 percent more likely to receive favorable judgments from their officers when it came to their supposed "inner," psychological qualities, including their potential as future leaders. Physical attractiveness, in other words, embellished these men with added credibility. "The correlations," wrote Thorndike, "were too high and too even."

The psychologist called this phenomenon the halo effect (or the halo error), and it proved to be the springboard for a succession of modern studies that have sought to analyze the culture of the changing world with such concepts as "beauty bias," the "attractiveness factor," and "erotic capital"—such as teachers giving higher credit to attractive students and jurors assessing the credibility of witnesses on the basis of their looks. Hair dye manufacturers would carry out surveys to demonstrate how different shades of hair commanded different levels of salary according to male preferences—blondes have more funds.

In the second half of the twentieth century, feminist thinkers would come to critique this monetizing of beauty. They labeled it "lookism," and condemned model agencies for encouraging the sexual "objectification" of women. Yet no such reservations were voiced in the mid-1920s.

"Beauty is a greater force in human affairs than steam or electricity, than economics or engineering," wrote advertising guru Earnest

Elmo Calkins, founder of the Calkins and Holden agency, in *Atlantic* magazine for August 1927. "In beauty, the sky is the limit."

Virtually stone deaf from a childhood attack of measles, Calkins had honed his visual senses the more keenly on what he called "Beauty—the new business tool." In his eyes, the most significant event of 1927 was the fact that General Motors' stylish Chevrolet saloon car had, for the first time, outsold the less-than-beautiful Model T Ford, even though the Chevrolet cost two hundred dollars more. Affluence, he argued, was changing the sensibilities of Americans, who now bought a new car "not because the old one is worn out, but because it is no longer modern. It does not satisfy their pride."

People were starting to define themselves by the look of the goods they chose to purchase, and Calkins cited the immense success of a recent trade show at Macy's where New Yorkers had lined up for hours to study modernistic French furniture in the hope of adding "style" to every corner of their homes, from parlor to bathroom. "We demand beauty with our utility," Calkins wrote, "beauty with our amusement, beauty in the things with which we live."

For all his aesthetic evangelism, the adman had no sentimentality about the role that advertising was coming to play in the creation of purchasing needs—particularly among the increasing number of emancipated working women. Beauty was a commodity like any other. "There is behind all these changes," he wrote, "simply the desire to sell."

How better to advertise a new car or sofa or perfume than with the help of a pretty model? In the course of the 1920s, beauty became the tenth-largest U.S. business category. Retail sales of cosmetics and toiletries reached $378 million in 1929, and as both advertising and editorial coverage expanded, it was not surprising that John Robert Powers encountered competition—from Walter Thornton, another resting actor, who set up his own modeling agency in 1930, a matter of months following the Wall Street crash. The onset of the Great Depression might have seemed a bad time to start something as frivolous as a modeling agency, but Thornton proved able to secure work for his models thanks to the so-called lipstick effect. While cosmetics sales as a whole fell to three hundred million dollars in the four years up to 1933, with many companies going out of business, sales of some products held up, and were anecdotally reported to have risen in certain sectors, as women spent their diminished incomes on relatively inexpensive, morale-boosting items of makeup.

"It's up to the women," proclaimed *Ladies' Home Journal* for February 1932. Wives and mothers were the "purchasing agents of twenty-nine million American families," and it was their job to help restart America's "wheels of progress and prosperity" by purchasing food, clothing, and the millions of cakes of soap, tubes of toothpaste, and cosmetics needed "for the sake of the good looks that, depression or no depression, must be maintained."

Glossy magazines actually flourished in the Depression years as, for a few cents a month, they nurtured readers' dreams of the good life—the print version of the lipstick effect. *Apparel Arts* (which later became *GQ*), *Esquire*, *Mademoiselle*, *Glamour*, and *Brides* all got their start in the early 1930s, while the glossy brand leaders, *Vogue* and *Harper's Bazaar*, enjoyed a heyday under their eccentrically creative editors, Edna Woolman Chase and Carmel Snow, respectively. These rival female popes of American fashion went on handing down their edicts as to what was "in" and "out" with blithe indifference to the economic Armageddon around them.

"Why don't you wash your blond child's hair in dead champagne, as they do in France?" suggested Diana Vreeland, who became *Bazaar*'s fashion editor in 1936. Critics derided her notorious "Why Don't You?" column, yet *Harper's Bazaar* nearly doubled its circulation between 1932 and 1938.

In this curious atmosphere of insouciance, the Walter Thornton modeling agency managed to thrive. As proud of his Shakespearean knowledge as John Robert Powers, Thornton took to describing himself as the "Merchant of Venus" on the strength of discovering the sultry Betty Perske in a Greenwich Village beauty contest and relaunching her as Lauren Bacall, then pulling off the same trick for

Edythe Marrenner of Brooklyn—Susan Hayward. It was small wonder that would-be models beat a path to his door, and one day in 1938 a starry-eyed hopeful from Great Neck, Long Island, presented herself at Thornton's plush office on Lexington Avenue, its walls covered with photos of well-known models and film stars.

"A sixteen-year-old heart began to pound with excitement," she later wrote, "as the agent glowingly sketched the career he envisioned for the girl. Magazine covers and screen tests were practically assured within six months! She would, of course, have to spend the insignificant amount of $60 to have photographs taken, but the money would be made up in a day or two. The girl could hardly wait until she arrived home to tell her parents of the fairy tale that was about to come true."

The fairy tale never happened, of course. The Merchant of Venus extracted a further forty dollars for prints of the nondescript test shots of the teenager—"then promptly forgot," she later recalled, "that I ever existed. He never booked me for one single modeling job, and looking at the picture, I am not surprised. I had a nice, pert nose but a plain round face and a mop of curly brown hair. That was not the photograph of a successful model."

Eileen Ford was able to be as brutally honest about herself, the starry-eyed wannabe from Great Neck, as she would prove to be about the thousands of young women she would assess in her long career as a model agent. But her painful first contact with the fashion business did teach her a valuable lesson. When it came to money and modeling, it clearly made more sense to be behind the camera than in front of it.

CHAPTER 2

ORIGINS

People are like a cat when it comes to their lives: they have
at least nine, and they . . . pick out the one to write about
that they think will look best.

—*Will Rogers, 1928*

I REMEMBER MY FINNISH GRANDFATHER TELLING ME, 'YOU'RE
lucky to be born in America. Never look back.'"

Eileen Ford liked to explain herself in terms of her family origins: a quarter Finnish, quarter Irish, quarter German, and quarter
Russian—though she preferred to conceal the fact that both her German and her Russian grandparents were Jewish. "My Finnish grandfather didn't like to talk about his past. Most immigrants didn't come
here to reminisce. There were a lot of things, I imagine, that they
preferred to forget."

The few facts that Eileen ever discovered about her grandfather
Laine's history were that he used to make sails in Finland and was
a sailing ship captain who came to America to study the winds. He
decided to stay, so his Finnish relatives sent him his meerschaum pipe
and his mink fur hat, and he never heard from them again. The U.S.
Census for 1900 lists Andrew Laine as a "dock builder," living with
his wife, Margaret, and his children—Arthur, Loretta, Annie, and
Walter—at 362 West Forty-Fifth Street, Manhattan. Soon afterward
the family moved to Brooklyn.

"He didn't get rich, but he used to make wonderful model sailing ships with sails and rigging as a hobby. He built me a whole doll's house with little electric lights that sparkled, and on Sundays he'd let me sip at his beer and have a puff on his cigar."

Andrew's wife, Margaret—Grandma Laine, Eileen's grandmother on her mother's side—was born Margaret Nixon in County Longford, in the center of Ireland, one of seven brothers and sisters, and she kept her Irish accent till her dying day. Eileen remembered Grandma Margaret enjoying a glass of whiskey after Mass on a Sunday, and describing how, as a child in Ireland, she had worn shoes only when she went to church.

"Grandma came across the Atlantic with one of her brothers, who got a job in New York as a hod carrier, transporting bricks on his shoulders to the bricklayers on the upper floors. He died when he fell off the scaffolding at the Savoy Plaza hotel—so that was my great-uncle that I never met. I am very proud to be descended from hard-working immigrant folk."

Margaret Laine's daughter Loretta, Eileen's mother, was born in 1892, the second of four children, and went out to work in 1905, aged only thirteen, at one of New York's smartest new department stores, Best and Co., located on Twenty-Third Street, close to Lower Sixth Avenue, the so-called Ladies' Mile. The subway under the river was not yet completed, so Loretta spent more than an hour every morning walking to work across the mile-long span of the Brooklyn Bridge. "It was some time before my mother could afford a warm coat," Eileen recalled. "She told me she got very cold crossing that bridge every morning and every night."

Once Loretta reached Best and Co., however, she entered a different world. America's new department stores offered a warm and comfortable environment to working women—and even more seductive comforts to their largely female clientele. The brightly lit dream palaces of the Ladies' Mile competed to offer women the goods they desired in a sensuous environment, and to fulfill needs they had not known existed until they entered the store. With their monogram-crested carpets and elevators and their orgiastic displays of buyables stacked floor upon floor, these overgrown drapers' shops—"Ladies' Paradise," as Émile Zola described them—were taking the mundane act of shopping into a different universe.

"My mother knew about shopping and fashion," Eileen recalled, "so that world was never strange to me. She had a great sense of style—she wore beautiful clothes—and I imagine that contributed a lot to my path in life. Right from the start I knew about models and what they did."

The teenage Loretta became a model, in fact, for a short spell, her striking good looks earning her a promotion to the ranks of Best and Co.'s mannequins. Wearing dresses from the shopwindows, she would parade them on the sidewalk outside. Yet this was colder still than walking over the Brooklyn Bridge, and Loretta used to relate how she spent much of her working day in tears.

Loretta's travails were nothing compared with those suffered by the young women who labored behind the scenes in the New York rag trade in the early twentieth century. Then, as now, fashion models were the fortunate faces of an industry that was guilty of some appalling labor practices. The seamstresses who had stitched for Dolley Madison and her friend Sally McKean at the end of the eighteenth century may not have been well paid, but they did, at least, manage a respectable living as dressmakers.

A hundred years later, mass-market clothing had led to mass production by what was effectively slave labor. The poverty in the sweatshops of the Garment District around Seventh Avenue existed in a different world from the glittering emporiums of the Ladies' Mile. In March 1911 a fire in the factory of the Triangle Shirtwaist Company near Washington Square resulted in the death of 146 workers, 123 women and 23 men, most of them recent immigrants—the deadliest disaster on the island of Manhattan until the destruction of the World Trade Center ninety years later. Many of the Triangle Shirtwaist victims were trapped in the upper floors of the building and jumped to their deaths. The factory's safety exits had been locked and chained to prevent the workers from slipping out during working hours for unauthorized rest breaks.

BY THE TIME OF THE TRIANGLE SHIRTWAIST TRAGEDY, LORETTA
Laine had moved on from the rag trade. She had secured herself em-
ployment as a switchboard operator in an uptown Manhattan hotel,
where, in the spring of 1909 and still only sixteen years old, she attracted the attention of a young Brooklyn-Irish mechanic, James J.
Forsythe, himself just eighteen years old and already a wheeler-dealer
in the developing trade of used automobiles.

Out of his overalls, James Forsythe cleaned up very plausibly. He
was of medium build, according to his 1917 draft papers—five foot
nine, with brown hair and blue eyes—and he lavished presents on
the pretty girl in the headphones, who responded positively to his
advances. After just four months of courting, James and Loretta
eloped to Plainfield, New Jersey, a small township twenty-six miles
from Manhattan, where they were wed on June 27, 1909, in the office
of Plainfield's famous "marrying justice," Hezekiah Hand, who advertised his Rent-a-Reverend services in the *Daily Press*—"Couples
married while you wait; day or night; rain or shine."

Justice Hand did not ask his customers awkward questions about
their age. The sixteen-year-old Loretta, legally too young to marry
without parental consent, claimed that she was nineteen, while James,
age twenty on June 27, 1909, wrote down his age as twenty-two.

A few months later, back home and now living with James Forsythe's parents in the Flatbush district of Brooklyn, Loretta found
that she was pregnant—and that her husband's ardor was suddenly
on the wane. In June 1910, a year after her wedding, she gave birth
to twins, a son whom she called Thomas and another child who died
after only two days. But James Forsythe's reaction was not to comfort
his young wife. Instead, the car salesman disappeared from home,
telling Loretta on his return that he had, in his absence, "committed a
great wrong," but proffering no further explanation. Then, a few days
later, he vanished, never to be seen by Loretta again.

For six months the abandoned bride waited in vain for her husband, until a girlfriend reported that James had been spotted living

with a woman on the Upper West Side, at West 144th Street. There Loretta discovered *another* Mrs. Forsythe, the former Caroline G. Higgins, who claimed that *she* had married James only weeks before—as recently as February 12, 1911. James Forsythe was a bigamist.

To add insult to injury, Caroline G. Higgins had been working as a hotel telephone operator, just like Loretta, and had married James in the grand surroundings of St. Patrick's Cathedral—though none of this proved of much comfort to the second Mrs. Forsythe. At a subsequent encounter, Caroline reported that James had deserted her as well, and had taken all their furniture with him.

It was at this crisis point in her young life that Loretta Laine Forsythe met a stylish young Jewish debt collector, Nathan Ottensoser (pronounced Otten-saucer), a commercial lawyer in his mid-twenties who had started work in his father's debt collection agency and was now in the process of striking out on his own.

"My mother was very, very pretty," Eileen recalled. "My father used to say that he fell in love with her the moment he set eyes on her. He spotted her buying vegetables in the market at Washington Heights, and he followed her around for weeks. She just ignored him. When she eventually agreed to go with him for a drive, she got dressed in a pale lavender dress and hat. His car got stuck in the mud. But it *was* a beautiful touring car, she told me later."

The driver of the enticing touring car was a cut above any suitor who had approached Loretta before, and he represented a charmed escape from the mess in which her impetuosity had landed her. Nathan Ottensoser, "Nat" or "N.O." to his friends, was a man with connections. His father, Lippmann "Louis" Ottensoser, was a grand master of the Ancient and Accepted Scottish Rite, Thirty-Third Degree (the highest attainable rank in Masonry), and it just so happened that one of New York's most high-powered divorce attorneys, Herman L. Roth, belonged to the same fraternity, and was only too happy to assist the forsaken young telephone operator in her plight.

Roth loved getting his name in the newspapers—"Ninety of every hundred respondents in divorce cases are blondes," ran one of his headline-catching pronouncements. "Blondes are vain. Blondes are fickle. Blondes love no one well but themselves." Loretta, of course, was a brunette.

On July 4, 1912, the *New York Times* reported Herman Roth's success in securing a divorce for Loretta Laine and an annulment for Caroline Higgins, albeit at the cost of seeing their embarrassment splashed all over the popular press. Suddenly Loretta had might on her side—and new career possibilities. On September 25, 1914, the State of New York Department of State Records listed Loretta Forsythe and Nat Ottensoser as fellow directors of FAPA, the Fifth Avenue Protective Association Incorporated, a newly founded debt collection agency whose profits were to be the making of Nathan Ottensoser—and, indeed, of Mrs. Loretta Ottensoser, when the couple married a few years later.

"One of the things I learned from my parents," remarked Eileen, "was how well a husband and a wife could work in harness together."

CHAPTER 3

THE MOST TALENTED CHILD EVER BORN

Beauty is not in the face. Beauty is a light in the heart.

—*Khalil Gibran*

THE NAME OF OTTENSOSER MEANS "SOMEONE FROM OTTENSOOS," a Black Forest village near the neighboring but sharply contrasting Bavarian towns of Nuremberg and Fürth—Nuremberg being notorious for its anti-Semitism (and later for the Nazis' mass rallies), while Fürth, by contrast, was actively welcoming to Jews. The home of Germany's first Jewish hospital (1653), orphanage (1763), practicing lawyer (1843), and judge (1863), the town of Fürth (whose name means "ford") was the cradle of such eminent Jewish Americans as Levi Strauss, the inventor of blue jeans; and Julius Ochs, whose son Adolph purchased and rebuilt the ailing *New York Times*. In the twentieth century the fourteen-year-old Henry Kissinger played on the junior team of SpVgg Fürth, Fürth Playing Association, the town's successful soccer team.

Zevi "David" Ottensoser was one of several notable Ottensoser rabbis and scholars raised in Fürth. In the early nineteenth century, Zevi helped spread the revolutionary ideas of Moses Mendelssohn, the driving inspiration of modern Reform Judaism, and Ottensoser's famous treatise *Amerika* encouraged German Jews to make their way across the Atlantic to build a new life for themselves in the freedom of the New World.

Lippmann Ottensoser was among those who heeded the call. One of seven brothers and sisters who all traveled to America between 1863 and 1874, Lippmann helped organize the family migration on a shuttle basis, raising funds to bring over his siblings in installments. As he got settled in his new country, he changed his given name to Louis, and in 1887, aged thirty-four, he married the dark-haired Fannie Lesser from Syracuse, New York. Ten years his junior, Fannie was the daughter of a well-to-do local wholesale jeweler of Russian-Jewish descent, and a liberal arts graduate of Syracuse University. Their only son, Nathan, Eileen's father, was born in August 1888.

Eileen's grandfather Louis tried his hand at just about anything: real estate, insurance, clothing manufacture, bankruptcy adjustment, and even as a dealer in Native American hair. In December 1909, Louis Ottensoser of 611 West 111th Street, New York City, took out display advertisements in the *Times* of Muskogee, Oklahoma, a town close to several American Indian reservations, offering cash payments for "long hair and good combings."

His enterprises met with varying success—at the end of 1907 he had debts totaling $637 ($16,000 today). A few years earlier, after Louis and his wife repaid eighty-five of their one hundred mortgage installments to an Ocala Savings and Loan, the bank had collapsed, and in a case still cited in the law books, the Ottensosers were overruled in their attempts to seek legal redress.

Louis paid off his obligations, faring better than his younger brother David, Eileen's great-uncle, a manufacturer and importer of jewelry, who gave notice of bankruptcy in January 1913, owing creditors a total of $126,227, the equivalent of some $3 million in 2015. Great-uncle David was eventually vindicated—in terms of his honesty, if not his good sense—when court proceedings revealed that he had been tricked by a con artist who paid him for the use of his name, then embarked on an elaborate fraud involving forged receipts from nonexistent Woolworth stores around the country.

All these business misadventures in the family seem to have taught an important lesson to Eileen's father, Nathan Ottensoser. In the midst of financial disaster, there is one person who never fails to make money from bankruptcy proceedings: the liquidating, or "adjustment," agent, who has first call on the surviving assets and gets his fee paid in full. "Take advantage of your disadvantages," ran an old Jewish saying that Nat liked to quote. So bankruptcy, debt collection, and credit rating became his chosen path in life, starting in 1914 with the incorporation of his Fifth Avenue Protective Association, FAPA. The dunning agency listed his recently acquired sweetheart, Loretta Laine Forsythe, as one of its directors.

The fact that the twenty-six-year-old Nat, educated at the prestigious Moses Brown Quaker school in Providence, Rhode Island, could kick off his adult life by incorporating his own business indicated a family background of some substance. In 1910, while he was completing his commercial law studies at New York University, the Ottensosers were living at 611 West 111th Street, a fashionable new Morningside Heights apartment building, and a few years later they had moved to 20 Morningside, where the census showed Nat still at home with his parents, along with one live-in servant. By 1915 the family had upgraded again, to 302 West 109th Street, where there was now room for *two* female servants, one French and one Italian. The Ottensosers were comfortably off.

Loretta's significantly less prosperous Finnish Irish family, the Laines, meanwhile, remained stuck in West 25th and 116th streets, on the seedy side of Brooklyn, moving from one shared property to another. It was the sort of area from which the Ottensosers' live-in servants might originally have come, and Fannie Ottensoser seems to have taken a dim view of her only son, Nat, getting mixed up with a poverty-stricken and apparently gold-digging young woman from the wrong side of the river, with her fatherless three-year-old son, Thomas, in tow.

Loretta responded to her mother-in-law's hostility with similar disdain, and even a certain degree of anti-Semitism. According to her granddaughters, Loretta thought that Fannie spent far too much time going out to highfalutin concerts and recitals, to the neglect of her family, and she was especially contemptuous of one particular

Ottensoser family oddity: even in later life, Fannie had a fondness for taking off her upper garments and requiring that her beloved son Nat wash down her naked back.

When Nat and Loretta got married in March 1916, they chose a Lutheran church across the Hudson River, in Jersey City, and moved as far away from the back-washing practices of the Upper West Side as possible—to the eastern corner of Queens, at 2210 Lincoln Place, Far Rockaway, in the company of Loretta's son, Thomas, now aged five and bearing the surname Ottensoser.

A modest boardwalk beach enclave, Far Rockaway was in the process of transforming itself from a spring and summer resort into a year-round bedroom community serving Manhattan, complete with modern schools and hospitals. Yet when, in the summer of 1921, Loretta found that she was pregnant, there was no question of the Ottensosers' first-born child being born locally. Nothing but the best would do, and Nat booked his wife into Manhattan's prestigious Woman's Hospital, at the junction of 110th Street and Amsterdam Avenue, the first dedicated women's hospital in the United States.

SO EILEEN CECILE OTTENSOSER ENTERED THE WORLD ON MARCH 25, 1922.

"My parents doted on me," she liked to recall. "They'd waited a long time for me. I was the cure for cancer, the answer to everything. So far as they were concerned, I was the most talented child ever born—the answer to all the world's problems."

Neither parent had an Eileen or a Cecile in the family, and Eileen's explanation of how she came by her name was that Loretta, during her pregnancy, had met a woman at the theater—a total stranger, apparently—whose cute little daughter impressed her mightily. On discovering that the little girl's name was Eileen, Loretta declared that Eileen would be the name of her own daughter, if she had one.

Named on impulse and later famed for her impulsiveness, the newly arrived Eileen was taken home by her parents, briefly to Far

Rockaway, then farther south and east, to 14 West Walnut Street, Long Beach, a block from the Long Beach railroad station. Eileen later recalled a broad, unpaved, and rather muddy main street down which she was once led on a pony—and the clinging discomfort of sitting in her sodden wool bathing costume after swimming at the beach.

Eileen's memories of Long Beach are perfunctory, however, since her parents moved again as she approached the age of five. Nat and Loretta wanted a good school for their daughter, and they considered Long Beach "kind of seedy." So in 1927 the Ottensosers made a complete break from the creeping urbanization of New York. They moved twenty miles north, to the up-and-coming suburb of Great Neck.

CHAPTER 4

GREAT NECK

It was a matter of chance that I should have rented a house
in one of the strangest communities in North America.

Nick Carraway, in The Great Gatsby

I N THE SPRING OF 1924, TWO YEARS AFTER EILEEN OTTENSOSER
was born, F. Scott Fitzgerald was searching for a commuter community that embodied the go-getting spirit of Jazz Age America,
and he found it just half an hour east of Manhattan, on Long Island
Sound, "where there are," as he wrote " . . . two unusual formations of
land . . . a pair of enormous eggs, identical in contour and separated
only by a courtesy bay [Manhasset Bay] . . . They are not perfect ovals
. . . but their physical resemblance must be a source of perpetual wonder to the gulls that fly overhead."

Fitzgerald christened his oval headlands West Egg and East
Egg—in real life, the affluent communities of Kings Point, Sands
Point, Port Washington, and Great Neck, less than twenty miles from
New York—and here the novelist set his cautionary tale *The Great
Gatsby*. Great Neck was the gateway to the fabled "Gold Coast" of
glamorous lawns, boat docks, and estates that were attracting the up-
wardly mobile young families of the Jazz Age—among them Eileen's
parents, Nathan and Loretta Ottensoser.

"I remember it as just a little town around a station with one main street," Eileen would later recall, "with a lot of big, old trees. There was still a great deal of countryside around."

By chance, the Ottensosers' home at 2 Hilltop Drive, Great Neck Estates, was only a few minutes' stroll from the house that F. Scott Fitzgerald rented from 1922 to 1924 while writing his famous novel. Yet Eileen had no knowledge of this as a child. Her memories were of farms. "Beyond our garden wall there was a hill that fell away to a brook. You could see a farm on the other side with two or three cows and a huge barn. I could walk along the brook through the woods, and pick violets. On the next street was my piano teacher who had an apple farm. We used to steal the apples when we went by."

The attractions of rural life drew many city-dwellers to Great Neck. As automobile use spread in the 1920s, new bridges and parkways linked New York City to its Long Island hinterland, and the area's population doubled. Great Neck embodied the dream of America's early suburbia, offering the best of town and country in one spot—"the rich aroma of nature's luxuriant abundance," as Broadway star Eddie Cantor put it in his bestselling memoir, *My Life Is in Your Hands*. Cantor also made explicit one particular attraction that Great Neck extended to new arrivals like him, born Israel Iskowitz and brought up in New York's Lower East Side, as well as to Nat Ottensoser and his family. Unlike its neighboring communities, Great Neck extended a welcome to residents who were Jewish.

Anti-Semitism was a building block of the modern American suburb. The prejudice was barely concealed. The property deeds of early twentieth-century U.S. housing developments routinely contained "restriction" clauses that limited homes' sale and resale to "members of the Caucasian race"—and as for membership in that ultimate and defining U.S. middle-class institution, the golf and country club, the discrimination was flagrant. A Jewish family might be able to build or buy a pleasant house in a high-toned suburb but had little chance of playing tennis or golf in one of the new country clubs being built all over the United States in these years. The number of these clubs exploded between 1917 and 1930, from 472 to 5,856, with most of them operating membership restrictions that were pro-WASP and anti-Jew (and, needless to say, anti-Latino and anti-black). Rare were exceptions such as Great Neck's Lakeville Golf Club, "one of the most beautiful and exclusive country clubs in America" according to Eddie Cantor—built on land provided by the Jewish banker and philanthropist Nathan S. Jonas.

Great Neck's inclusiveness was famous, and sometimes sneered at, beyond its borders. Picking up the biblical name for a Hebrew council of the elite, a 1927 article in *The New Yorker* slyly described the neighborhood as "the Sanhedrin of the successful," where building and decorating contractors were told, "Don't worry about the expense, old boy; go to the limit." But Hal Lanigan, editor and chief writer of the *Great Neck News*, felt that assimilation was the American way, and was proud to see it taking place in his community.

"*THE NEWS*," he wrote in September 1928, "is for every race and creed . . . We've got pals among the Great Neck Jewry by the dozens . . . We don't go out often, but when we do, it's at the home of Jewish friends, almost once out of every three times." Like Eddie Cantor, the editor was proud of his friendship with the banker Nathan Jonas: "And as for other Jewish folk who haven't Mr. Jonas' wealth, or are only in the medium class . . . we know dozens upon dozens whom we like equally as much as we like Irishers, the Scotch, the English and the rest. So that's that!"

Great Neck's racial harmony was more selective, in fact, than Hal Lanigan cared to acknowledge. In September 1925 several hundred members of the Ku Klux Klan had gathered from all over Long Island to parade, in full regalia, down the main street, Middle Neck Road, with bands and floats. This was an event that editor Lanigan chose *not* to chronicle in the pages of the *News*—no more than he dreamt of referring to the fact that the fame of Eddie Cantor, Great Neck's model of assimilation, was based on years of his playing burned-cork "Nigger minstrel" characters in the Ziegfeld Follies.

IN THE FIRST QUARTER OF THE TWENTIETH CENTURY, NEW YORK
City was still the headquarters of the American movie business.
Filmmakers might travel out to Arizona and California for their winter shooting, but the big studios' center of gravity remained on the
East Coast, with busy production lots in Brooklyn, Queens, Harlem,
and, across the Hudson River, Fort Lee, New Jersey. The great D. W.
Griffith got his start as an actor and director at Paramount's Astoria studio in Queens, where John Barrymore and the Marx Brothers
also made films. *The Cocoanuts* (1929) and *Animal Crackers* (1930)
were both shot by Paramount in Queens, so Groucho Marx made
his home in Great Neck, as did Griffith and Barrymore. Other show
business locals included comedian Ed Wynn; Molly King Alexander,
one of the vamps of the silent screen; and Oscar Hammerstein II,
whose *Show Boat*, composed with Jerome Kern, was the Broadway
hit of 1927.

Eileen Ford remembered the elegant Mrs. Alexander coming to
one of the parties that her mother, Loretta, gave after morning Mass
on Sundays: "I couldn't have been more than eight years old, and I
can still remember Mrs. Alexander's pale-blue chiffon dress with an
ostrich feather, and shoes and hat to match. But we didn't mix much
with the movie people. We reckoned that they were very sophisticated and arty. They lived their own glamorous life."

The *Great Neck News* kept its readers fully in touch with this
glamour, painting a picture of a community that was exploding with
showbiz excitement. To read the breathless accounts of every celebrity arrival in Hal Lanigan's weekly column was to see Great Neck as
the Beverly Hills of the East—with added decorum. "The many folk
of the stage who have bought and built here," wrote Lanigan in April
1925, " . . . are a much different type than those rattle-headed, silly
nuts and nuterinos that form Hollywood's movie colony. No murders
here; no disgraceful orgies; no wild motoring."

Lanigan did not welcome the image of drunkenness and debauch-
ery that F. Scott Fitzgerald portrayed in *The Great Gatsby*. "WEST
EGG NOT US!" was the headline over his report when the play of the

novel opened on Broadway. "The night revelry on Gatsby's estate," he wrote, "is just one of those things of which the playwright takes liberties. It's a most exaggerated scene."

His local readers agreed. When a pre-Broadway version of *Gatsby* opened in January 1926 at the Great Neck Playhouse, the audience reception was distinctly frosty, with scant applause and no curtain call. Fitzgerald had clearly scored a bull's-eye.

THE OTTENSOSER HOME, AT 2 HILLTOP DRIVE IN THE NEIGHBORHOOD known as Great Neck Estates, was a stretched-out and comfortable single-story house built of stone and brick, with a sharply pitched gable roof that gave it the air of a storybook cottage from "Babes in the Wood." There were rosebushes around the door, and one of the gables covered a garage that housed two of Nat Ottensoser's beloved touring cars: a silver-gray Cord with curving fenders and gleaming exhaust pipes that emerged from the side of the supercharged engine, alongside a cream convertible Cadillac with lacquered wickerwork around the rear.

"Our house had six bedrooms and six bathrooms," remembered Eileen, "including one service bedroom at the back where my half brother Tom Forsythe stayed when he was home from school."

Eileen felt that her father treated his stepson Tom as a fully equal member of the family, bestowing his name, Ottensoser, upon him, and sending him to the highly regarded Peekskill Military Academy in upstate New York. "My father," she maintained, "raised Tom like another son." Yet Tom did not see things that way, according to his own son, William Forsythe, the modern dancer and choreographer, who heard Tom's side of things from his mother, Katherine. She recalled her husband confiding in her that he found it painful to be sent off to military school "at the ripe old age of six."

"My father was so young," recalled Forsythe, "that a couple who lived at the school—I guess it was the caretaker and his wife or whoever it was—considered him too young to be at such a place and took him under their wing." William Forsythe got the impression that Nat was not particularly happy to have Tom around—that there was "some sort of primitive jealousy at play."

Nat and Loretta never told Tom about his parentage. He discovered the truth only when a meddling great-aunt, Grandma Margaret's elder sister, Mary, took it upon herself to tell him he was adopted. The teenager was furious with his mother and stepfather, insisting that he should cease to be an Ottensoser and revert to his birth name, Thomas Forsythe.

Eileen's memories of her childhood home were detailed and vivid. "We had a living room," she recalled, "that was big by most standards and a music room. I also remember when we got one of the first record players that would change the discs automatically. It had a beautiful wooden cabinet, and we got our own projector so we could watch movies at home—my favorite was *Felix the Cat*. There was a formal dining room and a breakfast room and a kitchen with a butler's pantry for china. Downstairs there was the laundry with a washing machine and also a mangle, with an oil burner to heat the house. All the houses in the street had heating. There was a milkman who brought milk every day and an iceman who delivered ice—until we got a fridge. At night we listened to *Amos 'n' Andy*."

A record player, home movies, central heating, roller skates, an electric icebox, and a comedy show every night on the radio—Eileen Ottensoser belonged to the first generation of Americans for whom these material comforts were part of everyday life. Prosperity was more widely enjoyed in the America of the 1920s than in any previous time or place on earth, and Eileen's father was in the vanguard of the new consumers whom Earnest Calkins identified as not just spending their wealth, but seeking to display it in style. In 1926 Nat Ottensoser was a member of New York's Art in Trades Club, which sought to "harmonize commercial activity with the growing art tendencies of the present time," and he was listed that year as a patron of the Art in Trades exhibition at the Waldorf Astoria, which displayed the latest elegant American taste to eager crowds.

The success of Nat's debt collection agency raised the lifestyle of his family an extra level. The aspirational Ottensosers employed a succession of governesses, together with two black servants who traveled in and out from Harlem every day. Cornelius, the family handyman, whose wife doubled as housekeeper and cook, would drive Nat Ottensoser down to the station each morning in style.

"Great Neck was a classy community," recalled Eileen. "It had its own Dancing Academy, and a movie house with a trained nurse on duty during the children's matinees. You didn't see *that* in many places. All the new houses in Great Neck were beautifully designed, and there was a planned village called 'Kensington' which had gate pillars just like the ones in Kensington Gardens."

From pseudo-royal London park gates to trained nannies at the movie theater, English gentility mattered greatly to the new rich of this community where every structure seemed to be half-timbered. "We call England the 'Mother Country,'" remarked Robert Benchley, the Algonquin Round Table snob who loved deriding others' snobberies, "because most of us come from Poland or Italy." Indeed, in Great Neck, there were a yacht club and polo club based on two English exemplars—Cowes and Cowdray—and even a small group of very rich inhabitants who rode to hounds. F. Scott Fitzgerald departed from Great Neck dripping with contempt for the pretensions of "this unprecedented 'place' that Broadway had begotten upon a Long Island fishing village." His narrator, Nick Carraway, dismisses the suburb as "a shortcut from nothing to nothing."

Yet the would-be English ladies and gentlemen of Great Neck did not see their "Wonder City" (Hal Lanigan's term) in this way. They had escaped from the tawdriness of the Lower East Side—or, in the case of the Ottensosers, from Far Rockaway and "seedy" Long Beach—to realize their dreams of ascent. They were moving on and moving up, pursuing the gentility that was the badge of the aspirational and style-conscious values that Eileen Ford would come to espouse and dedicate her life to promoting.

CHAPTER 5

THE BOBBSEY TWINS

Modeling is not just about luck and genes; it is also about having this sort of determination built into you—never giving up.

—*Erin O'Connor, Ford model in the 1990s*

YOUNG EILEEN OTTENSOSER HAD A PASSION FOR READING. "Books were my treasure. My mother read books to me from the earliest I can remember."

The first books Eileen could recall reading were the serial adventures of the Bobbsey Twins, an unrolling sequence of more than seventy juvenile novels with a strong mystery flavor. "I read every volume that I could get my hands on."

There were, in fact, two sets of Bobbsey twins—Bert and Nan, who were eight when the series started in 1904, and Freddie and Flossie, aged four. They lived close to the shores of an attractive stretch of water somewhere in the Northeast of the United States, where Richard Bobbsey, the children's father, ran a successful lumber business. The spacious family home of the Bobbseys lay "on a fashionable street and had a small but nice garden around it," and the twins were cared for by the family's man of all work, Sam Johnson, and his wife, Dinah, the cook, whose speech patterns were rendered in the style of Bre'r Rabbit and Uncle Remus: "Well, I declar' to gracious, if yo' chillun ain't gone an' mussed up de floah ag'in!"

A successful businessman father, a comfortable upper-middle-class home, and a couple of adoring black domestics—a scenario that was lapped up by the millions of American children who made best sellers of the Bobbsey Twins books was no more than the everyday reality of Eileen Ottensoser's childhood. Might the triumphal sense of entitlement with which she barreled her way through life have owed something to the fact that her favorite childhood stories could easily have been written about her—and invariably had happy endings?

"As I look back," she recalled eighty years later, "I have to say that my childhood was the most enchanted and privileged time."

Eileen did not have a twin, but her younger brother, Bobby, born in 1924 and only fifteen months her junior, was her natural sidekick, and he became her co-conspirator in all manner of adventures.

"Bobby and I were very close," she remembered. "We did everything together, and we ganged up, I'm ashamed to say, on our baby brother, Billy, when he came along [in 1928]. We tortured him. We created special clubs that he was not allowed to join. Billy had his own nurse, Dame Edith Pitt, who wore a little white hat and apron and a long blue dress. She wouldn't let us go near Billy, especially in his bath, which was in a folding tub on a wooden frame—'If you touch that soft spot on the top of his head, the boy will die,' she would say. Well, what could be more tempting to a six- and four-year-old than that?"

Eileen's confession of sibling rivalry, even to the extent of contemplating a fatal poking of her finger into her younger brother's skull, was a rare suggestion of a dark side to her "enchanted" childhood among the cows and apple orchards of Great Neck Estates. Her recollections were almost fairy tales. Eileen's success in adult life was as a merchant in fantasy, and her childhood memories are early examples of her talent for making things appear more beautiful than they actually were. Her mother and father might have been old-fashioned disciplinarians—the Ottensoser children ate separately from their parents, for example, and were expected to curtsey or bow to visitors—but in later life she could not recall a single instance of harshness or injustice.

"I never doubted that I was adored. My mother and father had been waiting six years before I came along, and I think their love for me was the source of my self-confidence. I never doubted that I could do anything, especially so far as my father was concerned. To my father I was heaven, I was always right. I had two brothers, but I was Daddy's girl—and it was a wonderful position to be in."

The qualities that would make Eileen Ottensoser an arbiter of style for a whole generation of American fashion derived from her close observation of the two parents she idolized. "My mother had such dress sense," she remembered. "She loved satin and silk above all. She didn't know what cotton was. I remember her bridge luncheons with all the ladies in their elegant dresses. They sat around in their finery while the staff brought them drinks and food."

One of the hallmarks of the Ford Modeling Agency in its heyday was the aura of perpetual entertaining that wreathed Eileen Ford and her husband wherever they went. No meal was complete without guests, no encounter worthy of the name without an exchange of good cheer—and on Eileen's side, the origins of that went back to Nat and Loretta Ottensoser.

"Both my parents were very social. I remember looking out at the parties when they moved all of the furniture out of the living room and entertained everyone on the terrace with steaks and ice cream. They did everything with such taste."

A modern witness to the elegant "Art in Trades" style of the Ottensoser household in the 1920s is William Forsythe, son of Tom Forsythe, Eileen's elder half brother. "My father inherited a lot of stuff from the family house in Great Neck," he recalls, "and I have some of it now in Vermont. Every so often I look at it and say, 'Wow, that is beautiful!'—like the hand-carved turn of an arm on an antique armchair. I have not had a lot of the old furniture reupholstered, because the choice of fabric was so divine—pale yellow silk brocades. It was all incredibly discreet."

In later life Eileen tried to play down her family's prosperity. Yet Nathan Ottensoser's Fifth Avenue Protective Association rode the nine-year bull market of the 1920s with panache—until it ended. October 24, 1929, notorious as Black Thursday, saw shares on the New York Stock Exchange lose 11 percent of their value at the opening bell. It was followed by Black Monday and Black Tuesday on October 28 and 29—and FAPA was affected, like everyone else. Nat Ottensoser came home on the train one evening at the end of 1929 to announce to the family that the good times in Great Neck were over. They would have to lay off the servants, shut down the house on Hilltop Drive (with the hope they might sell it or rent it), and move to an apartment in New York in the New Year.

Young Eileen Ottensoser was poleaxed. "I'll never forget my father telling us, 'We are going to the poorhouse.'"

To start with, eileen ottensoser just hated new york. "I cried and cried. My parents sent me to an Episcopal school called St. Agatha, where I had to wear a uniform. The long stockings were so painful. Every morning I begged and pleaded to be taken away."

The seven-year-old didn't have to cry for long. After just two days, Eileen was taken out of St. Agatha and installed in a Catholic convent school, the Institut Tisané, a junior academy for young ladies with just eight girls in every class and where all the teaching was in French. The teachers wore long black gowns with high, white lace collars and expected their charges to curtsey to them—*faire obéissance*—just as the little girls were taught to curtsey to every other adult.

Nathan Ottensoser might have told his family they were heading for the poorhouse, but the apartment he rented for them in Manhattan, on West 88th Street, was actually quite large and comfortable— and not far from his mother's home on West 103rd Street, where Grandma Fannie was now living with her brothers, William and Benjamin Lesser, the partners in Lesser Brothers, a commercial law firm that did business with Nat and his Protective Association. Economic stringency had made for something of a family reunion on the Upper West Side.

Fannie, Nat's mother and Eileen's grandmother, was now a widow, and getting frail. She was sixty-eight years old, and her son Nat may well have moved back to the Upper West Side to be close to her in her old age. Eileen and Robert, the two Bobbsey Twins from Great Neck, would visit Grandma Fannie in her apartment on West 103rd Street and march up and down while she played the piano.

The Upper West Side was a popular area with prosperous German Americans. George Herman Ruth, the acclaimed baseball star "Babe" Ruth, lived just across West Eighty-Eighth Street from the Ottensosers, and Eileen later remembered roller-skating along the tree-lined street with Ruth's daughter, Dorothy Ann.

Nat Ottensoser was presumably being ironic when he talked about the family's heading to the "poorhouse," since he was, in reality, far better placed than most to profit from the financial mayhem that followed the 1929 crash. Financial disaster was manna from heaven for a nimble bill collector, with some twenty-six thousand business collapses recorded in the United States in 1930, and twenty-eight thousand the following year. With the Fifth Avenue Protective Association taking first charge on every bankruptcy it handled, Nat Ottensoser prospered from the misfortunes of others. He also had the wit to formalize the database he was building on companies' payment problems to move beyond crude debt collection. He expanded FAPA into a full-scale credit-rating agency—some years later he would receive business approaches from Dun and Bradstreet, the leaders in that field—and as his business status thrived, his family lived better than ever.

For the seven-year-old, the great event of 1930 was the appearance of Nancy Drew, the heroine of a new set of juvenile novels from Grosset and Dunlap, the publishers of the Bobbsey Twins books. Nancy was a feisty sixteen-year-old girl detective who was never too busy to help her widowed father, attorney Carson Drew, solve cases that arose from his legal practice in the idyllic imaginary town of River Heights, locality unspecified. Like Lakeport, the home of the Bobbsey Twins, River Heights was nostalgically depicted as an old-fashioned country town, but the community bore all the characteristics of a modern American suburb.

Impossibly accomplished, Nancy Drew spoke French; played bridge, tennis, and golf; danced like Ginger Rogers; and was the driver of a blue convertible that she flashed into and out of the Drews' garage "with a skill born of long practice." She could turn her hand, if the need arose, to changing a tire or repairing a distributor head, and while solving every mystery, she created another: why was such a clever young lady of sixteen not attending school? "The books were seventy-five cents each," Eileen remembered, "and I'd save all my pennies to buy them—though my father would give me extra money whenever I asked for it."

In this respect, Eileen's relationship with Nat Ottensoser was not unlike that of Nancy Drew with her father, Carson, her continually approving single parent, who not only imposed no restrictions on his teenage daughter's movements, but, in at least one episode, entrusted her with his gun. As *Fortune* magazine remarked in 1933, reporting on the phenomenal commercial success of the new series, Nancy had "crashed a Valhalla that had been rigidly restricted to the male of her species."

Making her debut a decade after American women had won the right to vote, Nancy Drew would become a role model for a generation of high-achieving Americans, from Barbara Walters to Supreme Court justice Sandra Day O'Connor to Hillary Clinton. All three, and many more, have happily acknowledged the girl detective as a mythic influence in their lives, and Eileen was proud to join this regiment. Her politics, as she grew older, would veer several hemispheres to the right of Hillary Clinton's—but that was the particular magic of Nancy Drew, who managed to reconcile her radical forays in female emancipation with reassuringly well-scrubbed and conservative values, demonstrating to her young readers, as one academic study has put it, that they could strike forward in life as liberated women while always retaining the comfort of staying "Daddy's little girls."

Eileen Ottensoser had an advantage over Nancy Drew in having not just a father but also a mother who firmly trusted in her daughter's capabilities. "For some reason, I always expected that I would be earning my own living when I grew up. I never expected anything different. My father expected me to aim high—and so did my mother. 'One day you'll be a lawyer,' she'd tell me, 'and if you are, that means you can become a judge.'"

These were heady aspirations for a little girl in fifth grade at the Institut Tisané. Eileen Ottensoser celebrated her eleventh birthday in March 1933, and her father gave her the best birthday present she could have hoped for. Business had gone well, he was able to report. The worst of the financial crisis was over. He had not had to sell or rent the family home, and they could all return to Great Neck.

CHAPTER 6

YOUNG AND BEAUTIFUL

It's mighty nice to have a smart little daughter.

—*Carson Drew in* The Mystery at Lilac Inn,
by Carolyn Keene

S
O NANCY DREW WENT BACK TO GREAT NECK. EILEEN OTTENSOSER was eleven years old in 1933, and she plunged back into suburban life with gusto.

"My brother Bobby and I put on plays in the house," she recalled. "There was a wood-paneled room there with a bar. We set up a table, with curtains, and performed plays like 'Little Red Riding Hood.' The local governesses brought their children, and we made them pay a penny each."

Eileen loved to play card games—mah-jongg was the craze of the time for teenagers, and she also played blackjack. Yet she and her elder brother had to make sure that the churchgoing Loretta never found out. "My mother was very, very strict about no gambling, and when she said no, she didn't mean maybe."

If Loretta Ottensoser could instill the fear of God in her daughter, paterfamilias Nat could be just as intimidating. "I got home from school once," Eileen recalled, "and was chatting to a friend on the telephone. I didn't know that my father was trying to get through to tell the houseman that he had got back early to the station and needed collecting at once. I'll never forget the look on his face when he finally got home—and there I was, still speaking on the phone."

Nat Ottensoser's principal lesson in good behavior took place every Christmastime, when he would organize a lavish array of presents that he would give each of his children in a beautiful, purpose-built wooden box. "Then, after we'd opened the box and looked at every single present," recalled Eileen, "he'd make Bobby and me put half of them back, take the box to the local children's hospital, and give them away."

Nat Ottensoser's formative years in Rhode Island among the Quakers of Moses Brown (originally known as the New England Yearly Meeting Boarding School) clearly had an impact on his child-rearing practices. Republican though he was in his politics, the man who loved smart cars and smart furniture wanted to endow his children with more than things. The Society of Friends are Christ's own Buddhists, and their radical beliefs created such allegiance in Nat Ottensoser that when, in 1940, the U.S. government started asking Americans to list their religion on the census form, the fifty-two-year-old who had been born into Judaism wrote down "Quaker."

We don't know what led Nat's Jewish parents to send him to a Quaker school. Louis and Fannie probably wished to give their son a high-quality East Coast education, and Moses Brown, dating from 1784 and named for its radical abolitionist founder, did not impose a Jewish quota. Nat Ottensoser's time among the anything-but-prescriptive Quakers seemed to have left him with a deep skepticism toward organized religion. According to a cherished family legend, when Father Madden, Loretta's parish priest back in Brooklyn, came calling to advise her that her non-Catholic marriage to Nat meant she was living in sin, Nat had "offered to throw him down the stairs."

Nat Ottensoser was proud to have walked away from his Jewishness, displaying all the moral absolutism of those who pride themselves on shaking off the shackles of religion, and people who knew both him and Eileen would sometimes describe her self-assurance as a diluted version of her father's. When confronted with that comparison, she would happily accept it, adding a retort that encapsulated her own version of feminism: "When men make clear what they want," she would say, "they are called 'men.' When women speak their mind, they are called 'tough'—and worse."

Far from being cowed by her demanding father, Eileen wholeheartedly adopted his alpha-male assertiveness. "Mannish" and "domineering" were gibes leveled frequently at her in her adult life, and her taste for confrontation may well have derived from the way in which her father treated her—in many respects, as a son. On Saturday afternoons Nat would choose his tomboy daughter, rather than either of her brothers or any male friend, to be his companion at pro and college football games. "My father took me to see the Giants whenever they played at home," she would recall. "And in the summer, we went together to baseball games. I don't remember him ever taking my brothers. I might as well have been an only child so far as my father was concerned."

Eileen's drive and aggression were two keys to her adult success, and they were also the reasons some people in the fashion business could not stand her. As her career developed, people either loved Eileen Ford or hated her intensely—and she could not have cared less either way. At the peak of her success in the 1970s, she published a book, *Eileen Ford's Beauty Now and Forever* (1977), in which she offers a recipe for those not lucky enough to have had parents who boosted them as her parents did: "Envision yourself as you would like to be," she writes. "If you are firmly convinced of what you want, your inner self will take the suggestion and act upon it. . . . Your mental-emotional attitude will carry you to whatever life you are going to live from now on." Employing the imagery of Pavlov and his dogs, she goes on to describe this technique as a form of self-conditioning: "If you were conditioned as a little girl to think of yourself as pretty, vital and attractive, your mind will still project this image, and the image will reach other people's eyes; *pretty, vital, attractive.*"

By 1977, Eileen's proclamation of the power of positive thinking clearly bore the stamp of such self-help gurus as Norman Vincent Peale and Dale Carnegie. Yet at the heart of her gospel of self-propulsion were the memories of the little girl whose parents believed she was "always right" and "the answer to all the world's problems," who took her to football games, and who told her she could be not just a lawyer but a judge as well. Such children, wrote Sigmund Freud, who are brought up in the belief that they are *the* child of the family, keep "for life the feeling of the conqueror, that confidence of success that often induces real success."

EILEEN'S SUBLIME LACK OF SELF-DOUBT STOOD HER IN GOOD STEAD when, in the fall of 1933, she enrolled in Great Neck High School, on the corner of Arrandale and Polo roads. Very different in style and scale from the Institut Tisané and its select classes of little ladies curtseying to their lace-collared *mesdames*, the recently constructed redbrick high school bustled with more than 1,000 eager teenagers (1,228 in 1936). Eileen's distinguished fellow alumni in later generations— graduates, all of them, in the years after World War II—would include movie director Francis Ford Coppola, fashion designer Kenneth Cole, TV news correspondent Dan Raviv, and biologist David Baltimore, winner of the 1975 Nobel Prize for Physiology.

So far as her own school career was concerned, Eileen was proud *not* to have been a prizewinner—"I failed sewing twice"—but worked hard at the subjects she liked.

"I loved Latin—Caesar's Gallic wars, with all that fighting."

The devotee of Nancy Drew and the Bobbsey Twins loved her English lessons, and particularly her eighth-grade grammar teacher, Mrs. Briggs, a Shakespeare enthusiast who took her charges into Manhattan to see Orson Welles playing Brutus in Welles's production of *Julius Caesar* in Fascist dress. Eileen developed a taste for the romantic poems of Edna St. Vincent Millay, and as she matured, she proved a diligent club-joiner, becoming a member of the Theta Beta sorority and helping to organize its meetings.

Her best friend at school was Marie Louise Watts, who earned Eileen's undying admiration by burping out the full tune of the *1812 Overture* one day in music class. "We were sent to the office of Dean Anderson and just sat on the floor laughing." Dean Anderson seems to have been one of the earliest adults outside the adoring circle of the Ottensoser family to be unimpressed by Eileen's self-assuredness. "He wasn't laughing at all," Eileen remembered.

Marie Louise's father owned a small oil company and had built a home so grand that one entire wing was a hothouse dedicated to orchids, as Eileen remembered, with tame pheasant strutting across the grounds outside—"I ate pheasant so often at the Watts' that I grew tired of it."

The Ottensosers were able to return the Wattses' hospitality by taking Marie Louise with them on their annual summer holiday at Elizabethtown, in upstate New York, where Nat and Loretta liked to play golf together, and had a special set of miniature clubs and golf clothes made to order for Eileen. "It was not far from Saratoga," Eileen recalled, "and our father always took us to drink the spa water there. It was horrible. It tasted of sulfur and cost a penny a cup. Our father used to say, 'It's good for what ails you,' and Bobby and I were always ready with our response: 'There's *nothing* that ails us!'"

The Ottensoser code of polite behavior evidently tolerated retorts from the children if they were sharp and clever enough, arming Eileen with a gift for repartee that she would deploy to the full in later life.

After school, Eileen and Marie Louise would go to Kelly's Record Store and the ice-cream parlor across the street from the movie house to sip ice-cream sodas and flirt with the boys. "I remember the first day I met Bo Meyer—John Collier Meyer, Jr. He was a year ahead of me, very handsome, with brown hair and gray-blue eyes, and wretchedly unfaithful. All the girls were after him. Once I caught him coming out of Eileen Butler's bedroom. I forgave him. I couldn't help it. Bo and I didn't go to bed or anything, but he was my boyfriend, on and off, for three or four years."

The photograph of John Collier "Bo" Meyer, Jr., in *Arista*, the Great Neck High School yearbook for 1938, does full justice to Bo's firm features and film star good looks—he is described as "one of our most popular young men." Yet the "Senior Popularity Contest" on page 46 also makes clear his inconstancy: he was voted the class's "Biggest heart-breaker."

"I suppose I knew in my heart that 'Bo' would always be unfaithful," Eileen remembered. "Whenever I was upset about him, my mother told me, 'You may die of measles or mumps, but you will never die of a broken heart,' which just showed me at the time how she didn't understand."

By her final high school years, Eileen was firmly identified with her sorority socializing. In a facetious "Class Will" published in *Arista*, the sorority queen of the senior year, Carolyn Guild Bryan, bequeathed her "Greek Letters" to "Tot" Ottensoser, to carry on her good work organizing dances for the socialites in the new graduating class. The interschool fellowships would organize evenings at the local country clubs, and it was Eileen's job to select and book the bands. "I was very good at organizing. I was fifteen or sixteen years old when I started, and this was my first experience of the sort of thing that I would do later. I would get groups together, boys and girls, to go and see bands in about five different places. We would all go by train together, and when we got home our parents would meet us at the station."

By Eileen's final year at Great Neck High School, Bo Meyer was in the past. "Glenn Miller used to play at the Glen Island Casino in the summer, and one evening I met his latest young vocalist, Ray Eberle, who was *very* cute." Eberle and the seventeen-year-old high school band booker embarked on what Eileen later recalled as "a very nice romance"—until the singer made the mistake of calling the Ottensoser home for a chat at two o'clock in the morning. "The call woke my mother. She had very definite ideas about my future, and they did *not* include a big band singer called Ray Eberle."

CHAPTER 7

SOMETHING MELLIFLUOUS

But, sure, the sky is big, I said;
Miles and miles above my head;
So here upon my back I'll lie
And look my fill into the sky.
And so I looked, and, after all,
The sky was not so very tall.

—"Renascence," by Edna St. Vincent Millay, 1912

LORETTA OTTENSOSER HAD NO DOUBT. SHE WANTED HER ONLY daughter, Eileen, to attend a truly top-class college for women, and in her estimation, that was Barnard, whose magnificent Greek columns dominated the western sidewalk of Upper Broadway. Barnard College (founded in 1889) rivaled Vassar for leadership of the famed "Seven Sisters" group of elite female liberal arts colleges, which were located close to some of the finest Ivy League universities for men and shared academic activities with them to varying degrees. Barnard's "brother" college was Columbia, even more glorious than its sister, with its green campus and Greek- and Roman-columned buildings, its gates only a few yards away from Barnard, immediately opposite, on the other side of Broadway.

The problem for Eileen Ottensoser was that, like Harvard, Yale, Princeton, and all the Ivy League schools in the 1930s, Columbia and Barnard imposed the so-called Jewish Quota. The colleges felt they had too many Jewish students, and systematically sought to cut down that number. In 1935, for example, in his final year at high school, the future Nobel Prize winner Richard Feynman won the New York

University Math Championship by a huge margin that shocked the judges. Yet he was of Ashkenazi Jewish descent, and though his high school grades were perfect or near perfect in math and science, he was not accepted when he applied to Columbia. (He went to MIT instead.)

Many American academics in the 1920s were quite open about their implementation of the quota, which they regarded as a matter of racial fairness, not prejudice. "Never admit more than five Jews; take only two Italian Catholics; and take no blacks at all," was the maxim of the Yale School of Medicine, according to David Oshinsky, the biographer of Jonas Salk, inventor of the Salk polio vaccine, who ended up at New York University (alma mater of Nat Ottensoser) rather than at any Ivy League school. In 1935 Yale accepted just five out of two hundred Jewish applicants.

The dilemma facing the Ivy League was comparable to that faced today by educators in cities such as New York, where Asian students, less than 10 percent of the city's student population, routinely win more than 50 percent of the top high school places on merit. Until 1924, entry to U.S. colleges and universities was decided on the basis of an essay written in English, and Jewish students worked hard, often with special tutors, to practice and perfect their essay writing technique—as compared, say, with relatively untutored farm boys and girls from rural schools in the Midwest.

The introduction that year of the SAT (Scholastic Aptitude Test) was deliberately designed to counter this advantage by offering all intelligent pupils the equality of boxes to tick, and from 1924 the proportion of Jewish students in U.S. higher education started to fall, through dilution. The arrival of increasing numbers of strapping young men and women from the Farm Belt also did no harm to the record of the East Coast's varsity sports teams.

Yet "the quota" remained.

"We limit the number of Jews admitted to each class to roughly the proportion of Jews in the population of the state," said the dean of Cornell's medical college as late as 1940, citing a policy that was dignified with the name *numerus clausus*. At the Yale School of Medicine, applications by Jewish students were marked with an *H*, for "Hebrew," while Harvard requested passport-size photos to help identify Semitic facial features. Using questions about religious affiliation and giving priority to the sons of alumni (the so-called legacy preference), the Columbia University College of Physicians and Surgeons was able to reduce its proportion of Jewish students from 47 percent in 1920 to some 6 percent twenty years later—to the delight of alumni who deplored Jewish students as "damned curve-raisers" for working too hard and decreasing the value of the leisurely "gentleman's C."

Barnard, to its credit, tried to stand apart from such prejudice. The taboo-breaking college was largely the creation of Annie Nathan Meyer, a self-educated Sephardic Jew who had the clever idea of naming her all-female project in honor of a man, Frederick Barnard, the open-minded president of Columbia in 1889. Virginia Gildersleeve, the college's dean from 1911 until 1946, disdained religious and racial exclusivity, encouraging the admission of young African American women to the school and paying to support at least one through to graduation from her own personal funds.

Yet, in the interest of diversity, Gildersleeve did seek to dilute the 40 percent preponderance of Jewish students at Barnard in the 1920s, supplementing the traditional admission essay with psychological tests, interviews, and letters of recommendation, so that by the late 1930s only 20 percent of Barnard women were Jews. This did not totally eliminate Eileen Ottensoser's chances of gaining entry to Columbia's prestigious sister school, but by her own admission, she had scarcely been a serious high school student and she had a far better chance of securing one of Barnard's 80 percent of non-Jewish places.

The answer was simple: change her name. It was not as if her Quaker-espousing father and Roman Catholic mother had brought her up in any remotely Jewish fashion. Her two younger brothers, Bobby (age fifteen) and Billy (eleven), who would be facing the same college entry quota hurdles in the next few years, had already been the object of childish anti-Semitic sneers at school—classmates had changed Ottensoser to "Cup-and-Saucer"—and this experience had led the three children to devise a pact. Sometime in the months before Eileen's senior year in high school and her starting of the college entry process, Bobby and Billy banded together with their sister to tell their father that none of them would go to a university unless he changed the family surname from Ottensoser to Otte.

Nat Ottensoser revealed this juvenile ultimatum in the very human statement that he submitted to the New York Supreme Court, Nassau County, on September 16, 1938: "People have always encountered difficulty in the spelling of my surname," he declared.

The pronunciation of the name has been very difficult for people to grasp, especially over the telephone.

I am engaged in the business of credit checking and credit adjustments, and I am the general manager of the Fifth Avenue Protective Association Inc., 220 Fifth Avenue, New York City. During the day I may have as many as 100 or more telephone calls, and a goodly number of them are with strangers . . . A good deal of time is lost by me in trying to instruct these people with my name before I can undertake the discussion of the credit matter.

A graver problem has recently arisen. My children encountered the experience of being called "nick names" in their classroom. My children have told me that they will not attend University unless the University permits them to use the surname OTTE.

I personally have always been able to ward off the shocks produced by innocent missnomer or wifull [sic] missnomer. I make this prayer for a change of name at this late age to assist my children. I do not want them to harbor any resentment.

In Nat's petition, only this last sentence did not ring true, for the root of the problem facing American Jews in the late 1930s was not

their resentment toward others, but the open resentment and growing prejudice that others directed toward *them*. Starting in 1936,
more than thirty million listeners tuned in every week to the CBS-
syndicated broadcasts of the Detroit Catholic priest Father Charles
Coughlin, who preached that Jewish bankers were behind Bolshe-
vism, and propagated as true the notorious forgery *The Protocols of
the Elders of Zion*, which portrayed a sinister Jewish conspiracy to
take over the world. Also starting in 1936, and paralleling the rise of
Hitler on the other side of the Atlantic, the German American Bund
promoted fascist causes in America with camps, marches, and Nazi-
style rallies at which its leader, Fritz Julius Kuhn, would deride the
president as "Frank D. Rosenfeld" and denounce the socialist intentions of FDR's "Jew Deal."

"Tot" Otte, as Eileen now became for her final year at high school,
gloried in her new identity. In the Class Will for 1938, she had been
bequeathed the Greek letters that were the badge of her sorority work.
Now, in the Great Neck High School *Arista* yearbook for 1939, she
in her turn, as a departing senior, joyfully announced that "Eileen
Otte leaves her 'Nsoser' behind"—and proudly published her success
in achieving the elite academic destination that had been the object
of the whole name-change exercise: "Eileen Otte—Freshman at Barnard College (NY)."

EILEEN OTTE'S JETTISONING OF HER ANCESTRAL IDENTITY WAS NOT
an unusual step for a Jew in pre–World War II America. The process was called "assimilation" and it was almost commonplace.
The billboards of Broadway and Hollywood in that period and afterward were dominated by "assimilated" names that concealed or
camouflaged the Jewish origins of some of America's greatest actors
and entertainers: Edward G. Robinson (Emmanuel Goldenberg),
Danny Kaye (David Daniel Kaminski), Kirk Douglas (Issur Dan-
ielovitch Demsky), Jeff Chandler (Ira Grossel), Stubby Kaye (Bernard
Katzin), Jack Benny (Benjamin Kubelsky), Lee J. Cobb (Leo Jacoby),

Shelley Winters (Shirley Schrift), and Tony Curtis (Bernard Herschel Schwartz).

"Rosenbergs became Rosses and Cohens became Curtis," recalled a Hollywood producer from those years. "The idea was to reduce the number of consonants and syllables in your moniker, and to end up with something mellifluous that did not remind people too much of herring."

It was an aural version of the beauty culture to which the moguls of Hollywood themselves subscribed in order to become "real Americans": Sam Goldwyn was born Schmuel Gelbfisz, and if William Fox, born in Tolcsva, Austria-Hungary, in 1879, had not changed his name, the United States would have learned to love 20th Century–Fried, along with the modern Fried News Channel and Fried TV Network.

Nor was the world of music immune: Maestro Serge Koussevitzky, the conducting instructor of the young Leonard Bernstein, suggested that his protégé might smooth his career if he recast his surname as Leonard A. Byrns, or Burns, to fit in with the snobbish world of classical music. (The tenor Jan Peerce had been born Joshua Pincus Perelmuth—as, in more modern times, Beverly Sills was born Belle Miriam Silverman.) The composer stoutly rejected the idea—he was proud of his heritage—but his brother, Burtie, did catch him on one occasion fabricating a grand Harvard accent over the telephone when trying to book into an exclusive hotel at Virginia Beach: "This is Leonard Bernstein," pronounced the famous conductor, "of *Boston.*" Burtie never let Lennie forget it.

One small act of assimilation that can be dated from the very same month in which Eileen became an Otte was that of Heinz Alfred Kissinger, who arrived in America in September 1938 and changed his first name to Henry. The future statesman, then a fifteen-year-old schoolboy and amateur soccer star of Fürth, had escaped with his parents from Bavaria just in time to avoid the horrors of Kristallnacht, in which so many German Jews perished.

Fürth was, of course, the famous south German center of Jewish culture where the early Ottensosers distinguished themselves and from which they emigrated in the nineteenth century. Yet while Heinz/Henry Kissinger was always proud, like many assimilated Jews, to acknowledge his Semitic roots, Eileen Ottensoser/Otte sought to conceal hers entirely. She was to make her mark in a business graced by many entrepreneurs and artists of Jewish descent, but the former Eileen Ottensoser declined to admit that she was one of them, making much of her Finnish ethnicity (25 percent) and Irish genetic input (25 percent) when discussing her origins, but mumbling something about "German" relatives (50 percent) when it came to her father's side of the family.

As the years went by, Eileen Ford adopted an increasingly WASP identity that eventually won her a place alongside the Forbeses and Johnsons in the "Social List" of Somerset Hills, the horsey upper-crust corner of New Jersey to which she moved in the 1990s. Throughout her career her official CV and every Ford agency handout claimed that she was born Eileen Otte. So that was the incorrect starting point for all the obituaries published after her death in July 2014. There was not one mention of her Jewish lineage.

CHAPTER 8

MODEL STUDENT

Push yourself to the limit as often as possible.
There's nothing except what you sense.

—*Sayings carved in the stone of the Barnard campus bench*

BARNARD COLLEGE WAS AN EYE-OPENING EXPERIENCE FOR THE seventeen-year-old Eileen Otte. For the first time in her life she was expected to finish her papers and hand them in on time, fully annotated and with the grammar correct. "I had never done that in all my years at high school," she recalled. "It was a revelation to me. And it was even more of a revelation to discover that there were girls who actually did that automatically, week after week, paper after paper—without being nagged!"

Eileen always credited Barnard with giving her the mental discipline to succeed in her subsequent business career. "I feel very grateful to have been organized so wonderfully. Barnard made me work hard, and really taught me to enjoy learning."

Psychology, the subject in which she had signed up to major, turned out to be less gripping than Eileen expected. Yet she found that she loved the obscurities of constitutional law, along with history—and especially English. She wrote a well-received essay on Britain's World War I poets Siegfried Sassoon, Rupert Brooke, and Wilfred Owen, and sixty years later she could still recite the opening lines of John Masefield's "Sea Fever": "I must go down to the seas again, to the lonely sea and the sky." In the spirit of her father's patronage of the Art in Trades Club, she joined a design class and sketched out a modernistic bathroom in malachite, every surface bright green.

For her first year, Eileen stayed in a dormitory on campus, but she found it difficult to concentrate on her studies. She decided she would get more work done living at home, so she spent several semesters traveling in from Great Neck, where her commuting companion was a fellow Barnard freshman who lived along the Long Island Railroad line, at Douglaston.

"I remember that I met Jean Compo on my very first day at Barnard—on September 21, 1939. She asked me the way to the bookshop. So I walked her over, and we became fast friends. When we were both commuting on the LIRR we would arrange to meet up on the train and play bridge all the way into town, laying down the cards on top of a spread-out newspaper."

Jean Compo was a stunningly beautiful blonde with a pageboy hairstyle with straight-across bangs. From the start of her studies at Barnard she had been earning extra money as a spare-time young model for the recently created Harry Conover agency, so when she heard of Eileen's unhappy experience with Walter Thornton, she persuaded her friend to try her hand at modeling again. Conover, she assured Eileen, was different.

HARRY CONOVER WAS THE HOT NEW NAME IN NEW YORK MODELING at the end of the 1930s. Six feet tall, green-eyed, and wavy-haired, Conover had started as a model himself with the John Robert Powers agency, then defected in 1937 with his handsome flatmate and fellow Powers model, Gerald Rudolph "Jerry" Ford, Jr., the future Michigan congressman, vice president to Richard Nixon, and eventually U.S. president, who became co-owner of the agency for a few years. Like Walter Thornton, Conover liked to give his "Conover Cover Girls" exotic new identities, but in a slightly different style, devising coquettish nicknames to go with their otherwise routine surnames—

"Chili" Williams, "Jinx" Falkenburg, "Dulcet" Tone, and "Frosty" Webb.

When Jean Compo brought Eileen Otte to Conover's office at the start of her 1940 summer vacation, Conover could see she was no glamour-puss, but one of his skills was to pick out the "natural" or "authentic" face that advertisers sometimes preferred over stagier beauty. Eileen was a fresh-faced college girl, pert and eager, with an uplifted ski jump of a nose. As such, she filled a perfect short-term niche. Every summer *Mademoiselle* magazine ran a "college" issue to preview youthful fashions for the fall. Professional fashion models were remote and aspirational figures—fantasies, at the end of the day. College girls were a step closer to reality, and Eileen certainly looked like the girl next door. So Conover booked photo sessions with her for the advertising and editorial sections of *Mademoiselle*'s special issue.

It was unfortunate that Eileen's moment of glory, her sole appearance on an editorial page, was miscaptioned: she was labeled as "Helen Otte" on page 170 of the college issue for August 1940, which described her as "the brightest sophomore on her campus in Stroock's fleece-cloth reversible . . . $39.95, Lord & Taylor." But later that year she became a cover girl, featured on the outside of *Campus Classics for Knitters* for October 1940 with a dazzlingly wide smile that revealed an evenly balanced array of handsome teeth. As well as appearing on the cover, Eileen was depicted on the inside pages, parked cheerily on a stone doorstep in Heidi-style socks, holding a pair of ice skates.

"The skates were the reason why I got the job," she recalled. "I was the only person at the agency who owned a pair. I signed up with Conover again for the summer of 1941, and he got me still more work."

Once again Eileen featured in a range of college girl shots in the pages of *Mademoiselle*: she advertised a collection of dressy undergraduate outfits for Saks–34th Street, and also appeared in the hallowed pages of *Vogue*, advertising Enka rayon and also SporTimer dresses—"To See Them Is to Want Them!" The highlight of her modeling career was her appearance that September on the cover of *Lib-*

erty, the "Weekly for Everybody," which prefaced each of its articles with its famous "Reading Time" prediction—an estimate of the time that each article would take to read, down to the second. A diminutive Eileen gazed up admiringly at a huge, muscular Cornell Big Red football player, above the cover line "They Had Magic Then! A Short Story by Sinclair Lewis."

Looking back on her modeling career from her eminence as a successful agent, Eileen could not remember the details of her final college-era photo session as a mannequin, but she could recall one very important upshot: "Conover never paid me a penny for all the sessions that he booked for me." Might there be a niche in the world of modeling for an agency that actually treated its models decently?

Back on campus at the halfway stage of her college education, Eileen was tempted by her brief contact with the beauty culture to try an experiment in the power of attraction. "I had a bet with another girl that if I sat in the front row in class and did no work and showed my legs, I'd get an A. And if she sat in the back and kept her head down working, she'd get a C. I won the bet."

Barnard had not shaken Eileen out of her bumptiousness—it is doubtful any institution could have achieved that. "Eleanor Roosevelt came to visit the campus, and we were all required to attend her talk. She was dressed totally in black, with shoes that were so big that we were trying not to giggle. Then she started speaking in her strange voice, 'Girls and women of Barnard College . . .' and we all burst out laughing. I got the blame, and I got banned from going to the assemblies, which was fine by me. It meant I could go off to Tilson's drugstore and meet all the boys from Columbia."

Boys now loomed very large in the life of Eileen Otte. "The war started in December 1941, at the beginning of my third year, and from that point on I suppose you could say that I majored in men and minored in psychology."

CHAPTER 9

LE MEILLEUR MOMENT DE L'AMOUR

*Le meilleur moment de l'amour, c'est quand on monte
l'escalier.*
(The best moment of love is when you are going up the
staircase.)

—*Georges Clemenceau, French politician and
World War I premier*

I REMEMBER COMING OUT OF THE CINEMA AT BARNARD ONE EVE-
ning in December 1941 to see the headline 'Japanese Bomb Pearl
Harbor.' From that moment, everything changed."

Eileen would recall being involved in war relief work from before the start of her time at Barnard: "I had read about the Japanese
invading China [in 1937], killing so many people, throwing the Chinese up in the air and catching them on their bayonets. So I went to
shake a box at Penn Station, where the train used to leave for Great
Neck. Then I went to Chinatown to give them the money. It was the
first time I ever tasted Chinese food." Columbia and Barnard had
been preparing for war for some time. In June 1940, Roosevelt announced a crash training program for young naval officers, and two
months later, the U.S. Naval Reserve Midshipmen's School opened
on Columbia's Morningside Heights campus. By the time hostilities
commenced, the university was turning out several thousand young
officers per year, and Eileen signed up as a volunteer with the Navy
League, offering cups of coffee and sandwiches to the young arrivals
on campus. "I remember doing a lot of washing up."

A man in uniform was the coveted date in 1941, a fact reflected in the fashion magazines. Eileen's particularly elegant advertisement for Enka rayon in the August 1941 edition of *Vogue* displayed her standing beside a handsome young naval ensign in his blue dress uniform and white cap.

"It wasn't like nowadays, when girls and boys jump into bed together," Eileen remembered of her college flirtations. "I had a lot of romances with the young men, but most of them were very proper—just a kiss on the cheek. As the French like to say, 'Les meilleurs joies d'amour sont sur les escaliers.'"

In later life Eileen Ford would claim that she got engaged to no fewer than eleven young warriors, all of them naval officers, in the first two years after the United States entered the Second World War. She seemed to regard the encouragement of naval heroes as part of her contribution to the war effort—starting with Johnny Gifford, who was her date on the night of the attack on Pearl Harbor. Gifford signed up for the Marine Corps the next day, and became the first in Eileen's soccer team of wartime betrothals.

"I had all these fiancés, but I was not evil. It would have been different if they had not all been going off to war. It was an emotional thing. I wanted to make their lives just a bit sweeter. There was Hank Wheeler who was killed on the Murmansk run, escorting ships to Russia. Then there was Bert Manro, who was killed in Panama with another fiancé. Bert was stationed for much of the war in the naval air station in Norfolk, Virginia, where he met two other fiancés of mine. So they decided to invite me down, and I met all three of them at the station . . . When all the boys came home at the end of the war my poor mother had to deal with a lot of confused and perplexed young men."

Eileen *did*, in fact, finally make a commitment, in January 1943, when she went with Jean Compo to Charleston, South Carolina, to get some winter sunshine during their mid-January semester break. The two young women encountered daunting snow and ice—it was the coldest winter Charleston had known for many years—but Eileen rapidly located warmth in the shape of a handsome naval officer four years her senior, Ensign Charles Paul "Shep" Sheppard, who was about to sail on U.S. Patrol Craft 565 in pursuit of Nazi U-boats—and before he sailed, Eileen decided that she would do more than just add "Shep" to her list of fiancés. She would marry him.

At nearly six feet tall, Charles Sheppard boasted a dazzling smile, chiseled features, and a Robert Mitchum cleft chin. He hailed from the spa town of Sulphur Springs, Texas, to the northwest of Dallas, where he had starred as quarterback on the Sulphur Springs High football team. An Eagle Scout and an accomplished clarinetist, he had headed up his own band, Shep Sheppard and the Swingers, who made themselves a name in the Dallas area. After graduating from East Texas State University, he trained as a teacher and got his first job as band director at Kerens High School, south of Dallas, where he composed the school anthem, "All Hail to Kerens!"

Shep enlisted with the navy before Pearl Harbor, in October 1941, and was sent to the Midshipmen's School at Columbia. Yet that was not where he met Eileen. "We met in Charleston by chance," she recalled. "That is how things happened during the war. Back then everybody just sort of talked together."

To say the least, it was a whirlwind romance. "It was a matter of just twelve days or so," Eileen later confessed. "War, I think, turns people into creatures of impulse. You know there may not be another day."

Shep had already been at sea for six months, patrolling the perilous sea-lanes of the so-called Caribbean Frontier for Nazi U-boats, two hundred miles off the Florida coast. After training at the Submarine Chaser Training Center in Miami, he was assigned to duty with PC-565, a long, rakish 295-ton submarine chaser that was escorting convoys of merchant ships and oil tankers loaded with war supplies. When he met Eileen, PC-565 had put into Charleston for a refit on January 1 and was due to go out on patrol again soon.

The immediacy of the deadline pushed Charles and Eileen into each other's arms. They went to see the Reverend Albert Rhett Stuart, priest of St. Michael's, the beautiful eighteenth-century Episcopal church whose spire towered over Broad Street like a whitewashed St. Martin-in-the-Fields, and he agreed to marry the couple on February 1.

There was no time for parents to attend. Shep's mother, a Baptist, expressed relief that at least her son's new wife was not Catholic—the pope, she had no doubt, was an agent of the devil. As for Eileen's parents, Loretta, up in Great Neck, made clear she was not happy, but somehow a wedding announcement found its way into the classified columns of the *Brooklyn Daily Eagle*—well, two announcements, because the first one got the bride's name wrong, describing Eileen as "Cecile Otte." Then Ensign and Mrs. Charles Sheppard enjoyed a brief three-week honeymoon in Charleston, before PC-565 slipped anchor and headed back to pursue the U-boats in the sea-lanes of the Caribbean Frontier.

THE NEWLY MARRIED MRS. EILEEN SHEPPARD HAD MUCH TO REFLECT on in the course of her sixteen-hour train journey north to New York at the end of February 1943, and by the time she got home to Great Neck, she realized that she had made a terrible mistake. She sat down and wrote to her new husband at once. "I told him immediately," she recalled in 2013, "that I wanted to end the marriage."

Eileen had jumped in on impulse, and now she jumped out just as quickly. Shep was handsome and charming, no doubt—"a very, very decent man," was her verdict sixty years later—but as she now looked beyond the romance of a dashing young naval officer who was off to war, Eileen feared she had signed up for a lifetime in the kitchen as a teacher's wife in Texas.

At the age of twenty, Eileen Otte was remarkable for not having articulated a single defined ambition for herself. Her short-term collection of officer fiancés reflected how little she had contemplated what she wanted to do in the long term with her life. Still, she knew enough to know that her future did not lie in Kerens, Texas, smiling in the audience of the local high school band.

Charles Sheppard accepted his wife's decision like a gentleman—and as things turned out, he did not end up in Kerens, Texas, either. After brave and distinguished wartime service that saw PC-565 sink a U-boat in the Caribbean sea-lanes and participate in D-day action off the Normandy coast, where he was wounded and won his Purple Heart, Charles "Shep" Sheppard stayed in the navy and enjoyed a high-level career that took him to senior jobs in London with NATO and then to Washington, DC. He married again and had a family. His children knew nothing of his first marriage until after his death in 2000, when they were going through his "sock drawer" and discovered a photograph of a happy young couple getting married in Charleston, along with an annulment document and a set of yellowing newspaper clippings charting the progress of his wartime sweetheart, who herself went on to enjoy an exotic career.

Eileen also kept the marriage a secret. In March 1944 a friend took her along to the Nassau County Courthouse to apply for an annulment of the union on the grounds of "fraud and deceit," the only grounds for marital dissolution then available. Shep had been guilty of misrepresenting himself to her, Eileen maintained, and she broke down in tears in the courtroom under the strain of telling the lie. The judge took pity on her—America's divorce courts were overwhelmed in the early 1940s with the fallout from hasty wartime marriages—and from that point onward Eileen operated on the basis, as she told her daughters when they eventually discovered the story seventy years later, that the whole thing had been "a bad idea that never happened."

Eileen's on-the-fly marriage in charleston had academic repercussions. Her missed classes in January and February 1943 meant she did not have sufficient credits to graduate that spring, and she had to attend an extra session of the Columbia-Barnard summer school in July and August. Yet she made up her tally without difficulty. Barnard College records list Eileen Otte (not Sheppard) as a graduate in the Class of '43, and armed with her degree, she soon found herself war work.

The twenty-one-year-old's first paying job was close to home, at the New York City–La Guardia Flying Boat Base, where she worked in the offices of AEA, American Export Airlines, a freight transporter that had won government contracts to fly war supplies to U.S. bases in Europe and North Africa. Eileen was in charge of AEA's "rationing and provisioning priorities," securing gasoline coupons for the company, but she found herself fired after only a few months when she refused a request to secure extra fuel coupons for the private use of the owner's wife. The outraged young Eileen remonstrated with her boss, to no avail.

"Don't think that if you pull that thing down over your breasts you'll get to me," was her recollection of her boss's remark as he pointed to her tight sweater in the confrontation that followed.

So Eileen left AEA, but not before she met J. Hamilton Wagner, a handsome pilot with dark, wavy slicked-back hair who was working for Eastern Aircraft. Eastern was manufacturing FM-1 Wildcats and Grumman Avengers for the U.S. Navy in its factories on Long Island, and "Ham" was its test pilot.

"Ham was older than me," she remembered. "He had flown in Europe with the Armée de l'Air, and also in England, where he got wounded. My parents both liked him very much. He was so much more stylish and sophisticated than anyone I had met before." Eileen was a sucker for "style." "Ham had been to Europe," she recalled. "He knew about cocktails and all sorts of things I'd never dreamt of. I had never had French food when I was twenty-one."

Early in 1944, Eileen went out to Eastern Aircraft's headquarters in Cleveland to spend time with Ham. The days of chaste kisses and cuddles were behind her. Eileen was a married woman, not yet legally separated from Shep, and approaching twenty-two years of age. Her relationship with J. Hamilton Wagner was a full-blown affair that went beyond the top of the stairs—and came to a rapid and tragic end in a cornfield in Ohio.

"That's where he died just a few weeks later, though I didn't know it at the time. I wasn't registered as his next of kin, so the news took some time to reach me. Ham was working on a plane that was highly experimental. Everything was very secretive. I got a letter from him saying, 'It's very *Buck Rogers*. Now, if only it can fly.' And then he got killed. The plane dug a hole in the ground, I was told, that was very, very deep.

"Ham was only a very short time in my life, and I don't know whether I would have lasted in marriage with him, but I was quite desolate. I was twenty-one when I met him, and just twenty-two years old when he died. I'd known a succession of brave men, and I swear to you, I loved them all. All of them were going into the services, and if you weren't alive in the war, it's hard to describe the feelings that caused."

Ham died in April 1944. "But then, in July, I met Jerry. From April to July was a very long time that year."

CHAPTER 10

JERRY

What a day! Fortune smiled and came my way,
Bringing love I never thought I'd see. I'm so lucky to be me.

—Betty Comden and Adolph Green,
"Lucky to Be Me," from On the Town, 1944

ENSIGNS GERARD "JERRY" FORD AND CHARLES "SHEP" SHEPPARD were handsome young naval officers who never met, but who had much in common. Both were noted for the easygoing charm traditionally displayed by gentlemen from the South—Jerry was from New Orleans and Shep from Sulphur Springs, Texas—and both had been stars on their high school football teams; most important, in the patriotic and romantic gaze of Eileen Otte, both were wearing white caps and naval uniforms in the crisis years of World War II and were heading off to battle on the high seas.

At six foot two in his stockinged feet, Jerry Ford held a clear advantage over Eileen Otte's first husband, and his football record revealed him to be the more outstanding player. Charles Sheppard may have been the starting quarterback on his Sulphur Springs High School team, but Jerry Ford had won a football scholarship to join the Fighting Irish of Notre Dame, where he played defensive end to the great Johnny Lujack, his South Bend roommate for a year. One of Jerry Ford's specialties was the "end-around play," where, playing right end, he would take the ball surreptitiously and then run speedily left, wrong-footing his opponents, who were still running in the opposite direction. His end-around exploits earned him a letter from the Los Angeles Rams sounding out his interest in turning pro.

Big Jerry Ford turned Eileen weak in the knees when she first laid eyes on him inside the Gold Rail, a student hangout on the west side of Broadway known for its burgers and beer. "When Jerry stood up in his uniform," she recalled, "he was so handsome I almost fainted." She had gone there in the middle of July 1944 to meet Great Neck friend Dorothy Ann Riley, who had lived in New Orleans and who happened to have attended the same Jesuit high school as Jerry.

There was a Navy League dance coming up in a few nights, and Eileen got to work immediately. She persuaded Dorothy Ann to cold-call Jerry and invite him to the dance, with a rendezvous beforehand at Tilson's Drug Store. Also in attendance was another Great Neck friend, Hank Green, invited along ostensibly to serve as Eileen's partner.

"Dorothy Ann was supposed to go to the dance with Jerry Ford," Eileen later related, "and I was supposed to go with Hank Green. But guess who walked out of Tilson's Drugstore with Jerry?"

When it came to end-around plays, Jerry Ford had clearly met his match. "I was a baby-snatcher," Eileen later admitted with one of her gleeful smiles. "Jerry was only nineteen years old when we met. I was twenty-two. If I hadn't snagged Jerry quickly, I have no doubt at all that he would have been snapped up by someone else."

A FADED BLACK-AND-WHITE PHOTOGRAPH OF 1933 SHOWS JERRY Ford and his family gathered in their living room in the Holy Name of Mary Parish in the Algiers section of New Orleans, five sons and a daughter proudly displayed around their prolifically Catholic parents, Ermine ("Erm") and William ("Bill") Ford, the New Orleans general freight agent for the Chicago, Rock Island, and Pacific Railroad, the famous "Rock Island Line" that served the central Mississippi states from the Great Lakes down to the Gulf of Mexico. All the Ford boys are strikingly photogenic, with their direct gazes and clean-shaven, firm jaws—all of the five would volunteer for naval service when they came of age, four of them in the Marine Corps. Yet, in the photo, it is the eight-year-old Jerry, the second to youngest, who seems to radiate some extra presence as he weighs up the world with a quizzical glance, already style-conscious in his dramatically V-patterned tie and Prince of Wales checkered socks.

"Jerry dressed with great style all his life," Eileen would fondly recall. "He loved his Huntsman suits from Savile Row, he wore a bright blue cornflower in his buttonhole, and when he put on his tennis whites, he always looked like a gladiator to me. A Greek god!"

Jerry must have acquired some of his style from his father, Bill, a shrewd and loquacious Irishman who enjoyed a rare perk in the Depression years: an entertainment allowance of three hundred dollars per month (twelve hundred dollars today) to help persuade clients to book their freight consignments on the Rock Island Line.

"We knew times were hard in the rest of the world," remembers Jerry's younger brother Allen. "People would come to the back door of our home almost every day begging for a sandwich just to stay alive. But Father had a good job and he worked hard to make sure we all had a good life. Even in the middle of the Depression we had long holidays every summer in Biloxi, Mississippi, where we had maids to cook our meals—and free railroad tickets wherever we wanted."

Jerry Ford used to say he never realized he was poor until he met Eileen and got to know the Otte family of Great Neck.

THE FIRST MEETING WENT WELL, APPARENTLY—WHO COULD NOT like the handsome and soft-spoken young gentleman from St. Mary's Parish, New Orleans? Big Jerry Ford would, in due course, sweep through a fifty-year career in the bitchy world of fashion without racking up a significant black mark or word of criticism.

"Jerry was a *haimish* guy—always funny, wry and understated," recalled author Michael Gross, who interviewed him several times for his history of the fashion modeling business, *Model*. "You could rely on Jerry to be relaxed—the very type of guy you'd like to find yourself sitting next to in a bar."

Relaxation and understatement were not resources in Eileen's portfolio. Her impulsiveness injected heat into any situation—and so it proved in her courting of Jerry Ford. Eighteen months after she rushed into marriage with Ensign Charles Sheppard, Eileen Otte embarked on the same hasty course with Ensign Ford—though her mother, Loretta, who had run away with the bigamist James Forsythe at the age of sixteen, could scarcely complain about her daughter's penchant for elopement. "When you think about elopement," reflected Eileen many years later, "I guess you could say it was something of a tradition in the family."

Jerry Ford's midshipman training at Columbia lasted just three months, after which he was assigned as surface warfare officer on a command ship in the Pacific, and he set off early in November 1944 to report for duty in San Francisco. After a couple of days, Eileen decided to follow him, borrowing money from friends to buy a train ticket to San Francisco via Chicago.

"I left a note for my parents," she later recalled, "but I didn't agonize for a long time before I did it—in wartime you know there may never be another day."

"Dear Mother & Dad," she wrote to her parents, "I know that you think I'm wrong in wanting to marry Jerry . . . [but] I've argued the whole thing out with myself and I can't convince myself that you're right. I love him and there doesn't seem to be much I can do about it, except marry him—so I've gone to do just that."

It was a letter worthy of the daughter that Nat and Loretta had raised—perfectly polite on the surface, and utterly headstrong underneath. Eileen had "argued the whole thing out" with herself, so what more could be left to say? The Ottes' twenty-two-year-old daughter was as helplessly impulsive as she had been less than two years earlier when she married "Shep," and also so brave—or foolhardy—that she shrugged that debacle aside. Not for the first time, the domineering romantic in Eileen was staking all her chips on the emotional imperative of *love*.

"Please don't be too hurt," she concluded. "I know I'm right—and I'll call you from the coast—I love you both so much, but I just want to marry him so much."

The moment Nat Otte read his daughter's note, he was on the phone to Chicago, hiring detectives to intercept Eileen on the platform where, he guessed, she would have to change trains in Chicago. Yet nineteen hours on a train from New York was long enough for the runaway bride to have palled up with a couple of young ensigns who were also heading west. So Eileen was one of a laughing party of three when she crossed the platform in Chicago, not the single young woman for whom the detectives were searching.

On the second stage of her journey west, Eileen also made friends with a female buyer for a San Francisco department store, who, hearing the young woman's romantic tale, made her a wedding present of a pair of silk stockings. Eileen wore them to City Hall, San Francisco, on Monday, November 20, 1944, along with a frayed gabardine jacket, a gray flannel skirt, and a blouse missing some buttons.

"Jerry didn't know he wanted to get married until he was married," Eileen would later explain. "I followed him across the country, and the poor guy had no choice."

Both bride and groom were composed enough for some judicious deceit on their wedding certificate. Only twenty years old, Jerry falsely declared his age as twenty-two—presumably he did not want to appear baby-snatched by his new wife. The bride, when asked to specify "the number of this marriage," wrote down "1st."

This was technically correct, since her marriage to Shep had been annulled—as if it had never been. But it was not the truth, and Eileen knew it. Close inspection of the San Francisco marriage certificate suggests that she had started writing "2," but changed her mind, finally writing the numeral "1" more heavily on top of it.

"And so," as Eileen liked to sum up the whole escapade, "with his back to the Pacific, he married me."

When someone once asked Jerry Ford how he could have committed to marriage on the basis of knowing his partner for little more than two months, he answered with a question: "Did you ever try saying no to Eileen?"

CHAPTER 11

STYLIST

I am simply thunderstruck
At this change in my luck.

—Betty Comden and Adolph Green,
"Lucky to Be Me," from On the Town, 1944

WITH THE WAR AT ITS HEIGHT IN NOVEMBER 1944, IT WAS
hardly surprising that Jerry Ford should declare his profession as "Naval Officer" on his marriage certificate in San Francisco. His new spouse, however, set down an occupation that was
more unusual in time of war, "Stylist," and listed her employer as a
"commercial photographer." Earlier that summer, at the same time
the young couple first met, Eileen Otte had embarked on the career
path that would lead to her creation with Jerry of the Ford Modeling
Agency.

It had started not far from her Long Island home. Lying on a
towel on Jones Beach, Eileen was engaged in one of her favorite activities: perfecting her tan. Until her mid-forties, her sunbathing
technique involved placing a reflective foil ruffle around her face, as
if she were an animal who had just been to the vet, and slathering
her face with oil.

"I had just finished a hot dog, when this charming photographer
came up to me. He said he was called Elliot Clarke and that he was
shooting a magazine feature on the history of bathing costumes.
Would I care to pose, he asked me, in a historic bathing costume?"

Just one? Eileen jumped up and put one hand to her ear and the other to her hip to present herself as the perfect 1910 "bloomer girl." Then she put on a black-and-white spotted "dressmaker suit" from 1922 and waded out into the surf to show what a bathing belle looked like in the year of her birth. With her animated features and wide, toothy smile, Eileen made herself the star of the quirky color feature that Elliot Clarke put together on Jones Beach that day, completing her poses in a modern (1944) two-piece swimsuit—"the flowering of a half century of progress"—with children and other bathers gathered around a picnic basket in a family tableau worthy of Norman Rockwell.

The photographs appeared early in August 1944, in the *Saturday Evening Post*, under the headline "Yes, My Daring Daughter." They hardly prompted a flood of phone calls from modeling agencies. In fact, the session with Clarke would be the last one in Eileen's relatively modest career in front of the camera. Yet it did prove a crucial step in her progress on the other side of the lens.

"Elliot was looking for a secretary/personal assistant," she remembered, "someone to get in early every day and open up the office. He asked me if I could do shorthand, type, and take care of his bookkeeping, and I told him yes to all three. I was lying of course."

Eileen's typing was rudimentary. She had had all her term papers at Barnard typed up for her by stenographers in her father's office, and it was difficult to overstate her incompetence at math: "When it came to calculating the sales tax on the invoices, I could never work out how to add on the one per cent."

Yet Elliot Clarke, a courtly character who was seldom seen without a bow tie, recognized the potential in his energetic young assistant. At the time of their meeting, he had just won a major commission to help launch "a new kind of *young* magazine." Walter Annenberg, publisher of the moneymaking *Daily Racing Form*, and of the *Philadelphia Inquirer*, had noted the recent coining of the new word *teenager*, and had decided to take one of his show business titles, *Stardom*, and rebrand it to capture the advertising revenue being aimed at this new demographic: "All the clothes shown," promised the mission statement " . . . will be found in Teen Departments of the best stores in the country." Elliot Clarke got the commission to design the cover, so Eileen Otte found herself on the launch team of America's first-ever teenage magazine, *Seventeen*.

The beach recruit's role was minor—to create the large wooden numerals, 1 and 7, that would be held up on the jacket by the model selected and photographed by Elliot Clarke. Yet it was Eileen's idea to decorate the numerals with brightly colored Alpine flowers—Shirley Temple had been a juvenile hit as Heidi, after all. So the new studio assistant could claim some small role in the instant success of *Seventeen*, which sold out its first printing of four hundred thousand and was soon handling more advertising than any other women's service magazine.

The new young stylist's next bright idea was not so well appreciated by her employer, however. When Eileen set off for Chicago and San Francisco in November 1944, she failed to warn Elliot Clarke of her elopement plans—and also forgot that she still had the master key to his studio in her pocket. So by the time Eileen noted down her profession in San Francisco's City Hall on November 20, 1944, she was, technically, an ex-stylist.

LEFT ON HER OWN IN SAN FRANCISCO IN NOVEMBER 1944, FOLLOW-ing the departure of her new husband to the Pacific, Eileen Otte Ford was not afflicted by second thoughts. She felt no "Shep" moment of doubt about the wisdom of her hurried marriage—quite the contrary.

"I was lonely, of course," she remembered. "I wept when I said good-bye to Jerry. But I had never felt so right being with anyone. I loved Jerry Ford then with all my heart—and I loved him for the rest of our life together."

The dive-in-headfirst Eileen Ford had found the solid and steady partner who completed her. For all the drama and the gaiety, there had been something desperate in the single young woman who went bouncing from fiancé to fiancé. Jerry Ford brought gravity to her dilemma—"bottom." Jerry did not so much cancel out his wife's impulsiveness as harness it for the benefit of the wild and challenging life path that they would carve out together.

Eileen decided to start off her married life by visiting the family of her new husband in Dallas. The Rock Island Line had recently transferred William Ford to Texas.

"She impressed us," remembers Jerry's younger brother, Allen, "as a thoroughly independent and capable young lady." Allen was the only Ford boy still at home. His elder brother Richard had been killed the previous year in the bloody advance by the marines across Bougainville Island, and his other brothers, Ed, Lacy, and Jerry, were all in the Pacific—Jerry in the navy, Ed and Lacy in the Marine Corps. Allen was taking extra courses so he could graduate early from high school and join his brothers.

While she was in Dallas, Eileen decided she would also visit Ham's family—and got a nasty surprise. It turned out that "Ham" had a wife, Esther, at the time of his death, by whom he had a son, John Hamilton Wagner, Jr.—and that Esther was his second wife.

"Ham" was a bounder, and Eileen had had a lucky escape. Weighing up the relative merits of Shep, Ham, and Jerry, it had clearly been a case of third Texan lucky.

EILEEN FINALLY GOT HOME TO NEW YORK IN THE SPRING OF 1945, four months after her elopement, to be reconciled with her mother and father. "I don't know whether we had ever been actually *un*conciled," she recalled. "I'd spoken to my parents over the phone from time to time while I was away, but long distance was considered very expensive in those days—a real extravagance. When you were away, you were away."

If Mrs. Ford missed her husband, she did not let it distract her. Eileen's priority was to get back to work, and the gentlemanly Elliot Clarke proved willing to forgive and forget. He provided his runaway assistant with a reference that helped Eileen secure a job with Becker Studios, the largest commercial photography studio in America.

William Becker had started his career as a commercial artist producing fashion illustrations for the Sears Roebuck catalogue, but he had shifted nimbly with the advent of color photography and improved printing techniques. Early in the 1940s, the Becker Art Studio became Becker Photographic Studios, and after consulting with the U.S. Department of Agriculture, Becker located his main photographic operations in Tucson, Arizona, where the Weather Bureau told him he could count on 3,800 annual hours of sun. Every year, Becker would spend two sessions of ten or twelve weeks in Tucson, flying in teams of models, most of whom he photographed himself, in grueling eight-hour sessions on a huge, white circular stage that was revolved throughout the course of the day to keep it facing the sun.

"It was hard work for long hours at a time," remembered Lorraine Davies Knopf, one of the models flown out by Becker to stay in the nearby Pioneer Hotel. "We did nonstop shooting for catalogues, like a factory production line. Color film was still very slow, so we'd have to hold every pose for what seemed to be minutes, standing in winter suits and heavy coats in the blazing sun. If any model fainted—and some of us did—we'd get a whiff of ammonia, a cold cloth on the head, and get straight back to work."

Eileen Ford started work in the Manhattan headquarters of this hard-driving operation, on the top three floors of a building at 275 Seventh Avenue, in the heart of New York's Fur District. She would thread her way to work through the racks of minks, sables, and other garments being shuttled between the workshops in the neighboring lofts, where women toiled over sewing machines in sweatshop conditions that were not so different from those that prevailed at the time of the Triangle Shirtwaist fire in 1911.

Eileen's job was to coordinate, number, pack, and ship the clothes that would be photographed at the Tucson studio, and also to book the models to be flown out to Arizona. This was her first experience of serious negotiation with Powers, Conover, and Thornton, the principal agencies of the day, trying to beat down asking prices that had risen as high as twenty-five to thirty-five dollars per hour in America's wartime consumer boom. Becker Studios was famous for its financial corner cutting, negotiating bulk prices for group shipments from a single agency that would then supply its models in teams of ten or twelve at a discount.

Yet before she could get seriously engaged in the business of booking, Eileen fell afoul of Becker's penny-pinching ways. She had made some progress with her typing—but not enough to avoid mistakes; she was forever rubbing out her errors. Having bought herself a twenty-five-cent eraser one lunchtime, she went to see William Becker's secretary, Blanche, and asked to be reimbursed.

"Whadaya mean you spent our money?" came the angry response. "You pay for that eraser yourself!" Just twenty-three, and a long way from her husband's steadying calm, Eileen responded with equal aggression. She sarcastically drew a quarter from her purse, laid it on the desk in front of Blanche, and walked out of Becker Studios for good. "Blanche made Judge Judy sound like a lady," Eileen later recalled. "Besides, it's hard for people now to realize how easy it was to get work in those days."

Scarcely missing a beat, Eileen found herself a job in the advertising department of America's oldest department store, Arnold Constable, on Fifth Avenue, directly across the street from the New York Public Library on Fortieth Street. Reporting to Isaac Liberman, the owner of Arnold Constable, Eileen continued the apprenticeship she had begun with Elliot Clarke in the practicalities of the fashion business. She was a stylist again—and, more than that, working on the production of some of America's very first "story" catalogues.

"They were pages—whole sections in the catalogue—that had a

running theme with an editorial feel," she recalled. "And it was at Arnold Constable that I learned about accessorizing: what goes with what when you're styling photographs and presenting clothes."

Most of all, the young Mrs. Ford now dived deeper into the modeling business. "It was my job to hire all the models for Constable's advertising campaign and catalogues. So I was on the telephone a lot. I got to know how all the different agencies worked, and I made good friends with a lot of the models. I learned a big lesson when Mr. Isaac Liberman saw what I was paying for some models per hour. He was not happy, and he let me know it. So we had to work that much quicker in the photo studio."

Negotiating with photographers and modeling agencies, arranging photo shoots, and devising the marketing campaigns for one of the city's most eminent department stores, Eileen rapidly made a name for herself as she bustled around the high-pressure world of New York City's fashion business. Lively, self-confident, and efficient, the young Mrs. Ford was clearly a rising talent, and it was not long before the headhunters came calling.

"I made a terrible mistake. I let a recruitment agency, a lady called Betty Corwin, talk me into leaving Arnold Constable. It was partly the money, but also the idea that, in fashion terms, Arnold Constable was getting a bit homely and had become out of date."

In commercial terms, Eileen's new billet could scarcely have been more cutting edge—she joined the staff of Tobé (pronounced "Toe-bay"), whose newsletter was the bible of the fashion industry. Founded in 1927 by Miss Tobé Coller Davis, author of "Tobe Says" (without the accent), a nationally syndicated newspaper column, the Tobé report briefed the retail trade on fashion trends, helping to advise stores on their buying decisions. Eileen's job sounded ideal: to visit salons and workshops to sniff out the latest styles and designs. Yet she hated it.

"I was supposed to do *facts*," she recalled. "How many buttons and what colors they were. What was the weight of the material? But the facts were of no interest to me. I just wrote down, 'It's a gorgeous this or a gorgeous that.' Why should I describe the details when I knew how to persuade people to buy the whole thing?"

When Jerry Ford finally got home from the war in June 1946, Eileen joyfully handed in her notice to Tobé. "It was just as well you quit when you did," remarked her friend Carol Phillips, who had been commuting into Manhattan with Eileen to do work of her own in the fashion business. "They were going to fire you next week."

CHAPTER 12

AGENCY

What makes a great model is her need—her desire. And it's exciting to photograph desire.

—*Bert Stern, photographer*

A T FIVE FEET, TEN INCHES TALL IN HER SILK-STOCKINGED FEET, Natálie Nickerson had a pair of legs whose length and slenderness were scarcely believable—the undercarriage of a grasshopper. Successful fashion models, it would be observed in the 2002 movie *Men in Black II*, do not look quite like ordinary human beings: the impossible perfection of their good looks betrays the fact that they are actually extraterrestrials.

As peace returned to America in 1945, Natálie Nickerson stepped out at the head of a postwar parade of relaxed and modern fashion models who were different from their predecessors. They made you wonder, as you gazed upon their long and lanky frames, whether they were not magically floating an inch or so above the ground.

Instead of going to college, Natálie Nickerson decided to join the war effort in Phoenix, Arizona, where she went to work as a drill press operator in the local aircraft assembly plant, helping to build B-17 "Flying Fortress" bombers. Her specialty was the construction of altimeters, and she came up with an idea for improving the production process, which the company adopted. "But my supervisor took the credit for what I had suggested," she later recalled, "and he was a man. I decided there were better places to work than an assembly plant."

Natálie had some previous experience modeling, so she decided to splash her savings on a flight to New York—her DC-3 made seven stops as it hopped across the country—and she settled, aged twenty-two in 1945, into a humble church hostel in Lower Manhattan. By the time she made friends with Eileen Ford, who first hired her to pose for the Arnold Constable catalogue in 1945, she was doing well enough to have moved uptown to the fashionable resort for debutantes, the Barbizon Hotel for Women.

"I used to sleep on a camp bed sometimes in Natálie's room," Eileen later remembered. "I'd stay with her if I could not get back to Great Neck at night, or had an early morning start next day in Manhattan. She was a sweet, sweet woman. We spent a lot of time talking."

By 1945, Natálie had her own personal stationery, stylishly engraved without any capital letters: "natálie, the barbizon, 140 east 63rd street, new york 21." The accent on the second *a* of her given name was her cue to people to place the stress on the second syllable. That, she said, was how her mother had always pronounced it: Nat-*ah*-lie.

The model's lean and spare "postwar" look attracted the fashion business's top photographers. In the fall of 1945, Natálie posed for George Hoyningen-Huene wearing a striking backless dress by Claire McCardell, America's new sportswear queen, in *Harper's Bazaar*. A few months later, in January 1946, she was on the cover of *Vogue*, photographed by John Rawlings in his glass-topped penthouse at East Fifty-Seventh Street. Then, in the fall of 1946, she started work with Richard Avedon, the brilliant young protégé of Alexey Brodovitch, the art director of *Harper's Bazaar*, with his relentless quest for the novel. Avedon provided "novel" with his iconic first cover for *Bazaar*: a cool Natálie, athletically modern in shorts and a T-shirt, her long, bare legs akimbo, with a shirtless young male model lying on the floor behind her, his back to the camera, intended to resemble the young photographer. Brodovitch had worked with Jean Cocteau,

Chagall, and Man Ray, and Avedon's touch of surrealism seemed to owe something to them. Was it possible that fashion photography, a commercial mechanism for selling frocks, might one day be considered an art form?

By now Natálie was earning forty dollars an hour—making her, at that date, the highest-paid model in Manhattan, and hence the world, since no other country was paying models rates to match those in America. After a false start with a short-lived photographers' cooperative, the Society of Models Placement Bureau, she had moved to John Robert Powers, the doyen of model agents, still in business after nearly a quarter of a century and still capable of securing big bookings—though not as good at paying out on them. Powers owed Natálie thousands of dollars, but when she went in person to protest, the great man did not seem to know the name of his most successful model. "His secretary whispered it into his ear," Natálie later recalled to Michael Gross. "And that started things going in my brain."

Natálie decided she would take over her own billing, copying the voucher system that was already being used by models in California and the Midwest. She printed up her own numbered accounts book—it looked like a large checkbook, with carbon copies—from which she would write out a voucher that detailed her hours and her fee at the end of each session. She would then get the photographer to sign this mini-contract with the client, and leave it as her invoice for the job. When the money came in, she would forward the 10 percent agency commission to Powers.

Vouchers became the protocol by which models were paid for the rest of the century, but as Natálie put it to Eileen in their late-night Barbizon conversations, this protocol was back to front. "Models were treated as if they worked for the agencies," Natálie later recalled, "instead of the agencies working for them. There was too much sink-or-swim. I knew, because I was out there. Models need to know exactly where and when they were supposed to be for each particular booking, and what they're supposed to bring with them, and the big agencies were not efficient in making sure their girls knew even such simple things. There was no career planning, no special training or care, no help with hair and makeup—no real system at all."

So the two women decided to work out a system of their own. Eileen would act as secretary and booker to Natálie and to another model, Inga Lindgren, a Swedish beauty with high-arching eyebrows and meticulously manicured nails. Each model would pay Eileen thirty-five dollars per month for her secretarial assistance and for making phone bookings, while Natálie would act as a discreet publicist and drummer-up of business—a *rabatteuse*, to use the feminine form of the French term for a beater in the shooting of game birds— quietly recommending the energy and efficiency of Eileen's services to other models. "I realized," Natálie later explained, "that for any operation to be successful, they had to have at least one top girl [backing it]. And I was the model of the moment."

Natálie beat the bushes well. Eileen started working for her and Lindgren in September 1946, and by March of the following year, Natálie's word of mouth and Eileen's proven efficiency had attracted the signing of seven more successful models—high-flying women who were all fed up with how men were handling their business. Each newcomer paid Eileen a further $65 for her services, taking her monthly income to about $600—some $7,000 per year.

Yet Eileen did not put all this money in her own pocket. She split the extra revenue she received fifty-fifty with Natálie, since it soon became clear that the two women were partners in a flourishing commercial enterprise that could be described only as a modeling agency.

MR. AND MRS. JERRY FORD WERE IN SORE NEED OF MONEY AS THEY settled down to married life together, since the man of the family had no immediate job prospects. Jerry Ford had completed only two years at Notre Dame when he volunteered for the navy, so he arrived home in the summer of 1946 with two years ahead of him to finish his degree. In September 1946 he enrolled in evening classes at Columbia, in economics and business studies, while spending his days working in the Fifth Avenue Protective Association offices of his father-in-law, Nat Otte. By that September, however, it had become even more important for the young couple to stiffen up their economic security since Eileen discovered she was pregnant. As the Fords' firstborn daughter, Jamie (Margaret Jamison Ford) liked to say with only slight exaggeration, "I was born nine months to the day after my father returned from the war."

In the short term, Nat Otte and Loretta were on hand to provide. The newlyweds started their married life as guests of Eileen's parents in the family home on Hilltop Drive, but then found themselves being moved into Manhattan. Nat and Loretta had decided to wind up their life in the suburbs. With the conclusion of the war, the Ottes sold the family house in Great Neck and bought a retirement home in Florida and a little complex of buildings (part homes, part offices) in Lower Manhattan, at 142 Lexington Avenue and Nineteenth Street. There were two houses and a third house in back, where Nat built a bar to which he could invite his friends from out of town.

"God!" Eileen recalled one of their friends saying years later. "I used to go to some marvelous parties at your father's house!"

In one room inside this Otte family mini-campus, in the fall of 1946, Eileen set up her card table, address book, and telephone. "I wasn't so much of a booker," she later recalled. "I didn't need to be. The work just came in. The price was set already, and I just had to work out how many hours and the other details like time and place. So I was like their secretary."

Eileen was a secretary with a difference, however. Her work with Elliot Clarke, Becker Studios, and Arnold Constable meant she knew or could find out exactly what her girls needed to take with them—models in the 1940s were expected to do their own hair and makeup, carrying their hairpieces and curlers around with them in large circular hat boxes.

Also, Eileen had a different attitude. "The thing about Eileen," recalled Joan Pedersen, one of the earliest models to join her, "was that there was never any doubt that she *cared*. It was as if each booking she made for you was the most important in her life to date—so you felt that you should treat it that way too."

Eileen might have been working out of her family home, but she dressed up smartly every morning as if she were going to work in an office, even though she and Jerry had just twenty-five dollars in the bank. She bought herself a green maternity suit and top—maternity suits for office wear were a postwar innovation.

It had been Eileen's optimistic intention to carry on working without interruption right up to and through the arrival of her new baby in the maternity unit of St. Clare's Hospital, run by the Franciscan Sisters of Allegany. Yet she underestimated both the demands of childbirth and the capacity of the hospital switchboard. "I had so many calls that I tied up all the operators," she remembered. "After five days the sisters asked me to leave."

Cue the charming husband.

"Just before I went into the hospital, I had got Inga her first job with Irving Penn. We were all so excited because Penn was the rising talent, like Avedon. But the moment Inga arrived at his studio, Penn ordered her to take off, of all things, her beautiful nail polish! 'I don't like nail polish,' he said. Then he told her to lie down in a pile of sand in a circle with eleven other models in swimsuits, as if they were numbers around the dial of a huge clock—all facedown, with their faces into the sand. Inga was furious. She called the house howling with rage—and it was Jerry who picked up the phone."

Jerry Ford had found his job for life. With the arrival of firstborn daughter Jamie Ford on March 17, 1947—eight days before her mother's twenty-fifth birthday on March 25—Jerry stepped in to help his wife with the day-to-day problems of running her modeling agency, and he never stepped out. Jerry matched Eileen for efficiency and commitment, and he managed it all with a softer, less abrasive touch. "He would play good cop to her bad cop," said Michael Gross, chronicler of the American model business. "They made an incredible team. Eileen found herself a husband smart enough to revolutionize the way the business was done—and Jerry Ford didn't just stop at one good idea."

In the long term, Jerry's revolutionary ideas ranged from mechanized office efficiency to the restructuring of the perfume and makeup advertising contracts that would pave the way for the emergence of multimillionaire supermodels. In the short term, he soothed the rage of Inga Lindgren, and took a crash course in how to make model bookings and ensure that models' vouchers got paid.

At the end of March 1947, Eileen Ford had just turned twenty-five. Her husband was still twenty-two.

CHAPTER 13

NEW LOOK

We started when Dior started.

—*Eileen Ford, recalling 1947 in 2010*

NINETEEN FORTY-SEVEN WAS A YEAR OF FRESH BEGINNINGS. ON February 12, five weeks before Jerry Ford picked up the phone to join his wife in making bookings for her model clients, Christian Dior stunned the fashion world with the extravagance of his debut Paris collection: a parade of accentuated bosoms and sharply cinched-in waists above luxuriously full skirts. Wartime austerity was banished, and femininity was back. Women could be women again.

"It's such a new look!" exclaimed Carmel Snow, the editor in chief of *Harper's Bazaar*—and thus a fashion legend was born.

In fact, Dior's "New Look" was not new at all. His rivals Balmain and Balenciaga had both been offering long, wide skirts with petticoats back in 1939, while Dior had confided to his backer, cotton magnate Marcel Boussac, that his aim had been nostalgic—to recreate the lush, flounced skirts that he remembered his mother wearing in the years before the First World War.

The more serious problem was that while the New Look was marvelous on fashion models, it was a disaster on any real-life woman whose height was less than five feet seven: you needed those additional, extraterrestrial inches below the knee to avoid looking like a dwarf. In Britain, Norman Hartnell rapidly adopted Paris's long-skirted look for the princesses Elizabeth and Margaret Rose and condemned the petite royal ladies (five foot three and five foot four, respectively) to a decade of dumpiness—not to mention extreme personal discomfort. The New Look depended on an ancient and tyrannical substructure of a tight, whalebone girdle with a turreted bra and suspender belt, which did wonders for male fantasies but nothing for the ease of the lady who had to endure the apparatus. Christian Dior did not so much clothe his ladies, sneered his rival Coco Chanel, as upholster them—"What are you going to do with a coat that takes up an entire suitcase?"

Paris's New Look was designed by men. The true "New Look" of 1947 was designed by women—and by working American career women at that. Claire McCardell learned her craft by deconstructing Vionnet end-of-season, bias-cut samples in Paris, then returned to New York to shun French influences in search of the informal, affordable, and "democratic" styles that she saw as the essence of a truly "American" look. Working for Hattie Carnegie, but mainly for Townley Frocks, she used American fabrics such as cotton, denim, and seersucker, and modern synthetics such as rayon, to develop clean, loose lines of "sportswear" or "casual wear" that active American women could comfortably wear to the office, on a car trip, at a backyard barbecue party, or on a golfing weekend—anywhere, in fact, you might expect to bump into Katharine Hepburn.

Among the major department stores, Lord and Taylor was especially patriotic in its promotion of homegrown designers such as McCardell, Tina Leser, Clare Potter, Lilly Daché, Vera Maxwell, and Tom Brigance (a rare man in the pack). The elegant mass-market sports and casual wear produced by American designers at the end of World War II generated sales across the country and in Canada. By the end of the 1940s these designers had made New York a major fashion center in its own right—a fertile seeding ground over the years for Bill Blass, Halston, Calvin Klein, Donna Karan, Anne Klein, Ralph Lauren/Polo, Nike, Gap, Levi's, Wrangler, Tommy Hilfiger, and the other American ready-to-wear giants who would elbow French fashions aside to dominate the world's shopping malls in the second half of the twentieth century.

Paris would retain its cachet—American fashion editors continued to make their biannual pilgrimages to report on the French spring and autumn collections, as they do to this day. But in July 1943, the Seventh Avenue publicist Eleanor Lambert had organized a grand "Press Week" in New York to promote fifty-three American designers, headed by Norman Norell, at a series of runway shows and parties in the Plaza Hotel, inviting newspapers' women's section editors from all over the country. The gathering proved an immense success and became a regular event under the title of New York "Fashion Week," a name and formula adopted several decades later by the fashion communities of London and Milan—and, in 1973, exactly thirty years later, by Paris.

NEW YORK'S FASHION PHOTOGRAPHERS DID THEIR BEST TO MATCH the novelty of the casual new American aesthetic. Just decommissioned from the U.S. Air Force, for whom he had helped process the pictures of the atom bomb exploding over Hiroshima, Bill Helburn signed up for the classes that Alexey Brodovitch, the *Harper's Bazaar* art director, held in Richard Avedon's studio one night per week. "Milton Greene, Art Kane, and [Irving] Penn along with Avedon," he recalled. "There they all were—the cutting-edge photographers of the time gathered in one place, all sitting round discussing their work with Brodovitch. It was like a seminar in the new photography."

The intense and lugubrious Brodovitch had painted backdrops in his youth for Diaghilev's Ballets Russes, but since moving to New York in 1930, he had become a fervent believer in the aesthetic of the New World. "Lillian Bassman dropped in from time to time," remembers Helburn. "All of us photographers were in competition in one sense, but we swapped ideas with Brodovitch. It was an unbelievable collection of talent, and Brodovitch picked out the best pictures for *Harper's Bazaar.* We each paid twenty dollars for one lesson a week—maybe eighty dollars for ten sessions. It was a lot of money in those days, but it was worth it."

The young women whom Eileen Ford and Natálie Nickerson recruited for their new agency invariably reflected the Brodovitch New World aesthetic. Nickerson herself, in her own physical form—tall, slender, blonde, athletic, and straight-backed—offered a pretty accurate bodily stereotype of what the term *Ford model* would come to stand for.

Carmen Dell'Orefice was still growing into that look when, skinny, flat-chested, and barely sixteen years old, she attracted the attention of *Vogue* photographer Erwin Blumenfeld. He saw the potential in the teenager's huge almond-shaped eyes and made them the focus of his cover for the October 1947 issue. *Vogue's* youngest-ever cover girl, Dell'Orefice stares straight into his lens, wary yet self-possessed.

Before the cover appeared, the photographer took his model around to meet Eileen Ford. "This young lady is going to be a star," he announced. "Take my word, the camera loves her."

"If you say so, Blumenfeld," replied Eileen, not totally convinced by the shy bag of bones in front of her, but happy to poach another talent from John Robert Powers, with whom *Vogue* had previously placed the girl.

"I had been earning seven-fifty per hour with Powers," remembers Carmen, who also remembers plumping herself out for the encounter with tissues in her bra. "Eileen doubled my rate at once. In my first week, I worked five days at thirty dollars a day. But she also told me that she didn't mind if I took work from other agencies. She knew that my mother and I needed the money."

Dell'Orefice came from a broken home. Her father, a symphony violinist, had left the family when she was a baby, endowing her only with her extraordinary surname and her still more extraordinary cheekbones. The thin, sickly little girl—she was bedridden with rheumatic fever for most of a year—grew up with her mother in a fourth-floor walk-up beside the elevated railway on Third Avenue.

When *Vogue* needed her for a job, the magazine would dispatch a message via a runner, since her apartment had no telephone. Her mother earned pin money as a seamstress and made her daughter's clothes from precut *Vogue* patterns.

"It was deeply embarrassing," remembers Dell'Orefice today. "I still looked like a coat hanger, and they looked so homemade. But we could not afford anything else. When I got paid for a job, it meant we could pay the power bill for another month—and I was able to pay for my own braces."

Commercial school graduate Barbara Mullen came from a scarcely less impoverished background. "I never knew my father," she recalls. "My parents broke up shortly after they were married. Mullen was his name—Irish." After working in a hairdressing salon in Long Island City, Mullen got a job as a house model at Bergdorf Goodman, on Fifth Avenue and Fifty-Eighth Street, where the department store stands to this day. "It was like being in prison," she remembers. "We had to clock in before nine in the morning and go up by the back elevator to the couture salon, eight or nine of us house models, where we'd spend the day having the designers pin clothes on our bodies, then parade around for the smart lady customers so they could decide what they wanted. There was a bossy woman in charge of us called Gladys, who kept telling us not to make too much noise and not to talk to the customers. Visitors were strictly forbidden."

One day an enterprising emissary from *Vogue* managed to slip past the eagle-eyed Gladys. "How she crept through, I'll never know," recalls Mullen. "She said they'd been trying to get in for weeks. They had spotted this velvet dress that they really wanted to photograph, and had heard that it had been made and fitted on me. Could I come to the studio tomorrow?"

The "studio" turned out to be nothing less than the glass-roofed, white-painted penthouse of the fabled John Rawlings, a 1930s pioneer of the pared-down school of photography—Rawlings was one of the first fashion photographers to abandon tripod-mounted plate cameras for the flexibility of a handheld Rolleiflex. Rawlings also used the glass roof of his studio to shoot by natural light, and his color pictures of the dark-haired Mullen, headlined "The New Beauty Is Part Attitude," transformed her career.

"*Vogue* told me they had lined up this model, Bijou Barrington, that they had really wanted to use, but she could not get into the dress," Mullen remembers. "Normally they would have left the zipper unfastened down the back and got Rawlings to shoot her from the front. But they wanted to photograph how the straps looked."

Barbara Mullen thinks it was someone at *Vogue* who directed her to the Ford agency. "Powers and Conover were the big names, but somehow they had become bigger than the magazines—they had got too high-horsey for a lot of the editors. Eileen and Jerry were polite and friendly and very professional, so people started going to them."

Eileen happened to be away from the office when Mullen called in, but Jerry Ford agreed to take her bookings. "So you're the new model my husband's taken on?" asked Eileen a few weeks later when the two women finally encountered each other. "You've got a terrible profile and you must never show it."

Having demonstrated who was in charge vis-à-vis both her husband and his new recruit, Eileen then rolled up her sleeves and started working with her customary energy on Barbara Mullen's behalf, just as she did to promote the dozen or so other young women who made up the Ford stable by the end of 1947. With Nat Otte's agreement, Jerry had abandoned his brief foray into the debt collection and credit business to work alongside his wife during the day, making bookings and negotiating contracts—though, for the time being, aged only twenty-three on October 2, 1947, he kept up his economics and business studies at Columbia by night.

With the agency business doing better than either woman could have expected twelve months earlier, Natálie Nickerson thought it prudent to draw up a legal document formalizing their position. Dated October 9, 1947, a week after Jerry's birthday, it read:

Dear Eileen:

This is to confirm the arrangement under which we have been operating as partners since September of 1946 in carrying on the business of a Modelling Agency.

As you are devoting your entire time to the business and I am spending no particular hours in it, you are to have a reasonable salary as an expense of the business.

The net profits or losses are to be shared equally between us.

Neither of us can sell our interest without the consent of the other.

Signed: *Natálie Nickerson*
I CONFIRM THE ABOVE STATEMENT OF OUR ARRANGEMENT.
Signed: *Eileen O. Ford*

CHAPTER 14

GODDESSES AND MASTERPIECES

The model has to give you the moment. It's not you making it. They give it to you—and you capture it.

—Peter Lindbergh, supermodel photographer

I N THE FALL OF 1947, BILL HELBURN WAS WORKING OUT OF A SMALL set of rooms at the back of a gas station on Seventh Avenue. His improvised studio was down the West Side from Columbia University, and the photographer remembers Jerry Ford dropping in from time to time on his way back from his evening classes.

"Jerry was still wary about the fashion game," recalls Helburn. "When he was schmoozing, he made it pretty clear he didn't think that the model business was quite masculine—and he was a pretty masculine kinda guy, six feet four inches tall and built like a brick shithouse. He seemed very happy to let Eileen handle the girls and all that side of it. He didn't want the glory—he just wasn't convinced that running a girlie modeling agency could ever become a serious business."

Huntington Hartford helped Jerry Ford see otherwise. One of the richest men in America, Hartford had devoted the five hundred million dollars or so he had inherited from his family's A&P shopping empire to a number of ventures—among them a fashion model agency that he started in 1947, with chic offices in both New York and

Los Angeles. An unashamed playboy, the thirty-six-year-old Hartford made little secret of his motive for trafficking in beautiful women: he wanted to date them. The sheer volume of his money made him a formidable rival to the Fords, and to every other modeling agency, since he had adopted the voucher payment system with a difference. Hartford paid out his models on the invoices they submitted every week, whether he had collected the money from their clients or not. So the income of a Hartford model was paid promptly into her pocket, and was absolutely guaranteed.

"I switched from Conover to Hartford because of his voucher system," remembers Lorraine Davies Knopf. "There was not another New York modeling agency who paid you regularly by the week. It was unheard of. People talked a lot about Hunt's womanizing, but I have to say that I never had any trouble with him in that respect—and his agency was perfectly professional."

"For all that activity," Jerry Ford later mused to Hartford's biographer, Lisa Rebecca Gubernick, on the subject of the millionaire's rumored womanizing, there was "almost no consummation. [Modeling] is a small business, where everyone is very anxious to talk about what so-and-so does . . . and not much ever happened. Any model who was established and good wasn't bothered by him."

"It was a religious thing with him, just to be near them," explained Hartford's friend and adviser, fashion photographer Stephen Elliot. "Those girls were goddesses to him . . . masterpieces, natural wonders. He couldn't quite believe they could walk and talk, and that they actually had natural functions like the rest of us. For him they were a miraculous thing."

Gubernick traced Hartford's priapic tendencies back to the steamy communal shower rooms of St. Paul's, the elite prep school in Concord, New Hampshire, where Hunt's classmates, according to confidences he shared with his second wife, laughed at the size of his penis. Yet whatever the origins of Hartford's unhappy complexes, they had a dramatic impact on the world of the fashion model, for in devising the economic bait (hard cash) that he needed to lure his much-admired goddesses to join his agency, the multimillionaire pushed modeling into finally becoming a serious profession.

"A lot of very good models went there [to Hartford] simply because they got paid every day," recalled Jerry Ford to Lisa Gubernick. "He was a terrific threat to the rest of us, because none of us had the money." As Jerry Ford later put it to Michael Gross, "He had no idea how many of our models were thinking of going to him . . . He had the power to kill us."

NINETEEN FORTY-SEVEN DID NOT, ON THE FACE OF IT, SEEM THE ideal moment for Nat Otte to tell his daughter and son-in-law that he would like them to move their burgeoning modeling business out of the family home. "It was right at the beginning," remembered Eileen, "soon after Jamie was born. He told us that we would have to move the business. He was very happy for us to stay living at Lexington with the baby, and we did—for another year or so. But when it came to the business, he felt the time had come for us to grow up and stand on our own feet. Well, that was his meaning. He was very adamant about it."

Nat Otte was a family man. His granddaughter Jamie remembers him as a fond and committed grandfather. He enjoyed the bustle of the family around the house. Yet the founder of the Fifth Avenue Protective Association was also a shrewd and experienced businessman. He evidently sensed the need for his son-in-law to be nudged into a greater commitment to his still-fragile model agency project—and perhaps, in his judgment, the time had also come for his daughter, age twenty-five, to cease taking things for granted as Daddy's little girl.

"We had an old brown 1941 Ford that we could sell," recalled Eileen, "and we got nine hundred dollars for that. That was enough to put down a deposit on an office on Second Avenue between Fiftieth and Fifty-First Streets." Thus the Ford Modeling Agency's first commercial address became 949 Second Avenue, a walk-up between a funeral parlor and a cigar store. "It was two floors up," remembered Eileen, "and we painted the front door of our office red, to the horror of the owner."

Eileen brought the folding card table from home, Jerry got a bank of telephones, and Loretta provided an old red sofa for the comfort of models and visitors—one of the first of whom was a young model called Jean Patchett, who had been working for Conover until she encountered Natálie Nickerson on a shoot for *Ladies' Home Journal.* The *rabatteuse* did her job well. When Patchett heard about Eileen's expertise and efficiency, she was suitably impressed, and arrived at 949 Second Avenue expecting a plush office supervised by a woman of sixty—"very stern." But Eileen "turned out to be none of that," Patchett told the author Charles Castle in 1976. "I walked into this tiny, grubby office. There were six telephones on a card table, behind which sat Eileen Ford. She turned around, and I found that she was only about three years older than I was!"

Eileen Ford was equally surprised. "I was just stunned by the look of Jean," she recalled more than sixty years later. "I still remember the day she walked into our first office, on Second Avenue, wearing a long black coat with a black velvet yoke that her mother had made for her."

Coming from a humble background similar to Carmen Dell'Orefice's (as, indeed, did almost all Eileen's earliest recruits), Jean Patchett—"My name is Jean Patchett: don't darn it, I'll patch it"—relied for her wardrobe on a sewing machine, a devoted mother, and the *Vogue* pattern book. "Jean was just breathtaking," recalled Eileen; "tall, with great legs, a long neck, and a really beautiful face with dark brown eyes. She had a mole on her cheekbone, and she made it her trademark, three decades before Cindy Crawford. Jean knew what she looked like, and she knew how to make herself look even better—though at the beginning she did need to lose some weight."

The model herself recalled Eileen putting it more directly. "You're as big as a house!" was Patchett's version of what Eileen bellowed as she came through the red door. Having burst into tears, the new arrival thought further and decided that this opinionated and abrasive young woman was at least more attentive to her job prospects than was Harry Conover—"He had five hundred girls. I don't think he paid attention to any of them." So the 135-pound "house" set about losing more weight, while Eileen set about booking her stunning new client some cover sessions.

"Each of those early models was precious," recalled Eileen. "We worked very hard for all of them. But Jean Patchett was the first that we made into a star."

Keeping hold of a star could prove difficult, however, if Ford could not deliver her hard and reliable cash. When models linked up with agencies in the 1940s they were routinely signed to a contract that set out their rate of commission—uniformly, in those days, 10 percent—while also detailing who took care of a whole range of expenses, from bookkeeping (the agent's responsibility) to tax accountancy and special personal publicity (the model's). In the event of any conflict, the two parties tended to shrug their shoulders and go their separate ways. "There was no legal contract on earth," remembered Eileen, "that could tie down a girl who was unhappy and wanted to leave. We were not slave drivers or human traffickers. Our starting point was that we existed to help the girls—it was best to let them depart with a graceful smile."

The only way to dissuade Ford's high-earning models from defecting to Huntington Hartford was to set up a guaranteed payment system. Eileen and Jerry needed capital, and for that, Eileen turned to two of her friends from the North Shore of Long Island, the brothers A.J. and Charlie Powers. It was A. J. Powers who had given moral support to Eileen on Christmas Eve 1943, accompanying her to the Nassau County Courthouse when she went to secure the annulment of her marriage to Charles Sheppard. Now A.J. and Charlie, whose wealth derived from their father's flourishing photo-engraving company, supplied the funds that Eileen and Jerry needed to match the liquidity of the Hartford agency.

"Basically," Eileen later recalled, "A.J. and Charlie took out mortgage loans on their homes to raise us the money. We were all friends.

We would do anything to help each other. It's difficult to explain it, but that's what it was like in those days. We were young. We were naive. We were all working, and we were having a good time."

As a 50 percent partner in the business, Natálie Nickerson was a cosignatory to the note—a loan to the agency from "Augustin J. Powers, Jr. and Charles A. Powers in the sum of Thirty-five Thousand ($35,000.00) Dollars" (some $400,000 in 2015 values)—and Jerry Ford negotiated the technicalities. "It was a business deal between friends," remembered his daughter Jamie. "I believe that my parents first went to my grandfather for the money, and he said, 'Absolutely not.' So that's when A. J. Powers mortgaged his house to raise them the money. It was like an investment. My father agreed to pay a very high rate of interest, and managed things so the agency paid off the loan quite quickly—well ahead of time. But I know that he insisted on paying the full interest due for the full term to repay A.J. for his friendship. My father was always very proud of that."

Eileen and Jerry Ford now had the capital to expand their nascent modeling business. From January 4, 1950, the date of the cash injection by the Powers brothers, Ford models were guaranteed 80 percent of their voucher earnings, with the remaining 20 percent assigned to a reserve account that paid out when Jerry Ford had chased up the balance of their funds. The decommissioned young naval officer had become a serious player in the modeling game.

CHAPTER 15

MODEL TYPES

Give us little girls, and we'll make them into big girls.

—Arthur Elgort, photographer

IN HIS EARLIEST DAYS ON THE PHONE AS A MODEL BOOKER, JERRY Ford was delighted to negotiate a plum commission for Jean Patchett—a full two weeks in the Bahamas, travel and all expenses paid, in order to shoot a collection of beach and leisure wear. Patchett was already commanding twenty-five dollars an hour, close to the New York maximum rate, so at six hours a day for at least ten or twelve days, Jerry assumed he could clear fifteen hundred dollars or more for his rising star. When Patchett got back to New York, however, the voucher for her two-week trip showed only a few hundred dollars.

"It rained," explained the photographer, and the model glumly confirmed that the weather had been atrocious. In their two weeks in Nassau, they had been blessed with only a few days of sunshine for shooting. Those few days were all that went on Jean Patchett's time sheet—no work, no pay. Patchett would have made more money staying in New York doing regular studio work.

It was Jerry Ford's first encounter with the financial realities of the fashion business. Cancelled work meant cancelled checks. He and his wife might regard their models as "stars" to be cherished and rewarded for their very particular beauty, but in the eyes of the rag trade, models were just wage earners, another category of hired help.

"Back in those days," remembered Jerry's friend, the Swiss investment banker Roland Schucht, "the girls got paid nothing at all for the hours that they spent at fitting sessions, prior to a job. They were expected to do their own hair and makeup—in their own time, unpaid. And the clients could cancel at the last minute, or run on with a session as late as they liked, for any reason they chose, including bad weather. Successful models might ask twenty-five or thirty dollars an hour, but that was not the full story. At least the garment workers in the sweatshops had the union working on their behalf."

Eileen had always cultivated the style of the scrappy shop steward in her protective demeanor toward her girls. Now Jerry engaged in the same battle for better pay and conditions—in his own, courtlier fashion. "It was Jerry," recalled Schucht, "who introduced cancellation fees, fittings fees, and weather-permitting fees to the modeling business, without any shouting. He was very polite about it—and he also put in time and a half for overtime, in the event that sessions overran. But he was different from a shop steward: if the girls were late and held things up, then he would make *them* pay. The lost time was docked from their fee."

A few years later the young Dick Richards, the photographer and later film producer and director, was serving his apprenticeship as a photographer's assistant when his boss suddenly vanished from the studio. "I looked around," Richards remembered, "and there was Jerry Ford, who had just appeared from nowhere, all six foot two of him. My boss had fled. Jerry asked, 'Where's George?'—perfectly politely—and I said, 'In the back, I think.' So Jerry left without a fuss, but a few minutes later George came out with a check for me to take straight around to the Ford office. When you looked at Jerry, you just knew you had to pay; he had his own quiet way of saying, 'Hand it over.' It was partly because he was such a nice guy—you didn't want to let him down. And the bottom line was you knew that you couldn't get the top models from Eileen unless you paid Jerry."

This was the creative essence of the Ford partnership—Eileen had the eye that recruited the quality, and Jerry made sure that people paid properly for it. As for Eileen's eye, said Richards, "I remember the girls that Eileen used to send over for test shots. You could tell that many of them had never done modeling before. But they always had something special about them—you just yearned to put them in front of the camera. Eileen had a nose for quality."

By some happy instinct—taste, nose, eye, or however you might describe it—Eileen could pick out the best, and with her husband's help, "the best" would become her trademark. From the very beginning until her heyday in the 1970s and '80s, the title "Ford model" carried a cachet all its own. Ford models were seen as the aristocrats of their profession: thighs that stretched for miles; an expectation of blondeness, though not invariably so; and a general impression of extra sparkle, height, and slenderness—stature, in every sense of the word, including mental discipline and punctuality. They also became known in the business for turning up with every accessory needed in their model bags, from spare eyelashes to extra hairpieces—the result of Eileen's ferocious attention to detail.

There were three categories of model in the 1940s and '50s: "Juniors" stood at around five foot five in their stockinged feet and wore dress sizes five to nine—weighing 100 to 106 pounds, they were supposed to look like teenagers, and often were. "Misses" were a little taller and heavier, up to 110 pounds—they were sometimes described as "young mother" or "in-between." At the top of the range came the "high fashion" models, who started at five foot eight, ideally weighing little more than 112 pounds, with vital statistics of 32/34-inch bust, 20/23-inch waist, and 32/34-inch hips.

"There are two good reasons for these requirements," Eileen once explained. "First, photographic models must fit manufacturers' samples . . . Second, the camera really does add at least ten pounds to each subject."

There was no doubt which of the three traditional categories Eileen preferred—"the super-sleek models," as she lovingly described them, "who appear dripping mink and diamonds in the glossy fashion magazines . . . the epitome of sophistication." Unlike her competitors, who recruited all three categories of model and would book their girls for paying jobs ranging from Frigidaire ads to vaudeville tours, Eileen preferred to concentrate on the highest and purest of high-fashion commissions. Even for her models in the junior and miss categories, she spurned what she called "product" advertising. It was her proud boast that she had turned down the young Grace Kelly, quite a successful model in New York before she went to Hollywood, because Grace had done bug spray and cigarette commercials—one of Kelly's commercials featured her wearing a pinafore while wielding an aerosol can.

Thirty years later Huntington Hartford identified Ford's strategy of choosing the high-fashion route as the key ingredient in Eileen's success. "Eileen Ford had the inside track with the inside people in the fashion business," Hartford complained to Michael Gross in the 1980s. "[She] got all the best models."

Eileen herself liked to explain her "inside track" in terms of the fashion expertise she had developed in her months with Elliot Clarke, Becker Studios, Arnold Constable, and Tobé. "Let's say the Wool Bureau called," she would explain, "and needed someone who could wear Norell well. I knew who could."

Yet Eileen was hardly unique in this, and the inside advantage that really gave her the edge for more than five years was the succession of behind-the-scenes approaches made on her behalf by her 50 percent partner and undercover *rabatteuse*, Natálie Nickerson—who, while "not exactly honest and straightforward," as Natálie herself later admitted, was very effective. With one of America's most sought-after mannequins singing Eileen's praises in the changing rooms of Avedon, Penn, and Lillian Bassman on an almost daily basis, it was scarcely surprising that the Ford agency should find its stable filling up with some of New York's most elegant high-fashion models.

Jerry Ford capitalized on his wife's high-fashion priorities, following her lead in downplaying product advertising, and drawing up a list of commissions that Ford would not accept for its models in any category. For example, Ford girls would *not* pose for "True Murder" or crime magazine illustrations; they would not consent to brassiere, lingerie, or bathtub poses; the Fords would not supply bosomy heroines for steamy book jackets; and deodorant ads were discouraged as "not worthy" of their girls' "special talents."

This titillating list of taboos was published in *Life* magazine for October 4, 1948, in a five-page feature, "Family-Style Model Agency," which opened with a photo of the handsome young couple juggling phones in their Second Avenue office. "While her husband answers one telephone and hands her another, Eileen Ford, on a third, lines up a new job for one of her 34 fashion models."

The next spread displayed twenty-two of the Fords' thirty-four models, a charming collection of young women looking rather like a college sorority, all smiling and sitting informally on the floor in the office with Eileen and Jerry—"unlike most agency models," explained the caption, "the girls actually like to drop in after work just to visit." The balance of the photos showed Eileen in a sequence of humble and helpful poses, bending over to salve the blistered feet of model Sandra Nelson, or having her own shoulder massaged to alleviate the strain of holding the telephone receiver to her ear.

The most striking image showed Eileen down on her knees in front of the exotic Barbara Mullen, needle and thread in hand, repairing the hem of a ball gown Mullen wanted to wear to a party that night. It was Eileen's provision of these "extra services," explained the caption below the Mullen photograph, "which makes [the] agency popular with its models."

In reality, these "extra services" reflected some inventive stage management on the part of Eileen and the *Life* photographer Nina Leen. Recalling the 1948 photo session some sixty years later from her home in Switzerland, Barbara Mullen was quite adamant that Eileen never got down on her knees, before or after the *Life* visit, to wash her models' feet or to stitch the hem of anyone's dress, let alone hers.

Joan Pedersen, a two-time *Vogue* cover girl who was featured in the *Life* piece leaning forward to blow a bubble with her chewing gum for eighteen-month-old Jamie Ford in her best party dress, confirmed Mullen's recollections. "Yes, it all was staged for the public interest. Little Jamie did not come into the office every day, but we did see quite a lot of her, because Jerry and Eileen were doing all the booking themselves in those days. There were no other bookers, and the pair of them were working eleven hours a day, just like the article said."

Pedersen, now ninety and living in the California wine country, agrees with the main thrust of the *Life* article, which reported how "half the Fords' girls have come over to them from the big agencies like Powers and Conover, because the Fords have the time and the inclination to take a personal interest in their careers and to look after their personal welfare." It was true, in Pedersen's opinion, that the presence of the young Eileen and Jerry, working the phones together for eleven hours a day, made the place different—and fun. "The other agencies had a hands-off approach," according to Pedersen. "The Fords were hands-on, and that made them new. They were great friends to all of us. They really made the whole thing feel family."

"Eileen was like a mother hen," recalls Lorraine Davies Knopf, who came to work for Ford some years later as a junior model. "She used to give us advice on our makeup or personal life. She used to give us all Christmas presents—with presents for our children if we had any. That was unheard of."

Carmen Dell'Orefice remembers Eileen and Jerry's riotous Christmas parties, complete with balloons and streamers, at which Eileen would call out a name and fling her present across the room, with everyone cheering or jeering wildly depending on whether the recipient caught the present or dropped it. "Eileen and Jerry just loved entertaining," she recalls. "They worked hard and played hard, and they were very generous to all of us. Eileen organized a huge wedding shower for every one of my three marriages—until I worked out that I didn't have to marry the guy every time."

THE *LIFE* ARTICLE PUT THE FORDS' "FAMILY-STYLE" MODELING agency firmly on the map. The faded and predominantly black-and-white magazine looks quaint to the modern eye: "Adopt this new travel idea," reads an advertisement placed by the Hertz Driv-Ur-Self System. "Go by Train, Plane or Bus, and when you get there, rent a new car . . . *and drive it yourself!*"

In 1948 a five-page feature in *Life* was the equivalent, in modern terms, of appearing on both *Oprah* and *Good Morning America*, an immense publicity coup—and the images of the attractive young couple who were generating revenues of $250,000 a year for their attractive young models prompted still more mainstream articles. Before the arrival of Eileen and Jerry, there had been a certain hesitation in the media—a cough of apology, almost—when it came to coverage of the glossy, graying gentlemen who headed up the rival agencies. There was a lingering suspicion of seediness. Yet no one could be suspicious of the Fords with their baby on the floor beside them.

"The bookings came rolling in after that write-up," remembered Joan Pedersen. "There was an enormous upsurge in the business." Soon after the *Life* article appeared, Sherman Billingsley started inviting Jerry and Eileen to bring their girls, on his tab, to join the rich and famous at his fashionable Stork Club, on East Fifty-Third Street— "New York's New Yorkiest place," as the nationally syndicated gossip columnist and broadcaster Walter Winchell liked to describe it. Winchell had his own permanently reserved table, number 50, in the Stork's inner sanctum, the exclusive Cub Room (also known as the "Snub Room"), and as he name-checked the congregation, the expression "Ford Model" entered America's celebrity lexicon. One evening Winchell swept Eileen and Jerry off by limousine and police escort to sit beside him in the front-row seats at a championship boxing match in Madison Square Garden. The young Fords were suddenly the toast of Manhattan. They had arrived—and with their new fame, there arrived newer and even more stunning models.

Dorothy Virginia Margaret Juba grew up an ugly duckling, the daughter of a midtown patrolman. She was the butt of jokes at school (as many models relate that they were) on account of her skinniness—the result, in her case, of rheumatic fever in the days before antibiotics. Like Joan Pedersen, Dorothy Juba had had to abandon her dreams of being a ballerina because she grew too tall in her teens. Yet Eileen Ford knew exactly what to do with the twenty-two-year-old beanpole when she presented herself at 949 Second Avenue early in 1949. Eileen sent Dorothy directly to the studio of Irving Penn, who asked for her name. "Dovima," came the answer, a stringing together of the opening letters of her three Christian names: Do-Vi-Ma.

"Just look at that waist!" exclaimed *Harper's Bazaar*'s Diana Vreeland in delight when she saw the photos, and she whisked the young model off to Paris to work with Richard Avedon.

Avedon, Paris, and Dovima would prove a magical combination several years later, when the photographer took his willowy muse to the Cirque d'Hiver and got her to act out her dancing fantasies in time with the swaying of a row of elephants. Dovima swayed for an hour, Avedon clicked his shutter a good thousand times by his subject's recollection, and the result was an image that was considered for many years the very height of fashion photography—though modern sensibilities might view the picture differently: the apparent poetry of the huge beasts' endless swaying derived from the cruelty of having their feet chained to the ground.

Along with Natálie Nickerson, Barbara Mullen, and Jean Patchett, Dovima was one of the elite group of young women for whom Jerry Ford was able to negotiate earnings that made them, at various moments in the late 1940s and early '50s, the highest-paid models in the world—and early in 1949, they were joined by two more. Dorian Leigh had already made her name working both for Conover and on her own account when, dissatisfied with Conover's perpetual failure to pay, she had briefly set up her own modeling agency, the Fashion Bureau. Rather short (five foot five) and definitely on the old side for modeling—her thirtieth birthday fell in April 1947—Dorian Leigh was nonetheless a much sought-after cover girl, thin-faced and elegant, with *Harper's Bazaar*, *Paris Match*, *Life*, *Elle*, and half a dozen *Vogue* covers to her credit.

"Dorian knows what you want before you take the picture," remarked Irving Penn, one of her favorite photographers, and also one of her numerous lovers—"a neurotic lay," she later complained in one of the random barbs of indiscretion for which she was notorious. "Afterwards he'd drink bottled water. Sex dehydrated him."

With the closure of the Fashion Bureau, Dorian Leigh was not only in need of a new agency. She was eager to advance the career of her much younger sister, Suzy, fifteen years her junior. So she phoned Eileen Ford with a proposition, offering to join the Fords immediately and on standard terms, provided that they also sign up her kid sister, Suzy—sight unseen.

"Dorian was wild," remembered Eileen, "and she was really too small for a model. I wouldn't have picked her myself—for the very same reason that I wouldn't have picked Kate Moss. Rejecting the shorter girls was often a bad mistake I made."

By the time Dorian Leigh approached the Fords, her track record had made her a prospect they could not pass up—but what about her unknown sister?

The couple arranged a meeting with the two sisters at an Italian restaurant, Mario's Villa d'Este on East Fifty-Sixth Street, and waited anxiously amid a sea of white tablecloths to behold the petite Dorian walk in followed by a towering, carrot-haired teenager—the fifteen-year-old Suzy Parker was already five foot ten—with pale green eyes and freckles.

"Oh, my God!" Eileen remembered hearing her husband exclaim in dismay. Yet on this occasion Jerry Ford got it wrong, and Eileen's preference for height was vindicated. In just a few years, Suzy Parker would become even more famous and successful than her sister Dorian. The star model of the 1950s, Parker was also one of the inspirations that Richard Avedon used to cite, along with his first wife, "Doe," and also Dorian and Dovima, for his idea that became *Funny*

Face (1957), the stylish contribution made by *Singin' in the Rain* director Stanley Donen to Hollywood's largely undistinguished roster of movies about models.

Funny Face starred Fred Astaire as fashion photographer Dick Avery (the similarity in the names was no coincidence), who spots the modeling potential in Jo Stockton (Audrey Hepburn), a Greenwich Village beatnik. Though contemptuous of fashion—"chi-chi and an unrealistic approach to self-impressions"—Jo yearns to sit at the feet of French philosophy professor Emile Flostre, a Jean-Paul Sartre–style guru, so she accepts Avery/Avedon's invitation to travel on a fashion shoot to Paris, liltingly filmed by Donen in all its 1950s innocence in the bright new color technique of VistaVision. Once ensconced in Flostre's philosophy class, however, young Jo discovers that the professor is a lascivious groper, unlike her thoroughly decent, twinkle-toed photographer, with whom, after the requisite number of frolicking Astaire song-and-dance routines, she falls in love. All's well that ends well.

The happy ending of *Funny Face* is as predictable as those of *The Powers Girl* (1943) and *Cover Girl* (1944), two earlier model movies that featured the young ladies of the John Robert Powers and Harry Conover agencies respectively. Yet those earlier projects were essentially "girlie" movies for the proverbial tired businessman—"virtually every nook and cranny," sniffed Bosley Crowther in his *New York Times* critique of *Cover Girl*, "is draped with beautiful girls." They were happy-go-lucky troop shows on celluloid, with beauty contests and lines of high-kicking girls reflecting the vaudeville backgrounds of both Powers and Conover.

Funny Face aimed higher and came from a different age and sensibility. While gently satirizing the pretensions of the fashion industry in the person of a Diana Vreeland figure ("Think Pink!"), edgily played by the talented singer, vocal arranger, and author Kay Thompson, the movie took models seriously.

"What's wrong," asks Avery/Avedon as he plans his shoot in Paris, "with bringing out a girl who has character, spirit, and intelligence?"

The underlying message of *Funny Face* was the same as the gospel according to Eileen Ford: the face, funny or otherwise, was key to the highly serious creative process of fashion photography, along with discipline and a certain mental attitude. Getting the right model was everything—and it was only appropriate that Eileen's prize models Dovima and Suzy Parker were allotted cameo roles in the film. Sunny Harnett, noted for her shock of blonde hair and her huge red lips, was the third real-life model featured by Stanley Donen in the movie, and she, too, worked for Ford.

CHAPTER 16

SCOUTS AND BOOKERS

[How can anyone] be silly enough to think himself better
than other people, because his clothes are made of finer
woolen thread than theirs? After all, those fine clothes
were once worn by a sheep, and they never turned it into
anything better than a sheep.

—*Thomas More*, The New Island of Utopia, *1516*

FRESH DECADE, FRESH BUSINESS. THE EXPLOSIVE SUCCESS THAT
followed *Life* magazine's promotion of Eileen and Jerry Ford's
"family-style" modeling agency posed a dilemma. Eileen was at heart
a scout; her joy lay in finding new faces. So how could she and her
husband travel and enlarge their agency in the 1950s while still retaining the hands-on, "family" style that had been such an important
ingredient of their image and their success to date? Half the answer
lay in Eileen's ability to retain some essence of her quirky personal
contact with her girls. The other half involved hiring good bookers.

Bookers are the secret heroines, and occasionally heroes, of the
fashion modeling business. They book the dates and make the deals
that constitute day-to-day survival for both model and modeling
agency—then, as now, spending most of their days on the telephone,
wearing one earpiece or (usually) more. For nearly two years, from
1947 to 1949, Eileen and Jerry Ford had done all this booking work
themselves, chattering for hours down their bank of telephone lines
at 949 Second Avenue to fix dates with photographers, magazines,
and commercial clients that ranged from advertising agencies to
catalogue publishers, then calling their models to make sure they

got to the right place at the right time the next day. Everything was supposed to be squared away the previous night, but there was a "morning list" of checkup calls to be made by whoever was first in the office.

"You'd make that call at eight thirty," Eileen remembered, "and would get no answer. There were no answer machines or cell phones in those days. So then you'd wonder if the girl was still asleep, or was up and out already and on her way to the job."

In most cases with Ford girls, the answer was the latter. A stable of forty or so working models could involve several dozen different assignments every day, and hundreds of phone calls from early morning until late into the night—with the success of the whole operation depending ultimately on trust.

"A good booker puts in the long hours she works because she loves her job and she loves her girls," remembered Monique Pillard, Eileen Ford's booker of bookers, who left Ford to join John Casablancas in 1977. "People would ask me if I had any children, and I'd say, 'No. Only two hundred and fifty of them.'"

Bookers are seldom noted for their obvious beauty. Ruth Walters, the first booker the Fords hired in 1949, was distinctly dumpy and physically uncharismatic. Yet the dedication of the successful booker often surpasses that of the models she represents, and this was certainly true of Walters. She doubled as the agency bookkeeper, and set a caring style that was followed by Camilla Park, Rusty Zeddis, Judy Laine, and the others who joined Ford in the early years.

"They all knew their models well," said Joan Pedersen, recalling Ford's start-up bookers. "They kept that family atmosphere, and they knew how to give you the feeling that you were talking to a friend—which they were."

There was no little calculation to this. "Sorry, dear, I've got to go. I think that might be a job coming in for you" was one of the standard phone ploys that bookers developed to shake off models who demanded too much phone-time mothering—and Eileen would regularly remind her staff that while there were new faces and young careers to foster, there were always *two* people who generated money for the agency in any job transaction.

"As well as the model, you had to please the client—the editor, photographer, advertising agency, or whoever," remembered Dottie Franco Solomon, who worked as a Ford booker for more than a decade. "When the call came in, you would look at the girl's time card and see how you could juggle her sessions around. But sometimes it was just impossible to give the clients the girl they wanted at the time they wanted her. So then you would have to sell them another girl that fitted the bill, with the same sizes and style and everything, and somehow give them the feeling that they had actually got a better deal by taking the second-best. That was the heart of good booking. At the end of the day the best booker was always the best saleswoman."

EILEEN AND JERRY FOUND THEIR SALESWOMEN. IN 1948 THE BUSIness had taken in $25,370—10 percent of the revenues the couple had generated in bookings, with a further 10 percent paid by the clients. In 1949, with Ruth Walters on the payroll, bookings nearly doubled, earning Ford $40,648.20 in commission, and by the end of the following year, with extra bookers on the phones, income had virtually doubled again, to $70,164.97. The time had come for Eileen to go scouting.

The couple started in London, where Anne Gunning, an Irish model who had worked for the Fords in New York, booked them a room at the Connaught, the Mayfair hotel that took reservations only on personal recommendation. But *Life*'s article on the "family-style" modeling agency had been syndicated in Britain, by *Illustrated* magazine, and word soon spread of the arrival of "American millionaire agents" looking for talent. Would-be models started calling the Connaught switchboard, and even loitering seductively in the hotel lobby—which gave quite the wrong impression. After two days, the American "millionaires" were asked to be on their way.

"We tried the Hyde Park Hotel," recalled Eileen, "but they were just as snooty. I remember the maître d' telling me, 'Madam, we do not serve tea in the dining room. If you wish, you may take tea in your own room, or in the tea room—but, in all my years, I have to tell you that I have *never* heard of tea being served with *ice*.'"

Eileen and Jerry moved down to Chelsea, where Anne Gunning lent them her Walton Street apartment, and also introduced them to the London equivalent of Powers, Conover, and Thornton all wrapped into one—the long-established Lucie Clayton Charm Academy. Founded in 1928 by an enterprising Blackpool beauty, Sylvia Lucie Golledge, the Lucie Clayton agency had made its name in the 1930s on the basis of the tall, thin girls Sylvia/Lucie recruited from poverty-stricken areas such as the mining valleys of South Wales.

When the Fords reached London, the agency had recently been taken over by Leslie Kark, a multitalented South African lawyer who, in addition to writing novels, had served in the RAF and wrote theater reviews for the *New York Herald Tribune*. With his secretary and later wife, Evelyn, Kark was moving his agency upmarket, promoting well-bred girls in the style of the aristocratic Barbara Goalen, Britain's archetypal 1940s model. Kark's expansion plans included a secretarial college and cookery school, and in his eagerness to generate publicity, he was happy to let Eileen take his protégés to New York for less than the usual "mother agency" commission of 10 percent.

The difference in recruitment policy was striking. Eileen Ford never met an aristocrat she did not thrill to—one of her excitements of 1950 was the marriage of her model Janet McMillan Stevenson to the British war hero and Tory MP, Tufton Beamish (Sir Bufton Tufton of *Private Eye* fame). Yet for all her snobbery, Eileen never picked her models on a social basis. Her "eye" was not class-conscious.

"Eileen's models all *looked* brilliantly classy," remembered Polly Ferguson, who was models editor of *Vogue* in New York for most of the 1950s. "They were long-necked with high cheekbones—they were like elegant roses. But many of them came from very, *very* humble backgrounds. Carmen, Dovima, Barbara Mullen, and Jean Patchett definitely came from the wrong side of the tracks—and it gave those young women an edge, in my opinion. In those days at *Vogue*, the requests were always coming down to me to book society girls or the daughters of society women. But I preferred the fresher alternative that Eileen offered."

Squeaky-voiced Dovima—"Her voice was so high," Eileen liked to recall, "that a dog could not hear it"—liked to make her lack of education a trademark, playing up the stereotype of the beauty with the ditzy bird brain. "Af-ri-ka?" she exclaimed as she touched down in Cairo for a photo assignment with Richard Avedon. "If I'd known Egypt was in Af-ri-ka, I'd have asked for double the rate." Dovima used her hotel bidet as a flowerpot, and according to Avedon, the huge bulk of her personal luggage, a capacious steamer trunk, far outweighed his photographic equipment as they loaded up their camels for a safari into the desert. He presumed that the trunk contained the model's makeup and dresses, but when she lifted the lid, Dovima proudly revealed her "books," piles of dog-eared picture magazines and comics.

The Ford girls' humble origins wreathed them with the excitement of discovery—the girls from nowhere who were making good—and it gave Eileen's bookers a fresh story when they picked up the phone to call jaded editors and photographers: "Eileen's found a new face!" Selling the Cinderella syndrome was hardly original, but Eileen Ford's emphasis on active scouting was rapidly copied by rival agents, establishing a trend in the postwar model business that would culminate in the late-twentieth-century fever of model competitions and television's rags-to-riches talent shows.

THE FORDS' FIRST INTERNATIONAL SCOUTING EXPEDITION RAN INTO difficulties the moment they crossed the English Channel, for there was no such thing as a modeling agency in France. The Code Napoléon frowned on any commercial arrangement whereby someone could sequester a portion of somebody else's earnings at source, and French law enforcement officials viewed the notion of trading in beautiful young women as akin to prostitution. Paris's fashion models had to book their own jobs or, more usually, work on relatively low-paid retainers for the prestigious but parsimonious fashion houses. French models were paid dramatically less than their equivalents in New York—for which reason their employers were not inclined to see them lured away by ugly Americans.

"Someone had advised Jerry," Eileen remembered, "to take along a blue-striped seersucker suit to save on hotel laundry bills. So we were kept awake all night in the Crillon by this drip, drip, drip from the bathroom—and then, when he put on the suit to go out in the morning, everyone looked at him as if he had landed from Mars. They thought he was wearing pajamas."

Still, Paris beckoned. Eileen had a Great Neck friend in France, Marvin Buttles, a hedonistic and cheerily overweight character fortunate enough to have inherited twenty-five thousand shares in General Motors. Buttles devoted the dividends to an extravagant, transatlantic lifestyle that had him flitting between the Waldorf Astoria in New York and the Ritz hotel in Paris, and he was delighted to initiate his young friends into the joys of the City of Light.

"When we were with Marvin we drank nothing but Dom Perignon," remembered Eileen. "He showed us the town. We would stay up all night, then go off at dawn to Les Halles, the vegetable market, to drink onion soup. It was broad daylight, and we'd go straight off to work."

The "work" did yield some interest in Ford models from France's flourishing fashion and current-affairs magazines. Eileen and Jerry made friends with Daniel Filipacchi, who was then a young photographer on the recently founded *Paris Match*. With Filipacchi and other French photographers, they established the channels by which, over the years, young Ford models would travel to Paris to build up the "tear sheets" (published photographs of themselves torn out of magazines) that they needed for their portfolios. Traveling in the opposite direction, Sophie Malgat—"Home Town, Paris," according to the "Ford Stable" list for 1950, "Height, 5' 8"; Bust/waist/hips, 34/23/34;

Rate/hour, $25.00"—left Jacques Fath to flourish with Ford and eventually apply for U.S. citizenship.

Still, the immediate dividends of the expensive scouting trip were thin—and the Fords arrived home to discover trouble. While they were away, their founding partner, Natálie Nickerson, had heard stories that Eileen and Jerry had amused themselves in Paris by lighting cigars with hundred-dollar bills, and she put the accusation to them angrily.

The story itself was preposterous, but the image of burning dollar bills contained more than a kernel of truth. From 1947 to 1952 Eileen and Natálie, the agency's two founding partners, had divided the profits on a fifty-fifty basis, but that 50 percent dividend had been calculated *after* the payment of expenses—and most of those expenses had been greatly to the advantage of Eileen and her husband.

Much more of the revenues had ended up in the Fords' pockets: they were both on the payroll; they were both paid full salaries as agency executives; and on top of that, they also claimed their travel and entertaining expenses from the business. So while Eileen and Jerry may not literally have set fire to any money in Paris, their trip to Europe—during which they stayed in luxury hotels such as the Connaught and the Crillon and entertained contacts such as Filipacchi and Leslie Kark—certainly consumed a profusion of hundred-dollar bills, which came straight off the profits that Eileen divided with Natálie.

"I never received more than $20,000 from the Fords," Natálie complained to Michael Gross in the 1990s about her total income from the five-year partnership—and the accounting figures bear out the justice of her complaint.

In fact, the neatly typed stacks of figures dated June 1, 1953, make clear that Natálie received a grand total of $27,207 as her share of profits from the Fords over the course of five years, 1948–1952. However, this was on a total business turnover in model fees that yielded a commission income of $303,794. So after the deduction of expenses, Natálie's share had not been half, but less than 10 percent over the five years—and when the figures are further analyzed, the picture becomes even worse than that. Natálie's profit share increased quite regularly to start with, from $1,991.35 in 1948 to $6,521.01 in 1949, and to a very respectable $9,905.32 in 1950. But then it started to *fall* in the following two years, even as the agency business kept expanding.

How could the *rabatteuse* be getting paid so badly—a third of her income in 1950—when the business was evidently doing better than ever? "I felt cheated and betrayed," Natálie told Michael Gross, "and in my mind everything between us changed."

Natálie's own priorities had shifted, as she herself was the first to admit. In 1948 she had fallen in love with the portrait and fashion photographer Wingate Paine, whom she married the following year, changing her professional name to Natálie Paine and quitting most of her modeling jobs to help develop Paine's photography business. But whenever a promising model came through the Paine studio, Natálie told Michael Gross, she would encourage the young woman to join the Fords. "Everybody wanted to be with them."

The Fords felt otherwise. Natálie had *not* been recruiting with sufficient energy since her marriage, in their opinion, and, bottom line, they had come to regard the agency as exclusively their own.

"On behalf of my clients, Gerard and Eileen O. Ford," read a registered letter from Jacob F. Gottesman, of 295 Madison Avenue—the Otte family attorney who had previously fixed such matters as the change of name from Ottensoser and the 1943 annulment of Eileen's marriage to "Shep"—"notice of termination and dissolution of partnership is hereby given to you, effective December 31, 1952." Natálie had just two days to get out of the business: the letter was dated December 29, 1952.

Natálie fought back, and in the course of six months of tough negotiations secured a severance payment of $11,750 from the Fords and a further $7,000 in two agreements, dated March and June 1953, which revealed that, while their business might have been flourishing, the couple were short of ready cash. The Fords' settlement payment of $7,000 under the agreement of June 1953 was parceled out into installments of $1,000 and $500, with thirteen monthly promissory notes for $400 and one for $300, stretching out until September 1954, at an interest rate of 4 percent.

Eileen and Jerry also agreed to surrender to Natálie the partnership mailing list and "the full and complete list of the names, addresses and telephone numbers of all models and customers and clients for the years 1951 and 1952"—as well as the right to "enter into competition with [Eileen] Ford, Gerard W. Ford, 'The Fords' or any corporation, partnership, firm or other entity with which she, he or they are or may hereafter be connected, directly or indirectly, anywhere, either alone or in conjunction with others."

Natálie had been making plans, and the following month, in July 1953, she opened her own model agency, Plaza Five, which offered an array of top models—including Dovima and two other successful faces from the monthly Ford "head sheet" of available talent, Sandy Brown and Ruth Neumann.

"I couldn't think of a name for the agency," Natálie later related—and, as at Ford, she wanted to be unpublicized and "very behind the scenes." So she sent out notices "that Dovima would be at Plaza five-five-eight-nine-three or whatever it was, and the same went for Sandy Brown, and that's where the Plaza Five came from. I had given Dovima twenty-five percent to come with me because I, like Eileen, needed a top model, a big name." To "sweeten the pot," as Jerry Ford later put it, Natálie offered an accounting job to Dovima's husband, Jack Golden, her childhood sweetheart, who was then working as a bank clerk.

Eileen went into "conqueror" mode. In retaliation for the opening of Plaza Five, she instructed her bookers to refuse all calls and bookings from Natálie's husband, Wingate Paine—effectively strangling his photography business. "Nobody could exist without Ford Models at that time," remembered Natálie, who retaliated by calling all the New York photographers she could think of and asking them to intercede with Eileen. "Look, I'm not asking you to do this for Wingate," she would argue. "But who's going to be next? You? Should she be allowed to have the power to shut down a studio?"

Questioned sixty years later, Eileen had no recollection of being contacted by any studios or photographers about the Wingate Paine embargo—which was quietly lifted after a matter of months—just as she found it impossible to recall or acknowledge Natálie Nickerson's huge contribution to her agency's early success. "Natálie got too greedy," was her ungracious response to this author. "So we had to cut her off."

Eileen's standard narratives of her agency's early development either failed to mention Natálie at all or gave the impression that the model was a very nice woman with no particular business sense who had enlisted Eileen's expertise for a year or so, at most. As recounted in numerous TV and magazine interviews, the glorious history of Eileen Ford totally failed to mention her Jewish roots, her first marriage—or the role of the model who first devised Ford's voucher system and who worked for a full five years on the creation and growth of the agency.

By the end of 1953, however, Plaza Five was up and running and had established itself as New York's principal competitor to Ford. The models would come and go—Dovima was back with Ford again by 1955—but Plaza Five would flourish for another decade before Natálie Nickerson sold it at a profit, which suggested that she knew a thing or two about how to create and grow a good modeling agency.

CHAPTER 17

IDEAL FOR ENTERTAINING

In every generation, certain women seem to emerge as archetypes, and Eileen Ford selected and promoted more of them than anyone else.

—*Harold Koda and Kohle Yohannan,* The Model as Muse

EILEEN FORD COULD TAKE CREDIT FOR INSPIRING THE CAREERS of more than a hundred of the twentieth century's leading fashion models. The roll call of her "girls" from 1947 onward—and particularly the listings on her agency's "head sheets," the illustrated rosters of models Ford presented monthly to the market—make clear that Eileen discovered and promoted, on average, one attractive new face every three or four months for more than fifty years.

It was a sustained feat of fostering that could never be matched in the international melee of fashion modeling today. Yet all Eileen's discoveries counted for nothing, she used to say, compared with the satisfaction she derived from her personal mothering of the four Ford offspring, three girls and a boy, to whom she gave birth over the decade 1947 to 1957.

"Bringing up my children," she would frequently declare, "was the most important thing that I would ever do. And I am delighted to share the secret of raising good children when you are running a business—get good help."

Two caring parents and a succession of governesses had been the system that operated in the Ottensoser household, and that was the pattern Eileen embraced for her own children's upbringing. "In those early years," she recalled, "when Jamie and then Billy were born, I reckon that I hired forty-two nannies and nurses before I found the one who was right."

Remarking on this today, her children question the precision of that number—and dispute the size even more. "Mother multiplies the numbers of governesses by the tenth power every year," said her first-born, Jamie (Margaret Jamison Ford, born March 17, 1947). "I think you should regard the forty-two nurses in the same way that scholars view the forty days and nights in the Old and New Testaments. It means a long time."

Jamie can, in fact, recall just four domestic helpers—Nana Spafford, the nursery nurse who looked after each new arrival; Sonny from Norway; a nanny from Belgium; and a Scottish governess—before the appearance, in 1957, of her German governess, Centa Mayer, the "good help" for whom Eileen had been searching, and who stayed with the family for the following nine years. By that date all the remaining young Fords had joined the parade: Billy (Gerard William Ford, Jr., born August 5, 1952); Katie (Mary Katherine Ford, born September 28, 1955); and Lacey (Ann Lacey Ford, born August 2, 1957).

The names of the four young Fords were derived from beloved aunts and uncles—John Lacy Ford was Jerry's war hero elder brother, while "Margaret" commemorated Aunt Margaret Ford McNeeley, who had welcomed the young elopers to San Francisco in 1944. There was a second Jerry, of sorts, but no attempt to mint a second version of Eileen—and no tributes at all to the Ottensoser lineage. The Ford children's names carried a rather WASP-y flavor, set out, as they were, in traditional Social Register style, with a routine Christian name that was effectively jettisoned after the christening, followed by a second, middle name that was drafted into service as the child's "real" name, often in diminutive form.

With formal, old-fashioned names went formal, old-fashioned behavior.

"Eileen's children were always so polite," remembers Kay Bour-land, a longtime family friend. "When I first met Jamie, she must have been about seven. She came up and bobbed me a beautiful curtsey."

"Eileen and Jerry were the most organized and dedicated parents I ever worked for," remembered Centa Mayer, who stayed with the family until 1966, before leaving to get married when Jamie went off to college. "Every morning, without fail, they always took the children to school. I would pick up the kids in the afternoon and take them to their skating and dancing lessons, and then Eileen and Jerry would try to get home in the evening for homework and dinner. If they couldn't get home, I would say a prayer with the kids and put them to bed."

From 1955, the year of Katie Ford's birth, home base for the Fords was a tall, narrow, five-bedroom town house at 160 East Seventy-Eighth Street, just off Third Avenue, down the center of which still loomed the ugly girders and rattling tracks of the "El," the elevated railway that transported commuters, day and night, between Harlem and Chatham Square. "The 'El' was closed and was torn down within twelve months of us moving in," remembered Eileen. "So suddenly Third Avenue became quite a pleasant place to live. And our house quadrupled in value—there were some really beautiful houses on our block."

The Fords had started house hunting in 1951, after they left their free digs with the Ottes for rented accommodation, which, together with the expense of the nannies, may have been the reason for their shortage of ready cash to pay off Natálie Nickerson in 1953. At their first stop, the family, still only three in number, had crammed into a single-bedroom apartment on Central Park South—Jamie and her governess shared the bedroom, while Eileen and Jerry occupied the living room, courtesy of a Castro convertible sofa bed—before moving to a duplex at 829 Park Avenue with the arrival of Billy. "It was a beautiful apartment with a forty-foot-long living room," remembered Eileen. "It was ideal for entertaining."

Among their guests for a few weeks one summer was an almond-eyed Italian brunette, Elisa Tia, just nineteen years old and modeling in New York on a temporary contract with Ford. "She slept in my bedroom," remembered Jamie, "and had the most glamorous, hand-made, high-heeled satin sandals from a shop called Dal Cò in Rome. She sent Mother another pair to say thank you."

One of the assignments that Eileen booked for Elisa was for the cover of Britain's *Picture Post*, and it caught the eye of the actor Kirk Douglas, who happened to be looking for a fresh face to feature in a Western he was planning. So Elisa Tia found Hollywood fame as Elsa Martinelli, playing the role of Onahti in *The Indian Fighter* alongside Douglas, Walter Matthau, and Lon Chaney, Jr.

Sleeping in seven-year-old Jamie's bedroom at 829 Park Avenue, the teenage Elisa/Elsa was the first model to lodge with the Ford family. The move to the town house at Seventy-Eighth Street now meant there could be many more for breakfast.

EILEEN AND JERRY FORD WERE A GREGARIOUS COUPLE. THEY HAD both grown up in families where entertaining was part of life— underwritten at company expense in both Great Neck and New Orleans—and they kept up that tradition energetically. The young Fords were renowned for their parties. They gave Christmas and birthday parties at the office, together with baby and wedding show-ers; they threw frequent cocktail parties both in their rental homes and at Seventy-Eighth Street, where they would eventually acquire a cook and a butler to help them entertain in style; and they also hosted groups quite regularly at the Stork Club.

As time went by, certain models and their companions became particular friends. "We used to see a lot of Mary Jane Russell," re-membered Eileen, "and her husband, Ed. He was a creative director at Doyle Dane Bernbach, working on the Volkswagen account with that famous slogan 'Think Small!' Nan Rees's husband, Tom, was a great guy and a great doctor—one of the first plastic surgeons. Over the years he gave some of the girls a lot of help."

Then there was Barbara Mullen, the lively brunette whom Jerry had first hired on his own initiative and who had been photographed by *Life* magazine with Eileen at her feet, sewing up the hem of her ball gown. In 1949 Mullen had married James Courtney Punderford, Jr., a handsome and well-connected young man who played polo and sold château-bottled wine to exclusive restaurants. With his old-school connections, Jim was just the type of man of whom Eileen approved, and like Jerry, he had done his duty as an officer in Japan. So the Fords and the Punderfords found they had much in common and would go out together as a foursome, two young couples on the town.

Barbara Mullen considered that she herself was very happily married—"Jim was just the answer for me"—but she came to the conclusion that Jerry Ford was not. "They'd sit at a long table in the office," she remembered, "and Eileen would 'bark' at him, like he was her maid or something. I suppose that was OK if you were at home, but in front of the girls, that was not very nice. She was verbally horrid to him—woof, woof! It gave the impression he was more like a slave than a partner."

Rusty Zeddis, who joined Ford as a booker in the 1950s, expressed it in psychological terms. "For all her talent and success," she remembered, "it seemed to me that Eileen had this streak of insecurity. She knew perfectly well how to be pleasant and charming, but sometimes she needed to make other people seem little in order to make herself feel big. I saw her doing that quite often in restaurants—snubbing the staff for no reason at all."

A legendary tale of Eileen's insensitivity involved a new booker who was delighted one day to be invited by her boss to accompany her for lunch at a restaurant Eileen had not visited before—only to discover, on arrival, that she had been assigned a single table in a distant corner of the room, while Eileen got on with her business lunch. The mystery was solved when Eileen took off the expensive coat she was wearing and handed it to the young woman to guard. "It may be a great restaurant," she told the booker, "but I don't trust the hatcheck girl." Some of the waiters at McMullen's, the Upper East Side restaurant owned by the Ford male model Jim McMullen, refused to go near Eileen's table because of such behavior.

"And when it came to how Eileen talked to Jerry sometimes," recalled Rusty Zeddis, "you just had to feel that her husband was a saint." Not entirely, as it turned out. Dancing one night in 1954 with Barbara Mullen at the Stork Club, Jerry Ford leaned down and whispered in her ear, "I love you."

"I laughed and thought no more about it," remembered Barbara Mullen sixty years later. "We went back and sat down at the table. But then poor Jim fell ill a few months later."

CHAPTER 18

SHOES UNDER THE BED

What lips my lips have kissed and where and why, I have
forgotten.

—*Edna St. Vincent Millay*

IN THE LATE SUMMER OF 1954, JIM PUNDERFORD STARTED SEEING
double and acting in a confused fashion.

"We had just bought this marvelous house in Long Island," remembered Barbara Mullen. "We'd been in it for about two or three
weeks, and someone came around to do a small item of repair work—
just a little thing. And when the guy had finished and packed everything away, Jim asked him, 'When are you coming back here to
work again?' And I thought, 'What's going on here?' I started noticing these random things."

It was over Labor Day weekend that the double vision started, and
the moment the Punderfords got back to Manhattan, they headed for
Presbyterian Hospital, where a batch of tests disclosed a diagnosis so
horrifying that the specialist kept Jim in the hospital and contacted
Barbara Mullen privately to explain. "Your husband has inoperable
brain cancer," he told her. "You should put him in a ward, Mrs. Punderford, and try, if possible, to go on with your own life. I am sorry to
tell you that Jim is just incurable."

Distraught at the news, Mullen called Eileen and Jerry
immediately—they were still living in their duplex at 829 Park

Avenue—and they, in turn called Nan Rees's doctor husband, Tom. "Tom came over and gave me some sleeping pills," remembered Mullen, "while Jerry and Eileen poured me some stiff drinks. That was the solution to things in those days."

The model slept two nights on the guest bed in Jamie's bedroom, then checked into the all-female Allerton House at 130 East Fifty-Seventh Street, a slightly less chichi version of the nearby Barbizon Hotel for Women. Her resolution was to keep on working—and working.

"I thought 'I'm damned if Jim is going into a general ward like the specialist suggested,'" remembered Mullen. "I wanted him to have his own room with a day and night nurse. So I worked every day from nine to four thirty to pay for that private room—and Eileen and Jerry were very helpful. They could understand how I felt, with Jim being just gaga. He went downhill very fast. I think they got me extra work, maybe work that I wouldn't have done before."

Working all day, then spending every evening at her dying husband's bedside, Barbara Mullen scarcely ate for six months. "I lost so much weight," she recalled with black humor. "I looked better through the lens than I had ever looked before. The one place I could find freedom and relief was in front of the camera."

Inside, however, the widow-to-be was lonely and desperate. The emotional strain was intense—working all day, going back to her little apartment at the Allerton House to try to get some sleep, trying to both ignore and confront the terrible reality of her husband's imminent death. One night she cracked.

"It was impossible to bear. So I called up Eileen, and she wasn't there. She'd gone away somewhere with the children. But Jerry was. So he came and took me back to their apartment to have a drink and a chat so forth, and, well . . . There are moments in life when you just have to be held."

It was the start of a poignant and deeply felt love affair.

"People didn't just jump into bed together in those days," remembered Barbara Mullen in her Zurich apartment in the fall of 2013.

"And for the two of us, it was not just an affair, with 'bed plans.' There was something more serious and important. We certainly felt there was a future for us somewhere, somehow. Jerry was having his problems with Eileen. She kept snarling at him. We didn't talk about it much, but it did seem possible to me that they were going to split up."

Mullen moved out of the Allerton House to the apartment of Nina de Voe, a friend and fellow model who had gone to work in Europe. "That made it easier for us to see each other. We were two lonely people who needed to be held. And I thought that Jerry was just a terrific guy. He was marvelous looking, but also kind, thoughtful, gentle, and considerate to other people—everything that Eileen was not."

For her part, Barbara Mullen was a catch for any man. "She had these beautiful almond-shaped eyes," remembers Carmen Dell'Orefice, "with a long neck and a laugh that seemed so sophisticated to me. She'd throw back her head and deliver this deep, throaty laugh. She had a lovely, easygoing nature. And long before Lauren Hutton made it fashionable, she had this beautiful little gap between her front teeth. Barbara had real charisma."

Barbara Mullen also had a conscience. When the affair started, sometime in March 1955, Eileen was pregnant with the Fords' third child, Katie, who would be born in September of that year. Then Jim Punderford died in July—both Fords attended the funeral, along with other friends—and as his widow looked ahead, she decided that she had to talk things through with Jerry.

"I felt that decisions had to be made," she remembered, "that we just couldn't continue this way. Did Jerry want to stay married, or would the two of us stay together? It was time to fish or cut bait. I loved him as much as ever, but what we were doing now was getting uncivilized, as far as I was concerned."

Jerry Ford did not seem too happy with the ultimatum. "He wasn't terribly pleased. He was a quiet man. But, credit where credit is due, he did speak to Eileen."

And to Eileen's credit, she spoke to Mullen rapidly and directly. "'I hope you will stay with the agency,' she told me." But that was all she said. Now well advanced in her pregnancy, Mullen's boss gave no indication of what she and her husband had discussed together, let alone decided, and for two weeks, the model had no contact at all with either of them.

"I was quite frankly in a terrible shape," Mullen told Michael Gross. "But I got my eyeliner on, and I went to work."

She heard that Jerry Ford was taking flying lessons. "I can spend most of my time in the air," he told Mullen, "where nobody can get me."

Then one evening in the fall of 1955, Mullen answered a knock on her door—to be confronted by an aggrieved Nat Otte and one of his sons, both of whom she had met socially in happier days. The two men pushed their way past her without ceremony and into the room, looking around the apartment, then heading for the windows, where they pulled the curtains aside as if they expected to find somebody hiding there.

Foiled in their expectations of catching Eileen's errant husband in flagrante, they turned angrily on his lover. Her behavior was "disgusting," they wanted her to know. And what were her "intentions" toward Jerry?

"I told them that I would go along with whatever decision Jerry made," Mullen recalled. "It was so awful. What else could I say? I told them that it was really in his hands."

IN LATER YEARS EILEEN FORD FOUND IT UNDERSTANDABLY DIFFI-cult to talk about Barbara Mullen. Her "eyes still go red and her hands start to tremble," reported Michael Gross in 1995 when he tried to broach the subject with her. According to one senior figure at the agency, Eileen felt things so badly that she threatened at one point "to jump out of a window" if Jerry did not end his affair.

"My mother is very old-fashioned," commented her eldest daughter, Jamie Ford Craft, in 2010. "There's no doubt it was the low point in the marriage."

The whole subject was something that Eileen preferred to address obliquely. "'Never have a best friend' was one of the pieces of advice that I used to give to the models," she said in 2010. "It was one of my favorite 'Sayings of Eileen.' 'Don't go away and tell your husband to take care of your best friend—or *she* will take care of *him*.' As my mother used to say, 'Absence makes the heart grow fonder—for someone else.'"

In the end it was a visit to the divorce lawyer that produced some sort of closure. The Fords had switched their legal business from Jacob Gottesman, the Ottes' longtime legal adviser, to the high-profile Aaron Frosch, who, as lawyer to such show business celebrities as Marilyn Monroe, Richard Burton, and Elizabeth Taylor, had run up many a client hour on the subject of divorce.

"It's quite a simple thing, Eileen," pronounced Frosch, according to family folklore, eschewing complicated legal advice on the rights and wrongs of Jerry's behavior for a grandfatherly statement of the obvious. "You have to decide: whose shoes do you want to have under your bed?"

Eileen confirmed that the story is true—which would suggest that her husband's infidelity made her angry enough to seek legal advice on ending her marriage, but that, on reflection, she drew back from the brink. The new baby, the family, the new family home, the growing business—love and loyalty aside, there were a lot of practical reasons for the Fords to stick together, and Jerry Ford decided to stay with his old life.

Barbara Mullen, for her part, decided to strike out boldly for the new. She crossed the Atlantic to work in France, signing up in 1957 with the pioneering modeling agency opened in Paris by Dorian Leigh—who, a few years later, sent her top-earning model on a holiday to Switzerland. There Barbara Mullen met Fredi Morel, the handsome ski instructor and entrepreneur to whom she has been happily married ever since.

Mullen looks back on her months with Jerry Ford more with fondness than regret. "Jerry Ford loved me," she says with a nostalgic smile. "He brought me comfort at a moment in my life when I desperately needed it."

NOT SURPRISINGLY, EILEEN FORD HAS NEVER FELT ABLE TO VIEW THE episode so benignly. "If Jerry Ford left me, I'd kill him!" she spat out in 1983 to the journalist Judy Bachrach, who had raised the question of marital difficulties in the course of an interview for *People* magazine.

Bachrach was startled by the violence of Eileen's reaction, but later in the interview she noted her subject's mood mellowing. The ever-attentive Jerry had brought his wife a chilled glass of aquavit, and after a few sips of the 40 percent liquor, Eileen became positively expansive.

"Once Jerry was really mad at me," she confided to Bachrach. "He told me I had to mend my ways or we'd be divorced."

"I told her she was too bossy," interjected her husband, confirming the remark, but not specifying when he made it.

"So . . ." said Eileen, "so I mended my ways. That's why I'm so docile now."

Eileen smiled demurely at the journalist. Jerry made no comment.

CHAPTER 19

BONJOUR, PARIS!

Beauty is a short-lived tyranny.

—Socrates

DORIAN LEIGH BUILT UP AN IMPRESSIVE PORTFOLIO OF LOVERS in the course of her long modeling career—the photographer Irving Penn; musicians Harry Belafonte, Dizzy Gillespie, and Buddy Rich; movie producer Sam Spiegel; and novelist Irwin Shaw, among many more. When Leigh published her memoir, *The Girl Who Had Everything*, in 1980, her sister Suzy Parker suggested the book would have been better entitled *The Girl Who Had Everybody*. By Leigh's own admission, the consorts came and went on a rapid basis, but the man she always professed to have loved most dearly was an aristocratic Spanish playboy and racing driver with a bulging suitcase of names: Alfonso Antonio Vicente Eduardo Angel Blas Francisco de Borja Cabeza de Vaca y Leighton, Marquis de Portago—"Fon" to his family and friends.

With his lineage, connections, and towering good looks, Fon had everything going for him except money. He lived in Paris in an apartment on the elegant Avenue Foch, next door to his mother, the dragon-like Marquesa Olga Martin-Montis, who controlled the family fortune—and thus controlled him. Pregnant with Fon's child, and creeping into and out of assignations via his garden gate in dread of the disapproving marquesa, Dorian Leigh pondered how she and her lover might gain some financial independence—she had already lent him more than fifteen thousand dollars to finance his car racing. She was now approaching her fortieth birthday, and her modeling career was nearly at an end.

Having run her own model agency briefly in New York, Dorian Leigh could see the opportunity offered by the absence of such agencies in France—the couture houses were awash with photogenic young women who were snapped up by the world's leading photographers at good rates. Yet how could she get around the legal obstacles that prohibited agents from deducting commission from the income of their models? Talking in 1957 with some Parisian friends in the fashion business, Leigh came up with a solution. What if she were to set up an agency where she worked on behalf of her models for no payment at all? She would make a point of not charging her girls any commission, but would take her profit instead from the money she charged the magazines and advertisers that booked her models for photographic sessions. The girls would get 100 percent of their fees, while she—along with Fon and Fon's newborn son, Kim—would live on the 15 to 20 percent commissions she billed the clients.

The French authorities did not at first approve of Dorian's bright idea. From the moment she set up her business in the elegant eighth arrondissement close to the Élysée Palace, Leigh received regular visits from the police. "They said I had a *bureau de placement clandestine*," she recalled. Within a few months she was summoned to court. "I went by myself," she told Michael Gross. "I didn't even have a lawyer! I didn't know it was important."

The tribunal found Leigh guilty, and fined her one hundred francs. Yet the judges were sympathetic to her attempt to work within the law. They suggested that she could keep her agency open if she found a way to adjust her business formula, so she went back to one of the friends she had consulted earlier, Hervé Mille, the editorial director of the magazines *Paris Match* and *Marie Claire*. Mille could see the advantages of native French models being more easily available for fashion shoots, and he provided the legal backup that eventually established that modeling agencies *could* operate commercially under French law—and even, in due course, charge commission to their models. So for more than two years, until the end of the 1950s, Dorian Leigh was able to operate the only modeling agency in Paris.

By then Fon was dead. He had been killed in May 1957, four months before Leigh opened her agency, in a tragic accident at the twenty-four-hour Mille Miglia race in northern Italy that took the lives of nine spectators (and contributed to the ending of the race on open roads). Leigh still had Fon's son, Kim, to support—along with four other children who were the product of varied liaisons—and she turned to Eileen Ford as the person with the cash and connections to help her now-legal agency move full steam ahead. Eileen Ford, she later wrote, was "one of the hardest working, most persistent persons I have ever known . . . [She] left no detail to chance."

Eileen and Jerry Ford, for their part, could fully appreciate the foothold that Dorian Leigh was offering them in Europe. "Dorian *was* Paris," recalled Jerry Ford. "There was nobody else."

Hooking up with the new Dorian Leigh agency gave the Fords the same entrée they enjoyed in London with Leslie Kark and his Lucie Clayton models, and the deal helped move modeling on both sides of the Atlantic into a lucrative new dimension. By the end of the 1950s, the Ford/Dorian Leigh/Lucie Clayton axis in New York, Paris, and London was generating a stream of mutually profitable business, and had also generated a new commercial phenomenon: the international model.

MODELS HAD TRAVELED AND WORKED ON BOTH SIDES OF THE AT-lantic for as long as fashion had been international—with the attendant cross-cultural misunderstandings: "She's wearing no underwear!" a Seventh Avenue designer had shrieked in horror over the phone to Eileen Ford in the late 1940s, after Sophie Malgat arrived in his studio for a fitting and made her way along his garment rack, dropping the dresses onto and off her body with Gallic insouciance.

Yet the transatlantic bridge created by Ford and Dorian Leigh in the years after 1957 was the start of something new. There was a sense in which Leigh herself was the first truly international model—she had been traveling from New York to model the French collections every season since 1950 and worked frequently with photographers in both London and Paris. Now her deal with Ford opened a career path that has been followed, in one way or another, by every major model since.

"Paris is the finishing school of modeling," explains Iris Minier, Ford's first scout in Europe, and today the international scouting director for Elite World in Paris. "Whatever they might like to think in New York, London, or Milan, Paris remains the true heart of fashion—Dior, Chanel, Saint-Laurent, Hermès—you can't argue with the sheer weight of it all. Paris is where a girl goes to learn how to pose and dress and then go home polished. All the best photographers from America or anywhere else go to work in Paris. New York takes you more seriously when you've been 'seasoned' there, and you can go back to your mother agency with prestigious French magazine tear sheets in your portfolio. You are ready to be sold."

It soon became routine for Eileen to ship her new girls to be seasoned in Dorian Leigh's French finishing school, while there was no shortage of models from Paris who were keen to travel in the opposite direction. It was a virtuous circle, with profit for everyone involved in the loop.

"We became the only importer in the United States," recalled Jerry Ford. "It was easy. Models were dying to come to America because they were paid ten cents an hour there, and a dollar an hour here."

Iris Bianchi, already a successful model in Italy, moved from Paris to New York in 1957 and settled in Manhattan with the help of the Fords. As she recalls, the hourly pay rates were not that different between the two cities, but New York offered more security and more regular work. "That was largely thanks to Ford," she recalls. "There was no running around on your own—and so much less uncertainty. Most of the time there was this nice secure feeling, 'I've been booked.' The Fords offered me an accountant, Mr. Sydney Felsen, who arranged all the working papers—the bank accounts, tax returns, and green cards and so on. Eileen booked me into the Barbizon for a month at her expense, then helped me find an apartment with another model. I always felt that Eileen was there for me."

Dolores Hawkins went in the opposite direction. The slender brunette from the Hudson Valley already had several dozen covers to her name, including *Harper's Bazaar* and *Seventeen* in the same month. Now Eileen Ford dispatched her to Europe to collect some more, starting in 1958—the year transatlantic travel was boosted by the opening of Pan Am's Boeing 707 jet service from New York to Paris. From Paris, Hawkins went across for a week in London, where she caught the attention of the *Daily Mirror*, which was fascinated that a twenty-four-year-old could be earning fifty dollars an hour and staying at the Savoy hotel.

Dolores Hawkins and Iris Bianchi were two of the new "international" faces Eileen Ford was promoting in the late 1950s. At five foot seven and five foot seven and a half respectively, the young women were significantly shorter than Jean Patchett (five nine), Carmen (five ten), and the other willowy stars of the early 1950s—Hawkins was actually classed as a "junior" model—but their lively, elfin style fitted the wide-eyed angularity that Audrey Hepburn had popularized in *Funny Face* in 1957. Jerry Ford characterized this late-fifties look as "soap and water" when he and Eileen arrived back from Paris at the beginning of 1958 and were asked to comment on new trends in modeling for the *New York Times*.

"The underfed, indoor, super-sophisticated fashion model is fading out of the picture," began the story by Phyllis Lee Levin on February 10, 1958. "For five years now she has reigned the fashion scene in all her haughty glory. 'Indoorsy,' unapproachable and unfathomable, she looks as if she emerges only at night to bask in the moonlight."

Europe was searching for something different, opined the Fords on the basis of their time in London and Paris. "Everyone there wants to look American," they reported, and the couple cited Iris Bianchi as an example of this ambition, with her "wide, sparkling eyes and 'all-American' page-boy hair-do." Here was proof that "the American look is international."

The *New York Times* deferred respectfully to the opinions of the Fords, who were designated as the owners of "the world's most successful model agency." The newspaper reported that the young couple, still only thirty-five (Eileen) and thirty-three (Jerry), had "re-vamped" the New York modeling scene, and were now conquering Europe. Following the lead of Dorian Leigh, Eileen Ford went scouting energetically in Italy and Germany—and also struck out in a new direction after a conversation in London with the quirky and debonair photographer Norman Parkinson.

"I was admiring some of Norman's latest pictures one day," she later remembered, "and was asking him where he found such wonderfully fresh faces. He said, 'Why don't you fly over to Stockholm?' He'd discovered some great models in Sweden, he said—tall and blonde with a fantastic work ethic. One of them was Nena von Schlebrügge, the mother of Uma Thurman. He said he'd found that the Scandinavians were very open when it came to business."

Dutch agents were difficult, Eileen had found. They liked to keep their girls and sell them to Germany, while German agents liked dealing with their own. "But Norman told me that the Scandinavians were different—and not only the Swedes, [but] the Danes and the Norwegians as well. So I started traveling every year to scout in all three countries, starting in Copenhagen usually, then going over to Malmö—and it was just like Norman said."

On her very first trip to Sweden in 1957, Eileen was invited by a local magazine to judge its annual modeling contest, where she picked out a tall and shapely teenager who was working at the counter of a cosmetics store. A few months later Anna Karin Bjorck was working in New York, and also staying as a house guest at 160 Seventy-Eighth Street.

"Anna Karin was the first Swedish model that we brought to New York," remembered Eileen. "She arrived that same summer, just a few days after Lacey was born, and she brought Victoria, a smooth-haired fox terrier who became our first family dog."

"It was a present for Billy," remembers Bjorck, today Lady Erne, the wife of Harry Erne, the Fifth Earl Erne of Crom Castle, Lord Lieutenant of County Fermanagh, in Northern Ireland—"a sort of consolation prize for having to put up with yet another sister."

As the years went by, tall blonde models became quite a trademark of the Ford agency—in fact, the term *Ford model* became synonymous with leggy blondes. Eileen made her Scandinavian scouting trip a twice-yearly event and she grew into something of a Nordic celebrity, dispensing advice in local radio interviews, while also judging the talent contests that provided her with regiments of ready-assembled recruits.

"For us," remembers Sandra Fosse, then CEO of Unique Models in Copenhagen, "it was a matter of knowing that someone would really take care of our models, and there was no one else who offered that service in New York. It quickly became clear to me that you had to be very strict in the model business, and I liked the way that Eileen was very strict. We had common ground on moral issues. I felt that I could send a girl to her with an easy heart."

Through the late 1950s and '60s, Ford developed a virtual monopoly of this fruitful northern nursery. Not until the advent of Johnny Casablancas did any of Eileen's competitors grasp the Scandinavian component of her ongoing success, and they left her, uncontested for nearly two decades, to forage beside the Baltic to her heart's content.

The mass influx of the Swedish models fortified Ford in two respects, since it strengthened the agency's new image of being suavely international, while also preserving the impression that its roster of models comprised the finest examples of American beauty. As Norman Parkinson once elegantly put it, how could you tell, just by looking at the picture, whether that alluring blonde with the lovely tits was reared in Malmö or in Minnesota?

CHAPTER 20

CELEBRITY MODELS

Do not choose your wife at a dance, but in the field among the harvesters.

—*Czech proverb*

I F DORIAN LEIGH WAS THE FIRST TRULY INTERNATIONAL MODEL IN fashion history, her younger sister Suzy Parker was the fashion world's first celebrity model. In 1956 the flame-haired Suzy was featured on Edward R. Murrow's TV show *Person to Person*, gracefully guiding prime-time America around her elegant Sutton Place penthouse, and soon after that she was the mystery guest on the top TV quiz show of the fifties, *What's My Line?* The panelists did not guess her identity, and they kicked themselves when they found out who she was. *Everybody* knew the girl who had helped inspire *Funny Face*—green-eyed Suzy, the first-ever fashion model to get on first-name terms with the rest of the world.

Her celebrity was not confined to America. When French *Vogue* wanted to publicize its coverage of the 1953 collections it chose the cover line "Collections—Suzy Parker!" Even in the chauvinistic and self-proclaimed capital of world fashion, the identity of this imported American model had become more important than who made the clothes (Dior, Givenchy, Balenciaga, etc.) or who had taken the photographs (*Vogue* eminence John Rawlings). When Suzy went out to lunch with Dorian Leigh one day in the course of what would later become known as Fashion Week, all the Frenchmen in the restaurant gave the young women a standing ovation. The Parker girls were celebrities on both sides of the ocean, so it was hardly surprising that the world's media flocked to Florida in the summer of 1958 when the lives of the two sisters were devastated by a tragic car accident.

Suzy had been staying with her parents in St. Augustine to celebrate her father Lofton's sixty-third birthday. She came every year, from wherever she might be in the world, for Suzy doted on her father, as he doted on her, the youngest of his four daughters, so much easier than his scandalous eldest child, Dorian.

When Dorian first embarked on her career as a model, her parents had refused to allow her to use the family name—she shrugged her shoulders and switched to "Leigh," one of her middle names. Yet they still took in and became foster parents to the succession of grandchildren she presented to them—one feature of Dorian's promiscuity was her indifference to contraceptive precautions. Her 1980 memoir recounts a bewildering succession of childbirths and abortions, along with five marriages and countless love affairs, culminating in the arrangements she made for the fathering of her fifth and final child over one Christmas holiday in Switzerland.

"I was completely calculating," she wrote, "in choosing four men I especially admired, and I managed to go to bed with each of them within one week's time." When her daughter, Miranda, was born nine months later, Dorian decided from her looks that her father must have been the ski instructor.

With the exception of Kim, her son by Fon, who was fostered by his grandmother, the Marquesa Olga Martin-Montis, all Dorian's offspring ended up in St. Augustine in the custody of Lofton and his long-suffering wife, Elizabeth, and it was a complication over the custody papers (an awkward letter from Dorian) that Suzy remembered discussing with her father in the last moments before the fateful car crash. The other thing she recalled was the silvery glint of a locomotive flashing through the trees on the railway track that ran parallel to the road, Florida State Road 207, along which they were traveling on their way to the airport.

The locals treated it as a sport—to race their cars alongside the whistling freight trains of the East Coast Railway for a mile or so, then swing across in front of the speeding locomotive when the road went sideways over one of the regularly occurring railroad track crossings, none of them gated in those years, and none with any warning bells or lights.

"Daddy raced trains all his life," Dorian later recalled.

But Lofton Parker badly misjudged his speed this muggy June afternoon. Suzy remembered her father accelerating as he swung his new Ford station wagon up and over the crossing tracks—then a sickening crash and a long, slow skid as the car was flipped in the air and ended on its wheels in a ditch.

The next thing she remembered was waking up with broken glass in her ears and her mouth, and the sight of her father looking as if he had been severed in two. George Lofton Parker lasted only a few hours after his arrival at the nearby St. Augustine East Coast Hospital, where, his wife, Elizabeth, was already lying in a nearby recovery ward following a mastectomy—she had recently been diagnosed with breast cancer. Suzy and her father had been planning to drop in at Elizabeth's bedside on their journey to the airport. Yet now Lofton was dying on one stretcher, while Suzy was lying on another with two broken arms and smashed shoulders, slipping into a coma that would last for several days.

"What is your name?" asked the duty nurse as the medics clustered around to attend to Suzy's wounds.

"I'm Mrs. Pierre de la Salle," came the answer. "Somebody tell my husband."

SUZY PARKER HAD FAILED TO SHARE WITH THE WORLD THE FACT that she was married. When Ed Murrow's cameras made their visit to her Sutton Place penthouse at the end of 1956, all evidence had been removed of her husband, Count Pierre de la Salle, a young Parisian journalist and unpublished novelist—"He wrote the same chapter for years," sniffed the designer Oleg Cassini. By 1956, Suzy and the count—he liked to be known as "Pitou"—had been husband and wife for just over a year, keeping the marriage secret, according to Pitou, for the sake of Suzy's career.

Yet this was only part of the story, according to Cassini and many of Suzy's supporters, who considered Pitou a "crumby snob." As they saw it, he was a philanderer—"Count de la Salle? More like Cunt de la Salle!" says one of Suzy's girlfriends, who recalls how Pitou flirted with her behind his wife's back and then tried to rape her. In their opinion, Pitou was a playboy and ne'er-do-well, happy to spend Suzy's money on sending his handmade shirts from Paris to England to be laundered ("because of the quality of the water"), but unwilling to accord his wife the dignity of his historic name and title.

"Coming from a fine old French family," Dorian later explained, on the basis of her own experiences with Fon's snooty Spanish relatives, "[Pitou] was somewhat ashamed of being married to a model: an heiress would have been acceptable, but not a woman who worked for her living—and his as well."

"No, I am not married to Suzy," declared Pierre de la Salle firmly when a succession of journalists telephoned him in New York at Sutton Place to ask about the accident. "I've never been married to anyone."

What are you doing in her apartment, then? came the next question.

"We only share it," lied the Frenchman robustly. "And don't jump to any conclusions. It's a tremendous apartment . . . Huge!"

Walter Winchell laid bare the deception in a matter of days. The couple had been married nearly three years before, in August 1955, in the Methodist church on Washington Square, he revealed in the *New York Mirror* of June 12, 1958, and the newspaper plastered the marriage certificate, no. 17281, all over the front page to prove it.

Pitou was compelled to admit the truth to the journalists waiting outside the little Florida hospital after he arrived from New York, and as Suzy slowly recovered from her injuries, she gave a series of bedside interviews seeking to control the damage—pointing out that the real scandal would surely have been if she had *not* been married to the man with whom she had been living for the past three years.

Yet the story did not leave the front pages until Eileen and Jerry Ford intervened. A few years earlier Jerry had rescued Suzy from a sixty-thousand-dollar claim for unpaid taxes by making her an interest-free loan—"that sweet angel," she said of Jerry to Michael Gross. Now, at the end of June 1958, the Fords whisked her away from the press to a secret location—the home that Eileen's parents, Nat and Loretta, had bought for their retirement in Ocala, in central Florida, eighty miles southwest of St. Augustine. There, beneath the oak trees hung with Spanish moss, Eileen and the Ottes cared for Suzy Parker for nearly a month.

"My parents did most of the work," remembered Eileen, "because I had to go back to New York. My mother was a very good nurse, and it was a total rest for Suzy. There were pieces of glass embedded all over her body, but none on her face—just one little scratch on her forehead. The newspapers were all over the story, but no one knew where she was staying until she appeared all healed up and healthy. By then the press had moved on to their next scandal."

Suzy Parker also moved on, having discovered that Pitou had not only developed a drug habit, but also started a dalliance with a Romanian armaments heiress. "Being married to a Frenchman is interesting," Parker later remarked; "you hardly ever see your husband."

The model's appearance in *Funny Face* had led to more substantial acting roles in other movies, and while working on one of them she met Bradford Dillman, a serious young actor who had made his name in a 1956 Broadway production of *Long Day's Journey into Night*. In 1960 the couple moved in together and got married in 1963, Suzy happily forsaking modeling to settle down as Mrs. Bradford Parker Dillman, raising children and baking bread in the hills of Santa Barbara, California.

"She had no more use for the business," remembered Eileen. "Bradford Dillman was a very good husband to her, a really nice man who supported her for the rest of her life. She had had enough of celebrity—and she had also had enough of Dorian after all the trouble with her parents and the custody of Dorian's children. They disagreed morally, and Suzy just didn't need it. The two sisters never really spoke again."

WHAT HAD POSSESSED DORIAN LEIGH AND SUZY PARKER, TWO OF the world's more beautiful, desired, and independently wealthy women, to hitch their stars to the likes of Fon Portago and Pitou de la Salle, a matching pair of titled deadbeats who were transparent in their idleness?

It was partly Americans' enduring weakness for titles, and partly the young women's personal reactions to their parents' disapproval. But it was primarily the dilemma created by the huge sums of money that Eileen and Jerry Ford had helped place in their pockets—a dilemma that was faced by all their successful contemporaries in the postwar generation of models. Earning a dollar per minute, sixty dollars an hour, fifty thousand dollars a year, made them the first group of working women in history to possess the power that rich men had enjoyed from time immemorial—the power to buy themselves a mate. It was hardly surprising that lacking guidance or experience, they bought badly.

"Those playboys saw these two girls coming," remembers Carmen Dell'Orefice. "Fon and Pitou were aristocrats with that old European instinct for family and the land—how to spot an heiress that could keep their boat afloat."

The Parker sisters were the equivalent of the turn-of-the-century "dollar princesses," who swapped their U.S. fortunes for the prospect of a European *de* or *von* in front of their names, plus a candlelit dinner.

"The American boys in the fifties were still very stiff and 'Brooks Brothers,'" remembers Carmen. "They didn't know how to romance a girl. So Pitou and Fon had it made. I spent a lot of time with Suzy and Pitou, and it broke my heart to see Suzy paying for everything. I did just the same, of course."

By the end of the 1950s, Carmen had experienced the ups and downs of two marriages (to Americans), in each of which she had been the principal breadwinner. "I desperately wanted my marriages to be *romantic*, and I think that a lot of the other models felt the same. Consciously or subconsciously, we knew that we were different from our mothers. We didn't have to marry for money or survival. So we had this wonderful opportunity to choose 'love.' And if that meant that we had to work to support our man, well, that made it all the more romantic—to start with."

When Dovima married her childhood sweetheart, Jack Golden, he soon gave up his job at the bank so he could travel with her—invariably, at her expense. In 1955 a reporter in Paris watched as Jack got drunk—a frequent occurrence—then vomited into a wastepaper basket, while Dovima waited patiently, ready to clean up the mess. "If I didn't have my husband," she remarked, "what would it all be worth? I think my husband is the only boy I ever met who told me I was beautiful."

The "New Woman" may have been on her way by the end of the 1950s, but her assumptions had not caught up with the new economic realities on which she was based—and the "New Man" was certainly yet not on hand to greet her. "We were all virgin princesses," observed Ford model Sunny Griffin, "and we all married creeps."

As feminists would warn in the following decades, it was not enough for the members of an underprivileged class to change their material status. What was needed was to change their thinking patterns.

Eileen had a simple solution to the problem she had helped to create, and it was of the traditional variety. "There is no reason," she would say, "why a girl who has made herself moderately rich should not marry an even richer man. It's a matter of securing the right *balance*. It has never been natural for a man to be supported by a woman. It's not good for his self-respect, and if he does not feel secure, she will not be happy, either."

It was in the late 1950s that Eileen started demonstrating how to achieve the right balance around her table at the "21" Club, where, every few months, she would invite promising young bankers and businessmen to lunch with select groups of her models. One of her businessman candidates was the immaculately smooth Robert Evans, a partner in the successful sportswear company Evan-Picone, who would shortly try his hand at the movie business, where he would progress to monumental success at Paramount Pictures as the producer of *Rosemary's Baby, Love Story, Chinatown,* and the *Godfather* movies.

"Eileen was a good friend to me," he remembered in Los Angeles fifty years later. "She introduced me to some of the most beautiful women in my life. But after a time she got wary of my track record. How shall I put it? I didn't prove to be the long-term stayer that she wanted for her girls—and the moment she realized that, the invitations just stopped. She remained perfectly friendly to me, but I remember once when I saw a really stunning girl and phoned Eileen to ask for her number, she refused me point-blank. I was blacklisted. I had to find another way."

Before she put Evans on her blacklist, Eileen had had her eye on the future film mogul as a promising partner for Anne de Zogheb, a poised blonde eighteen-year-old with a Lebanese surname, but a very English style and look, who arrived in New York from Paris in the winter of 1961. Her father was a diplomat who had settled in Egypt and lost everything in the Nasserite revolution. So his daughter was modeling to support the family, and while grateful to Eileen for her help and hospitality—Anne de Zogheb was another of the early guests at East Seventy-Eighth Street—the young woman had her own ideas about her boyfriends.

"Eileen would try to screen my dates," she remembers. "And I think she was running Bobby Evans as a candidate. But then, over my first Christmas and New Year, the agency booked me for a photo shoot in Puerto Rico."

There, on the beach in San Juan, Puerto Rico, the nineteen-year-old model met the twenty-year-old pop star Paul Anka, who was already famous for such hits as "Diana" and "Put Your Head on My

FIRST POSE.
Loretta Ottensoser with her only daughter, Eileen, age eighteen months, in the late summer of 1923.

Eileen, age two.

NAT. OTTENSOSER,
1305-6-7 Barclay Building,
299 Broadway, NEW YORK.

COLLECTING DEBTS WITH STYLE—and even a little wit. Nat Ottensoser advertised his services to the lingerie business (*far left, Corset & Underwear Review*, 1917); to art and antiques dealers (*below*, 1926 Art in Trades Club exhibition at the Park Avenue Armory, New York City); and to New York's garment trade (*bottom*, advertising blotter, circa 1937).

'Phones: 868 - 869 Mad. Sq.

THE COLLECTION SER-VICE WITH A BACK-BONE.   ::   ::   ::   ::

NAT OTTENSOSER

235 Fifth Avenue
New York City

I AM NOW LOCATED IN MY NEW QUARTERS IN THE MIDST OF THE TRADE. IF YOU ARE LOOKING FOR THE ONLY SHORT CUT TO THE DEBTOR'S POCKETBOOK —CONSULT ME ON DOUBTFUL ACCOUNTS. I PRODUCE REULT.

"Art in Collecting Accounts"

FIFTH AVENUE PROTECTIVE ASSOCIATION
(ORGANIZED 1911)
230 FIFTH AVENUE
ASHLAND 4370-1-2-3-4
NEW YORK CITY
NAT OTTENSOSER, *General Manager*

"Don't Be "Old Fashioned". Send us your "SLOW ACCOUNTS". The "RESULTS" *will convince you.*

Fifth Avenue Protective Association
220 Fifth Avenue
New York City

Collections
and
Adjustments

Ashland
4370-1-2-3-4

DADDY DARLING.
"How nice to have a clever little
daughter . . ." Eileen Ottensoser with
her father, Nat, circa 1927, in front of
their home at 2 Hilltop Drive, Great
Neck, Long Island, New York.

"The Bobbsey Twins"—Eileen and her
brother, Bobby, with their father on
their front doorstep.

EILEEN C. OTTE

Tot

Dashing, daring, debonair,
Describe Tot's distinctive flair
For pretty and becoming clothes
And attractive Amherst B(o)eaux.

YEARBOOK MEMORIES.
Eileen's first love, John Collier "Bo"
Meyer Jr., class of '38.

"Ottensoser" no more—Eileen
Otte, seventeen, debuts her newly
shortened surname in *Arista*, the
Great Neck High School yearbook
for 1939.

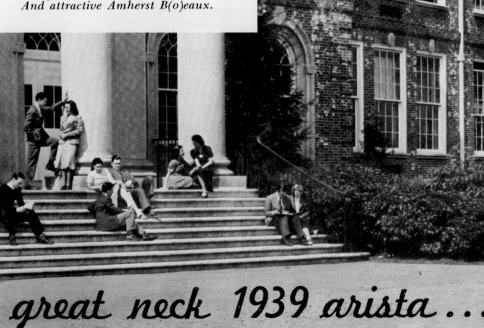

great neck 1939 arista . . .

COLLEGE GRADUATE.
Eileen at twenty-one in *Mortarboard,*
the Barnard yearbook for 1943.

The Barnard College Junior Prom
Committee with Eileen Otte (*fourth
from right*).

EILEEN OTTE

"all I ask is a tall ship—" . . . hopes
to buy a schooner and sail around the
world . . . besides the briny deep,
favors Princeton, sunshine, and bridge
. . . gets a kick out of life . . . always
beautifully dressed . . . has been a
commercial photographer's model . . .
worked hard for British War Relief.

MODEL AGENCY PIONEERS.
Above: Harry Conover
studies pictures of his
Conover "Cover Girls,"
December 1943.

Left: John Robert Powers,
founder of the world's first
modeling agency, crowns
Florida's Tangerine Queen.

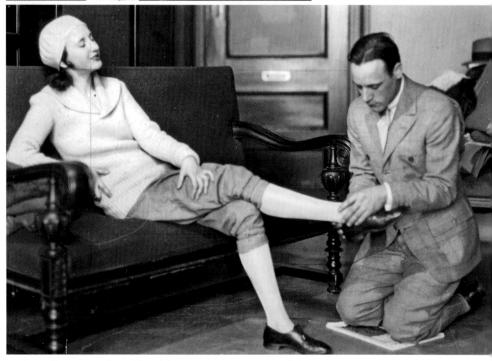

Walter Thornton, the self-styled "Merchant of Venus," founded his modeling agency in 193(

Macy's

"Velva-Teams"

NICE TEAMWORK IN COTTON VELVETEEN

Smoothest, lushest velveteens your money ever bought! Skirt and jacket ... hat and bag, all of a color or paired off, two by two. American beauty, brown, gravel gray, green, skyways blue. 12-20. Street Floor.

Hat___ **3.98**   *Bag___* **2.77**
Skirt___ **6.44**   *Jacket_* **8.44**

Spun rayon blouse in blue, gold, American beauty, flame. **2.98**

n prepaid orders, if you live outside Macy's otor delivery area, add 11c for shipping charges.

MAIL AND PHONE ORDERS ROMPTLY FILLED. *LA. 4-6000*

Campus Classics
FOR KNITTERS

VOL·10 **15¢**
(IN U.S.A)

ADVERTISING TALENT.
"I had a nice, pert nose but a plain round face and a mop of curly brown hair. That was not the photograph of a successful model." Eileen Ford was candid about her modeling potential when she appeared in advertisements on the pages of *Mademoiselle* in September (*right*) and August (*left*) 1941, and on the cover of the pattern book *Campus Classics for Knitters* in October 1940. She complained her agent, Harry Conover, "Never paid me a penny for all the sessions that he booked for me."

SAKS AT 34TH
BROADWAY AND 34TH STREET

5¢

Liberty

Sept. 6 · 1941
★

3 6

They Had Magic Then ! *A Short Story by Sinclair Le*
Pigskin Forecast *by Eddie Dooley*

MAGAZINE COVER GIRL. Eileen Otte on the cover of *Liberty* magazine: the pinnacle of her modeling career—and also the end of it.

NEW YORK GIRL WEDS IN ST. MICHAEL'S—Ensign and Mrs. Charles P. Sheppard, United States navy, are seen immediately following their marriage yesterday afternoon in St. Michael's Episcopal church. Mrs. Sheppard is the former Miss Eileen Cecile Otte, daughter of Mr. and Mrs. Nat Otte, of New York city and Great Neck, L. I.—(Photograph by R. A. Reilly.)

FALSE STARTS. Eileen's short-lived first marriage to Ensign Charles "Shep" Shepherd, February 1, 1943, and her next "fiancé," J. Hamilton "Ham" Wagner on service in England in 1941 with the RAF.

TRUE LOVE. Eileen Otte with Ensign Jerry Ford shortly after they met in the summer of 1944.

natálie
the barbizon
140 east 63rd street
new york 21

October 9, 1947

Dear Eileen:

This is to confirm the arrangement under which we have been operating as partners since September of 1946 in carrying on the business of a Modelling Agency.

As you are devoting your entire time to the business and I am spending no particular hours in it, you are to have a reasonable salary as an expense of the business.

The net profits or losses are to be shared equally between us.

Neither of us can sell our interest without the consent of the other.

Natálie Nickerson

I confirm the above statement of our arrangement.

Eileen C. Ford

NEW DIRECTIONS. *Above*: Carmel Snow (in hat, behind the editor's desk), directs *Harper's Bazaar* art director Alexey Brodovitch as he lays out the month's fashion pages.

Facing page: Natálie Nickerson, *Harper's Bazaar* cover for January 1947. (*Photograph by Richard Avedon,* © *The Richard Avedon Foundation*)

Left: Natálie Nickerson's October 1947 contract of partnership with Eileen Ford "in carrying on the business of a Modelling Agency."

BAZAAR

Harper's

January 1947

Fresh Style. Barbara Mullen shot by John Rawlings for US *Vogue* in 1952.

Jerry and Eileen Ford celebrate at the Stork Club, New York, with their friends Mr. and Mrs. A. J. Powers, who provided the money to help them fight off the challenge of supermarket heir Huntington Hartford, photographed (*right*) in Palm Beach.

Carmen Dell'Orefice, age sixteen, photographed by Erwin Blumenfeld.

"Family-Style Model Agency."
Pictures from the *Life* magazine feature of October 4, 1948, that made the Fords famous.

Eileen and Jerry Ford work the phones inside their Second Avenue offices situated on the second floor (*right*) above a funeral parlor and a cigar store.

LIFE ATTRACTIONS. When Suzy Parker (*right*) appeared on the cover of *Life* in 1951 fronting a lingerie issue, she wore a relatively demure one-piece nightshirt in leopard skin.

Ford model Joan Pedersen (*below left*) was photographed by *Life* in 1948 playing games on the floor with eighteen-month-old Jamie Ford while Eileen looked on.

Eileen Ford posed as a seamstress (*below right*) to mend the hem of Barbara Mullen's ball gown for the *Life* photo session of October 1948. But the pose proved embarrassing six years later when Mullen and Jerry Ford started a love affair that nearly ended the Fords' marriage.

LIFE

'I SAW THE BULLET THAT HIT ME'
A MARINE'S LETTERS TO HIS FATHER

BEST TOYS
TO GIVE
YOUR CHILD

CHRISTMAS
LINGERIE

20 CENTS
DECEMBER 3, 1951
CIRCULATION OVER
5,200,000

REG. U. S. PAT. OFF.

VOGUE

SUMMER
PLANS:

The Black and
White Idea

The Linen Life

Transparent
Fashions

Incorporating Vanity Fair
April 1, 1950
Price 50 Cents
in U. S. and Canada
$1.00 All Other Countries

THE BLACK AND WHITE IDEA. Ford model Jean Patchett used mascara to improvise her black lipstick in this striking cover by Irving Penn for *Vogue* in April 1950—American *Vogue*'s first black-and-white cover since the magazine switched to color in May 1932. On sale at all B. Altman department stores, the black coat-dress and white scarf were by the US designers Larry Aldrich and Kimball.
(*Photograph by Irving Penn © Condé Nast Publications*)

Shoulder"—and one year later Miss Anne de Zogheb became Mrs. Paul Anka. Beauty embraced fame, and riches were united, in a weighted love match of pop culture's new "talentocracy" that would be duplicated over the years by Ford models' marriages to other music stars: Sara Lownds and Bob Dylan, Barbara Bach and Ringo Starr, Jerry Hall and Mick Jagger, Rachel Hunter and Rod Stewart. They were not alliances in which Eileen placed great faith—she never lost her fondness for a good, old-fashioned aristocratic title or trust fund—but in terms of shared achievement from humble origins, these matches did represent some reflection of the marital "balance" she liked to recommend. At one stage in the 1980s every member of the pop group Duran Duran had a girlfriend who was on the books with Ford.

CHAPTER 21

IN THE EYE OF THE BEHOLDER

*Every woman can be her own sort of beautiful. All it takes
is know-how.*

—Eileen Ford

HUNTINGTON HARTFORD JUST WOULD NOT GIVE UP. OUT OF THE blue in 1959 the ever-hopeful billionaire made a million-dollar bid to take over the Ford agency, offering a deal that would have left the Fords themselves in full executive control of the business.

"We were very tempted," recalled Eileen, "because it was a gigantic amount of money. But then we got into negotiations, and Hunt started asking me these strange questions: 'What if I discover a girl that I want to be with the agency? Will you hire her?' and 'If I find that a girl is uncooperative, will you fire her?' Of course the answer to both those questions had to be No with a capital *N*. So that was the end of our one million dollars."

Unbeknownst to the Fords, the Hartford agency was running into trouble. The New York City Department of Consumer Affairs had been investigating claims of impropriety against its increasingly notorious owner. "An inspector called a few of the girls down for an interview," recalled one of the Hartford managers, "then asked, 'Has Mr. Hartford ever propositioned you?' . . . The girls started laughing and responded, 'Of course.'"

Toward the end of 1960, Aaron Frosch, the "shoes under the bed" attorney whom the Fords shared with Huntington Hartford, decided that the time had come to move his client out of the modeling business, and he quietly contacted Jerry Ford.

"Since he's not going to buy you," asked Frosch, "why don't you buy him?"

There was no purchase price, Frosch explained. The agency had run up losses to the tune of some $750,000, so the Fords could have the business for nothing if they agreed to take over those debts.

"It was a great deal for us," recalled Eileen. "Hartford had the best male model agency in the city—which was both sad and funny, when you think that he had done it all because of the girls. We didn't have a men's division at all. So Jerry renegotiated the debts for cents on the dollar, and we were stronger than ever, with all that solid income from the men's division. Girls earn more money, but boys go on longer."

In need of larger premises, the agency moved for a time to rental space on Fifty-Third Street, while Eileen and Jerry investigated the property market. "We put down the deposit on a building on Sixtieth Street," recalled Eileen, "and I assumed that Daddy would come up with the extra money that we needed to complete the sale. We were short of capital after the expenses of taking over Hartford."

Yet Nat Otte would have nothing to do with the project. "He said it was time we grew up and stood on our own feet," Eileen remembered. "He was very adamant about it. So we had to sell the Sixtieth Street building even as we closed on it. Luckily the price had gone up a little, and we made a profit without ever moving in."

Jerry had his plans better laid by the time Eileen spotted an old silver factory for sale in a scruffy and run-down industrial area on East Fifty-Ninth Street, facing the ramp of the Queensboro Bridge. It was by no means a fashionable area, but a number of photographers had their studios on the neighboring streets—*Vogue* had its studio nearby—and Jerry could see the potential in the tall redbrick building as the logical working headquarters he had long dreamed of creating.

"The place was full of garbage and overrun with rats," remembered Eileen. "So we had to gut it completely and do it up from scratch. We decided to keep the bare brick walls on most of the floors, but I wanted the main floor to feel like an Austrian ski lodge. We had some photos sent over, and I copied the lobby of the Zürserhof hotel in Zurs, with wood paneling and candelabras. I wanted the reception to give the feeling of a real homey place."

If the Tyrolean reception area was Eileen's flight of fancy, the rest of the building was her husband's carefully planned and systemized temple of work. "Jerry was very proud of his office systems," recalls his physicist brother Allen, the MIT graduate. "He was always trying to figure out more efficient ways of getting the job done. He loved to take me to the office and show me his latest ideas whenever I came to New York. One year, I remember, he had devised this big revolving lazy Susan system to keep all the models' folders together in the middle of the booking room—and when computers came in, of course, he was the first agency with that."

Terry Reno, Eileen's recently arrived "surfer girl" model from California, an icon of *Seventeen* magazine, remembers being reverently escorted to behold the Ford computer while the agency was still in its temporary lodgings on Fifty-Third Street. "The computer lived in its own dedicated office round the corner on the west side of Second Avenue," she recalled, "with a 'brain' and a printer that churned out spreadsheets and our pink pay sheet stubs—at a time when most businesses were still keeping their accounts in ledgers by hand. Howard Schein, the head of accounts, took me to see it. He was so proud of his baby."

Jerry Ford had organized the four floors of the agency's new home on Fifty-Ninth Street logically, from the file storage space in the basement up through the reception and separate booking floors for the women and the men—with a spare floor at the top for future expansion. The second floor contained Eileen's office, with a telephone operator sitting outside the door on one side and a row of bookers with their matching row of black telephones on the other. Their backs to the room, the bookers faced the wall and the sophisticated filing and calendar system that Jerry had devised to log and keep track of models' assignments—and to make sure that nobody was double-booked. One drawback of the system was that it made extensive use of metal staples, and Rusty Zeddis can still remember the network of cuts on the back of her hands from constantly reaching into the piles of stapled paperwork.

She also remembers coming back to the office one afternoon, past the untidy row of neighboring stores and workshops, to see smoke wafting out of the paint depository that was just a few doors away from Ford. "It exploded a few minutes later," she recalls, "and the windows blew out, shattering glass all over the sidewalk."

Next door to the paint shop was the local animal shelter of the Humane Society, and within minutes the street was alive with terrified cats and dogs. "Eileen insisted that everyone stop work immediately," remembers Zeddis. "She ordered us all to go outside and rescue as many animals as we could—especially the dogs. Jerry was furious."

The animal shelter was already a sore subject with Jerry Ford, since his wife had a fondness for dropping into the Humane Society to adopt some stray dog that caught her eye. She would then spend hours on the phone persuading a friend to adopt it, before getting the animal shipped off to its new home—often in some remote corner of the United States or even abroad—at agency expense. Now Jerry looked out the window to see Eileen and his best bookers scurrying around in the street trying to catch dogs and cats, while his beloved office building had become a madhouse of frightened animals.

"Somehow," recalls Rusty Zeddis, "one huge dog, a red setter, went sprinting through the men's division and came crashing down into the courtyard outside. Jerry was so mad; he brought his hand down on his desk with a smash you could hear around the building. It sounded as if he must have broken a bone. It was the only time in more than thirty years that I ever saw Jerry Ford get really angry."

WITH THE ACQUISITION OF THEIR OWN MEN'S DIVISION, EILEEN AND Jerry Ford quickly took steps to generate a third profit center along the lines already developed by two rival agencies: their own brand-name line in cosmetics. Jerry Ford had long dreamed of emulating the success of Cover Girl, the pimple cream that Harry Conover had marketed so successfully since 1938 with Noxzema. Conover had relinquished his interest in the business in 1959, when a combination of drinking and divorce problems had brought down his agency. But John Robert Powers, the granddaddy of them all and still very much alive, had recently been going from strength to strength in a similar field.

Like Conover, Powers had grown bored with the day-to-day details of fashion modeling. Having reached the age of sixty in 1952, the doyen of model agents had taken a break from his original core businesses, selling off the modeling and charm school rights to his name and moving to Beverly Hills for a few years. There he devoted his energies to developing new makeup lines and patenting brand names—Fluid Gold and Fluid Cosmetics in 1950; a countertop "Cosmetiscope" gadget in 1953, to analyze "your true skin tone"; and a "Beauty Tote," which appeared in 1957, to carry around your Powers beauty products. Powers recruited models from his own agency to advertise the products, and for some years he had been syndicating the John Robert Powers newspaper column "Secrets of Charm": "I have never met an unattractive woman" was his guiding theme; "only one who did not know how to make the most of her own, attractive self."

Eileen Ford Make-Up for Models went in a similar direction when it made its debut in August 1960—a practical-looking cosmetic kit that comprised liquid base, pressed powder, eyebrow pencil, eye and lip liners, mascara, lipstick, and lip gloss, all in a plastic zip bag that contained "a booklet of model make-up tips by Eileen Ford, who plans careers for the world's top models."

"Are you a Suzy Parker?" inquired advertisements in *Mademoiselle* and *Glamour* magazines that month, over a photograph of Parker, together with photographs of three other Ford models illustrating the kit options—blonde (Dolores Parker), brunette (Patsy Shally), light brown/"brownette" (Dolores Hawkins), and redhead (Suzy Parker).

For three dollars, a single kit guaranteed a two- to three-month supply of makeup "until now available only to Ford Models"—postage twenty-five cents extra.

Rusty Zeddis remembers Eileen's elder half brother, Tom Forsythe, coming into the office to help Ford design and launch the campaign. After an unsuccessful spell in the Otte credit business, Tom had created his own small agency, Forsythe Advertising, which specialized in artists and illustrators. "He was a charming guy," Zeddis recalled, "and he seemed to know a lot about advertising."

Eileen followed the example of John Robert Powers by syndicating her own monthly advice column in the newspapers—"Eileen Ford Answers Your Beauty Questions"—and she followed Powers's emphasis on practical self-help.

"Dressing, like beauty, starts from the inside out," she wrote in September 1960 in her first column in *This Week* magazine, a Sunday newspaper supplement with a circulation of some 14.6 million readers in thirty-nine papers around the country. "There is an exercise for drooping chins that may help you," she advised a reader who asked for her help with a sagging chin line. "Try to touch the tip of your nose with your tongue. You probably can't actually do it, but that doesn't matter. Trying 20 times every morning and 20 times every night will tighten the loose muscles around the jaw."

According to *This Week*, Eileen's first column attracted more than one hundred thousand letters—"she was deluged with sacks and sacks of mail from readers"—and the delighted magazine supplied her with a ghostwriter to sift through the inquiries and work out the answers with her over the telephone. The writer would then pass on Eileen's wisdom to her fourteen million waiting readers in a diluted version of the agent's trademark, shoot-from-the-hip style:

"What can be done about a small bust? The answer is 'nothing' unless you resort to often-unsuccessful surgery. But fashion models have very small busts and very happily so, because it means they can wear clothes better than anyone else. They have the figures that thousands of girls would love to have, so be happy! Lots of women envy you!"

On the perennial question as to why men seldom make passes at girls who wear glasses, Eileen revealed that she had made a virtue of her own short sight by building up a little wardrobe of spectacles: "For example, if I want to look intellectual, I have a pair of tortoise-shell-framed glasses. I have a few lighter pairs for summer dresses—and my luxury is a lorgnette for evenings."

These chunks of homespun wisdom proved a hit. In 1961, Eileen's columns were reorganized into an LP, *Learn to Be Beautiful: A Complete Course in Beauty by Eileen Ford*, with ten tracks running from "Skin Beauty" and "Face Makeup" to "Leg and Foot Beauty" and "Rules of Diet." Like her newspaper column, Eileen's one and only LP release was ghosted—both the script and the actress who read it were supplied by the production company.

"My own voice was pitched too low and sounded too gravelly," she recalled fifty years later. "I did not know how to project my voice."

Then ABC came calling. The radio network had recently devised *Flair*, a family-interest show hosted by an up-and-coming young comedian, Dick Van Dyke, and in 1962 *Flair* invited *This Week*'s young(ish) guru of beauty—Eileen was just forty years old that March—to share her wisdom as its women's editor. The afternoon program was repackaged into five-minute capsule reports that were broadcast around the country, and while some ghostwriting was deemed acceptable when it came to Eileen's scripts, the only voice that was possible was her own. The lady was seldom short of things to say, but now she needed coaching in how to say it, and for that she turned to the expert whom Ford already retained to coach models for their TV and radio commercial work: Betty Cashman.

Known as the "Queen of Carnegie Hall," where she delivered her voice-coaching lessons, Betty Cashman was a renowned trainer of successful actors. Jack Palance and Tony Curtis were proud to have been her pupils, and she had also coached the broadcaster Gene Shalit, as well as such prominent political figures as Congressman John Lindsay, the future mayor of New York; and William J. Casey, who finished his career as director of the CIA.

"She was the obvious person to turn to when we started our radio and TV commercial department in the 1950s," Eileen later remembered. "Ford always enlisted the very best available. So we sent the girls to Betty's classes at Carnegie Hall, eight or nine or ten of them, and they all came back really able to project. She gave them so much self-confidence."

Confidence training was at the heart of Betty Cashman's coaching technique.

"She deepened my voice and trained me to lose the flat *a*'s of my upstate New York accent," remembers Louis Licari, the Madison Avenue hairdresser whom Cashman helped turn into a star presenter on NBC's *Today* show. "But the main thing she taught me was courage—how to take control of my own life. Before I met Betty, no one ever told me that when it came to my own emotions, I did not have to be a brooder, that I was free to feel just however I wanted to feel."

Betty Cashman's recipes for success survive today in a bestselling series of self-help books that she published through the 1950s. "INTENSITY," she wrote in the concluding paragraphs of her book *Betty Cashman and YOU*, "is the burning of the heart, the brain, the nerves. It is desire aflame against the steel wall of failure . . . Dancers stretch, stret-c-c-h, stret-c-c-c-h their bodies to acquire physical flexibility for dancing, and singers stretch, stret-c-c-h, stret-c-c-c-h their vocal chords for flexibility in singing . . . To live is to have the courage of your convictions. To live is to think, to work, to play, to love, to laugh, and to be humane. Dare to fight! Dare to fail! Have the courage of your convictions . . . Remember, your yesterdays are memories, your tomorrows are visions, but your today *is reality*!!"

All this was either ham or Spam, depending upon your point of view—and for Eileen Ford it was pure, lean, unprocessed spiritual protein that she consumed avidly. Eileen became a devotee and friend of Betty Cashman for the remainder of her voice coach's long life.

"We all loved Betty and her New York accent," she reminisced after Cashman's death in 2001 at the age of ninety. "She got rid of everybody's funny accent, except her own. And she sure taught me how to project my own voice."

Eileen became a reasonably fluent public speaker, not only in the fashion and beauty reports that she delivered for ABC, but also in the hosting of charity fashion shows and luncheons organized by regional department stores, where she enjoyed the role of master of ceremonies and promoted the growing Eileen Ford Make-Up for Models line. Through the early 1960s, new products were added to supplement the basic three-dollar kit—"Night Miracle" cream, "Conceal" powder to lighten shadows, and "Disguise," a white makeup for the eyes. Sales grew, and it was not long before serious commercial interests came calling.

In the postwar boom years the Borden Dairy Company had started expanding beyond its core ice cream and evaporated milk range (along with Elmer's Glue and Krazy Glue—the by-products of rendering the bones of its dairy herds). By the early 1960s, with turnover approaching a billion dollars per year, the ambitious conglomerate had moved into chemicals and plastics, and in 1964, Borden opened negotiations with the Ford Modeling Agency, explaining that it was planning to expand into retail cosmetics.

Rusty Zeddis remembers Eileen and Jerry's excitement as they welcomed the Borden negotiator to their office. "But I knew," she says, "that I had seen the guy somewhere before. I had worked for a spell at John Robert Powers, and it suddenly came to me: I had seen the very same man at the Powers office, discussing some business to do with the Powers makeup line. Eileen and Jerry told me about their Borden deal one night going home in the car, and I tried to warn them about it. 'Be Careful!' I said. But they paid no attention."

Sometime late in 1964, Borden purchased Eileen Ford Make-Up for Models—but on November 20 the dairy company also acquired John Robert Powers Products and its line of beauty aids: Fluid Gold, Fluid Cosmetics, the Cosmetiscope, the Beauty Tote, and its recently patented Pearl Eyes, Up-Lift, Aquacel, and Grand Illusion.

In the flurry of the double takeover and the excitement of the huge financial windfall—the purchase price was a straight million dollars, according to Eileen Ford—Eileen and Jerry did not pause to consider the message conveyed by the technicalities of the different deals. While Borden bought Eileen Ford Make-Up for Models for a one-off down payment, Powers was assimilated into a joint stock- and profit-sharing agreement, with Borden establishing a dedicated John Robert Powers Cosmetics division inside its Borden Special Products Company. In other words, Borden had bought Powers as a business to develop, while it had bought Ford as a competitor to be shut down.

"Afterward, we realized that they wanted to eliminate their main competition right from the start," recalled Eileen Ford, ruefully reflecting on a rare commercial setback—albeit with the consolation prize of the million dollars they had failed to secure from Huntington Hartford.

With the abrupt closing of Eileen Ford Make-Up for Models, Eileen ended her regular newspaper column and ABC radio work; she also slowed down her schedule of regional department store appearances. Yet over the next dozen years she embarked on the creation of a sequence of bestselling books in which a series of ghostwriters cheerfully reshuffled her basic beauty advice among changing photographs of her models: *Eileen Ford's Book of Model Beauty* (1968), *Secrets of the Model's World* (1970), *A More Beautiful You in 21 Days* (1972), and *Eileen Ford's Beauty Now and Forever* (1977).

While her speaking engagements waned, however, Eileen still kept up her visits to Betty Cashman with surprising regularity—for more than thirty years, in fact. Eileen Ford's business appointment diaries through the mid-1990s show her visiting the Cashman consulting rooms at around eleven o'clock almost every Wednesday morning, whenever she was in Manhattan. Asked later about the purpose of these ongoing voice coaching appointments, at a stage in her life (her mid-seventies) when her public speaking appearances were virtually nil, she insisted that she still needed Cashman's professional help with the projection of her low-pitched voice.

Yet Eileen was seeking more than vocal improvement when she

went to see Betty Cashman—the closest thing she could allow herself to some personal therapy. Whether the outwardly invincible Eileen Ford acknowledged it, there was something in the psychological element of Betty Cashman's teachings that kept the agent of agents coming back for those self-esteem boosts week after week for more than a quarter of a century—the flame that Cashman offered to ignite in a woman's heart, brain, and nerves, to keep her personal willpower stretch, stret-c-c-h, stret-c-c-c-hing.

Dare to fight? Dare to fail?

Anything to keep the steel wall of failure at bay.

CHAPTER 22

YOUTHQUAKE 1965

Sexual intercourse began
In nineteen sixty-three
(Which was rather late for me)—
Between the end of the Chatterley ban
And the Beatles' first LP.

—Philip Larkin, "Annus Mirabilis," 1967

IF THE SIXTIES TOOK THEIR TIME TO GET A-SWINGING IN BRITAIN, they were delayed even longer on the other side of the Atlantic—till the very midpoint of the decade, according to *Vogue* editor-in-chief Diana Vreeland, who did not announce the arrival of what she called the "Youthquake" until January 1965.

"Youth," she wrote in her column "What's on Next?" at the start of the year, "warm and gay as a kitten, yet self-sufficient as James Bond," had already taken England and France by storm—"one of the exhilarating realities of life today." This same "exuberant tremor," Vreeland pronounced in her staccato style, "is now coursing through America . . . The year's in its youth, the youth's in its year. Under 24, and over 90,000 strong, in the U.S. alone. More dreamers. More doers. Here. Now. Youthquake 1965."

The Kennedy years that had opened the decade seemed stylish enough at the time. Yet the soigné tone set by Jackie and her "Secretary of Style," Oleg Cassini, with his couture-inspired dresses and signature pillbox hats, actually dated from an earlier era in Hollywood.

"I dressed Jackie to be a star in a major film—which she was," declared the pencil-mustachioed Cassini, who had made his name in the 1940s creating the looks of Veronica Lake, Gene Tierney, and Rita Hayworth for Paramount Pictures. The twinset and pearls "Jackie look" was positively nostalgic, not to say middle-aged, when compared with the raw exuberance of London's Carnaby Street and the King's Road.

Eileen Ford, forty years old in 1962, dressed in a businesswoman's adaptation of Jackie Kennedy's personal style, while being no special admirer of the woman—and even less of her husband's politics. She had a compact and wiry Jackie Kennedy frame, which she kept mean and lean into her late eighties with yoga and vigorous walking. Wound tight like a spring, Eileen Ford never had an issue with her weight. So throughout her life she was able to wear the trim, tightly tailored, Jackie O jackets with short skirts that showed off her shapely legs. Her friend Marion Donovan, the buyer for Woolf Brothers in Kansas City, would pick out dresses for her from Norman Norell, James Galanos, and Gustave Tessell, and for shoes she became addicted in later life to the hand-sewn, low-heeled court shoes that Henri Bendel brought to the United States from Belgium. The home she built in the 1990s in Oldwick, New Jersey, featured a wardrobe worthy of Imelda Marcos—an array of more than thirty pairs of Belgian shoes (at $360 or so per pair in 2015 prices), set out in a rainbow of shades from plum to lime green, with contrasted piping.

In terms of personal style and inclination, Eileen Ford was no "Mod" or "rocker," and she certainly didn't follow the hippie style that emerged toward the end of the decade. She did, however, adopt one of the fashion fads of the era, the craze for oversize spectacles, and armed with this accessory, framed in dark tortoiseshell and incorporated into her executive look, she set about spying out the faces that would define the look of the sixties.

At the very start of the decade, she welcomed to New York, and sometimes into her home, trendy London models such as Janie Blackburn, Sandra Paul, and Jill Kennington. In 1961 she hooked up in California with Nina Blanchard, a young Los Angeles agent whose West Coast business was based on the discovery and promotion of blonde

"Ba-ba-ba-ba-barbara Ann" surfer girls. Ford's top teen models, Terry Reno and Colleen Corby, notched up no fewer than twenty *Seventeen* covers between them in the course of the sixties, while Eileen's on-going Scandinavian trips continued to produce the Swedish models who *looked* like California girls—Maud Adams, the future "Octo-pussy," arrived in 1963.

When Melvin Sokolsky produced his revolutionary "bubble" pictures for *Harper's Bazaar* in March 1963, it was a Ford model, Simone D'Aillencourt, whom he used. Ali MacGraw was a 1960s Ford discovery—as were, briefly, Candice Bergen, Jane Fonda, and later style guru Martha Stewart before they moved on to their subsequent careers. Cristina Ferrare and *Hill Street Blues* beauty Veronica Hamel got their starts with Ford, and from Chicago, Eileen recruited Wilhelmina, a tall, high-cheekboned beauty of German and Dutch origin whom she packed off to Paris to lose twenty pounds and get herself "seasoned" by Dorian Leigh. The Ford agency's very greatest coup, however, years ahead of the general American fashion sensibility, was to become the U.S. agent of record from 1962 onward for a young Englishwoman whose face would become emblematic of the "Youth-quake" decade: Jean Shrimpton.

"We were so lucky," Eileen later remembered. "Jean just fell into our lap. She was on the books of Leslie Kark at Lucie Clayton, and we had the agreement to take his girls. So when Jean came to New York, she was a Ford model."

As a shy, middle-class charm school graduate with the look of a typical Circle and District Line secretary, Jean Shrimpton had the large, round, wide-spaced eyes and high cheekbones of many a 1950s model. Somehow, though, she deployed her component parts to star-tlingly different effect. She acted her own age, for a start, not her mother's—there was no wafting around in hat, veil, and gloves. She allowed herself to be young. When Shrimpton posed for the camera, she did not aim her hips at the chandelier. Her lower body undu-lated, rather, with a life of its own, in the way that models' nether regions have been overtly sensual to this day. "The Shrimp" had a looser, more available relaxation that reflected the tutelage of her boyfriend, the irreverent Cockney photographer David Bailey. "The model doesn't have to sleep with the photographer," Bailey liked to say, "but it helps."

Bailey had made his start as a studio assistant to John French, *Vogue* London's equivalent to the fastidious John Rawlings in New York. Yet whereas French, Cecil Beaton, and the other gay photographers of the postwar era were thinking about the clothes, Bailey was thinking about the feminine body parts inside them, giving his pictures a raw energy that he shared with London's other young photographers of the time, Brian Duffy and Terry Donovan.

"God, Duffy, I wouldn't mind a slice of that," Bailey remarked to Duffy when he first encountered Shrimpton at a shoot in 1960.

"Forget it," Duffy replied. "She's too posh for you. You'll never get your leg across that one"—an assertion to be proved wrong, according to Bailey, within three months.

The cameras of London's notorious East End trio lifted the extrovert fantasies of the King's Road into the popular consciousness. Long-haired photographers, like long-haired musicians, became part of the culture. In the 1950s there had been just one movie about fashion, *Funny Face*. In the style-conscious 1960s, the Swinging London movies never stopped coming—*The Knack, Alfie, Blow-Up, Georgy Girl, Kaleidoscope, Modesty Blaise, Darling, Morgan!*—with dolly girls on rugs obliging leather-jacketed photographers. In the 1950s Suzy Parker had tried to hide her relationship with her own husband, Pitou. Jean Shrimpton made no secret of her closeness to the married Bailey, and shrugged her shoulders when she was named as the "other woman" in his 1963 divorce.

"Of course, I was," she said—and never married Bailey.

When people looked at a photograph of Jean Shrimpton, they knew the backstory. She stood for a whole lifestyle, and the new realities of the post-Pill, free love era.

"Right at the beginning," remembered Eileen, "Bailey had taken these 'Young Idea' pictures with Jean for British *Vogue*. So when he brought her over to do the same thing in New York the following year—I think it was in 1962—Leslie Kark asked me and Jerry to handle the business side."

Bailey's moody images of Shrimpton with a teddy bear in a Brooklyn cemetery or wearing a spotted shower cap in the rain— "Young Idea Goes West"—seem pretentious to the modern eye. "But they were way ahead of their time for America," recalled Eileen. "I think *Vogue* New York only ran one or two of them at the time, quite small."

Jean Shrimpton's moment in America had to wait another three years. In April 1965, three months after Diana Vreeland bestowed *Vogue*'s imprimatur on the idea that serious American fashion could finally follow London and go youthful, *Harper's Bazaar*, whose inspiration Vreeland had been from 1936 till 1962, produced an extraordinary youth and pop culture edition that visually defined the Youthquake. Guest-edited by Richard Avedon, with the help of the young British designer Nicholas Haslam, the issue celebrated New York's pop art, the Beatles, Bob Dylan, space exploration, "and the Youthquake." Avedon daringly imagined Shrimpton as the first-ever woman astronaut, her face framed by a Day-Glo-pink space helmet, with one of her huge almond eyes covered by an optical illusion sticker, pasted onto each magazine jacket—a winking-eye hologram that blinked open and shut as you moved the page. The issue sold out immediately and remains, at five hundred dollars or more a copy, a collector's item to this day.

"That was the cover that really proved Jean had made it in America," remembered Eileen. "I was so happy and proud for her."

It was also something of a high point for Ford. Also featured in Richard Avedon's portfolio of "Youthquake" faces were two models of color whom Eileen had championed: Donyale Luna, an eccentric twenty-year-old from Detroit whom Bailey would photograph next year as the first-ever African American to appear on the cover of British *Vogue*; and China (pronounced "Cheena") Machado, who had been working with Avedon for some years.

"I met China in the late fifties," Eileen remembered, "soon after she came to New York. She had this fantastic, dark-skinned Eurasian look, half Portuguese, half Chinese. But when I sent her to *Vogue*, someone said, "She's too 'Chinky' for us." I was heartbroken. I just couldn't believe it. I was crying and crying. But Avedon said, 'Send her to me.' So I did, and Dick made China the great star that she became."

NINETEEN SIXTY-FIVE WAS THE YEAR EILEEN FORD GAVE UP SMOKING, in predictably stern and no-nonsense Eileen fashion. "I was forty-three," she recalled, "and I loved my cigarettes. Sometimes I smoked a pack or more a day. But by that date, everyone knew about cancer, and I came to see that I was crazy. So one day I just stopped. It was horrible. I suffered every possible withdrawal symptom. But if you want to do something, you can't go on talking and talking about it. That's a very boring song. So you just do it."

The withdrawal pangs were eased by the Fords' acquisition that summer of a dream house in the Hamptons—a cavernous, white-columned wooden mansion in the green and airy avenues of Quogue, beside Shinnecock Bay.

"It was huge," remembered Dick Richards, "with a circular drive and pillars with a pediment—like a country club or the governor's mansion. It must have been the biggest house in the village. There was eight feet of dining table, with a front hall like a ballroom, goddamn it! Jerry gave me a room there one summer. 'No rent,' he said. 'You've just got to paint it!' It took a helluva lot of painting."

"We called it 'Tara' when we first laid eyes on it," recalled Eileen. "We had rented a house in Quogue that summer, with Dave Garroway, who'd just retired from the *Today* show. Jerry was godfather to his son, and we were driving in Dave's lovely open sports car when we saw it—all derelict, with the grass knee high around the pillars like a scene from *Gone with the Wind*. It had a government lien on it. So we bought it for not much money and built a swimming pool."

Quogue became a new center of the Fords' social life, family and professional. "We'd go there on Memorial Day in the spring," said Eileen, "and shut it up in early October, a month after Labor Day. The children would spend their summers there, and every weekend, we'd bring out whatever models were staying with us."

By now, with daughter Jamie eighteen years old and about to go away to college, there were more and more young models staying at East Seventy-Eighth Street during the summer vacations. On Friday nights the Fords would pack all their houseguests into the family station wagon and head out to Quogue.

"I was the envy of New York," remembers Dick Richards, "staying out there with all those models. It was the sort of house that invites you to have a party—and a magnet for gate-crashers. But the crashers never stayed long. Eileen just fixed them with her beady eye, and everyone knew what *that* meant."

Eileen was strict in assigning household and kitchen tasks to the models—cleaning, serving food, and washing up afterward. "The sheets were given out as you arrived," remembered one model guest, "and you'd have to make your own bed. Then, when you left, you would strip the beds, put the sheets in the wash, and fold them up for the next person. The first time I went, I was assigned to wash the lettuce for the salad. Eileen tested every single leaf to make sure it was dry enough."

Eileen brought in a local staff to serve the meals, with a butler, Jack David from West Hampton, to supervise the entertaining. "Jack made a wonderful wine punch," she recalled. "Its chief ingredient was a whole bottle of brandy, and one weekend there was a communications breakdown. I put in a bottle, and so did Jack. Afterward, the Swedish contingent had to go outside and collapse on the lawn."

One neighbor complained at the noise coming from "Tara" by night—and also at the daytime indecency of young women lying out on the lawn in their skimpy bikinis. "I told him not to be ridiculous," said Eileen. "He could only have seen the girls by peeking."

Another neighbor, who never complained, was the Fords' lawyer,

Aaron Frosch. He lived two houses away and turned up at parties on the hottest days dressed immaculately in formal jacket and trousers. "Never wear shorts in front of your clients," he explained to Jerry.

Frosch's own weekend guests could be quite rowdy—notably his illustrious show business clients Richard Burton and Elizabeth Taylor, who got drunk one night and struck up one of their legendary quarrels. "You could hear every word," remembered Eileen, "coming clear through the air. They articulated so perfectly. It was like listening to *Taming of the Shrew*."

Summers at Quogue became the Fords' own version of the Swinging Sixties—hectic and hedonistic; wild, even, but incongruously corralled by Eileen's deeply conventional ideas of social propriety. The waitresses who came in to serve at mealtimes wore outfits from the Uniform Store in Southampton, a pastel or striped overall during the day, formal black with white trim for dinner—and the ballroom-size hall was too good an opportunity for Eileen to pass up.

"Nineteen sixty-five was the year that Jamie was eighteen and came out," she remembered, "so I gave a tea dance with an orchestra. It was just lovely."

EILEEN'S FINAL "HIT" RECRUIT OF THE SIXTIES FEATURED THIS VERY same mixture of wildness and the social calendar. In 1967 Penelope Tree became David Bailey's new muse—five foot ten inches tall (an inch or so taller than Bailey), gawky and angular as a grasshopper, with a pale, triangular face peeping out from beneath a thick opera house curtain of bangs and eyebrows.

"I always thought Penelope looked downright weird," remembered Eileen. "Jean Shrimpton would have been a great model in any decade. But Penelope could only have happened in the late 1960s. She came over like a waif, a little lost child—the right look at the right time. She really was 'way out.'"

Penelope Tree's "way-outness" embraced anorexia, student life at Sarah Lawrence, an interest in *Soul on Ice* and illicit substances, and, later, a jokey belief in unidentified flying objects—she had a

UFO detector installed the moment she moved into David Bailey's London flat. If Jean Shrimpton looked the sixties, Penelope Tree *lived* them—to the hilt. She and Eileen could hardly have broadcast from more different sides of the dial.

"I was quite bonkers," she remembers, "in the early 1970s."

Socially, Tree came out of the top drawer—her mother was the socialite Marietta Peabody, Adlai Stevenson's mistress and one of the first female delegates to the United Nations, while her million-aire British MP father was a confidant of Winston Churchill. Eileen positively purred when the elegant and patrician Ronald Tree came storming into the agency office in 1967, furious with the Fords for enticing his seventeen-year-old daughter down the slippery slope of fashion modeling.

"Sir Ronald was just seething," she recalled in an episode of cherished Ford folklore—erroneously bestowing on Tree a title he did not possess, and awarding her beloved husband an extra two inches in height. "So Jerry stood up, all six foot four of him in his Savile Row, Huntsman tweed suit, and he put out his hand. The two men shook hands and sorted everything out."

The young lady herself was less impressed.

"I loved working with Bailey and photographers like Avedon, who discovered me," recalls Penelope Tree today. "But I hated the other side of modeling—all those 'go-sees.' You are treated like a piece of meat because you *are* a piece of meat, and there was a definite element of regimentation about Eileen. I can now see that she meant well, but she was forever trying to 'steer' me. I just stayed away from the office."

As soon as she could, Penelope Tree went off to live in London and work principally with Bailey; she was a Ford model in name only. "I didn't want to be mothered by my own mother," she says, "let alone by Eileen Ford."

It was, arguably, more by luck than judgment that the Ford agency reached the end of the sixties having represented so many of the faces that defined the decade—Jean Shrimpton, for example, had fallen into Ford's lap, as Eileen herself put it, a gift from Leslie Kark and the Lucie Clayton agency in London. On the other hand, it was the initiatives that Eileen and Jerry took in their frequent scouting trips abroad that had made them the go-to address in New York for the leading foreign models, and they kept on looking for the best foreign sources. In 1969 they joined forces in London with two bright young Englishwomen, José Fonseca and April Ducksbury, whose quirky Models 1 agency would bring them fresh blood in the 1970s.

Eileen certainly made mistakes. On a trip to Paris in the early 1960s she administered the third degree to the flame-haired Grace Coddington. Why didn't Grace have a "waist cincher" (a wide elasticized belt) or a "sweater bra" (a seamless bra), she demanded of the willowy young English model, whose eighteen-inch waist and thirty-three-inch bust had been achieved quite naturally, without the help of these devices. And what about those *eyebrows*?

"This small, intimidating woman . . ." recalled Coddington in the memoir she wrote fifty years later. "She personally came at me with a pair of tweezers."

Eileen plucked the young woman's dramatic, heavy eyebrows into a thin arch, then pronounced the busy working mannequin unsuitable for either runway *or* photographic work—a verdict that was amply contradicted by Coddington's subsequent career as model, fashion stylist, and, eventually, creative director of *Vogue*.

Who said, "You'll never make a model" to Marisa Berenson, the woman *Elle* magazine would later describe as "the world's most beautiful girl"? "You just don't have the looks," Eileen confidently decreed to Berenson, a Models 1 client who would, in due course, come to command more than two thousand dollars per hour. When Berenson later started work in New York, she shunned Ford in favor of the less abrasive Barbara Stone of Stewart Models.

The majestic Countess Vera von Lehndorff also finished up at Stewart. When Eileen first laid eyes on the six-foot-one blonde, who was working in Paris for Dorian Leigh, she encouraged Vera to come over to New York. "You would be great for the States," she said, as Vera recalled the conversation, "because you are tall and blonde, and that's what we like."

Yet when Vera arrived in New York in 1964, Eileen instructed the new arrival to get rid of her blonde hair by dyeing it a darker shade—at one of Manhattan's more expensive hairdressers. "All the money I brought over with me was gone," Vera complained later to Michael Gross "—into hair! Then [Eileen] said: 'Never take a taxi because you will make no money here, so just walk and you'll lose weight, because you are too fat.' I was *never* fat."

The final straw for the countess came at the office of the immigration lawyer to whom Eileen sent her. "'Listen, it's too sad to see you always coming here,' said the lawyer. 'I must tell you that Eileen said, "Don't make a visa for her."' But she didn't want him to tell me! She was such a bitch! Every Friday she said to the booking girls, 'Throw her out!'"

Jane Hallaren, who trained and managed young models for Ford in the early sixties, remembers Eileen's Friday lists of girls to be let go.

"All through the summer Eileen and Jerry would head out for Quogue at three," she recalls, "and before she left, Eileen would hand me that week's list of girls to cut. She never had much time for niceties, and she was always ill at ease with women. She was so much better with men. I remember her saying, 'Get rid of the big Kraut! I don't like the cut of her jib.'"

Eileen had evidently forgotten that half her ancestors were supposed to be German.

"I didn't put it in that way to Vera, of course," remembers Hallaren. "With all the girls, I would sit them down somewhere outside the office—there was a greasy spoon–style diner right along the street from Ford's—and would try to find each of them a new path, or some fresh place to go, like Paris."

Vera von Lehndorff chose to go to Munich and Italy, where she reinvented herself as the statuesque and mysterious Veruschka, dressed all in black and featured in the coming years on no fewer than eleven

Vogue covers. When Vera returned to New York to work as Veruschka, it was with Stewart, where Hallaren had moved, and where in 1966 "the big Kraut" found herself selected by Michelangelo Antonioni to play David Hemmings's model in the famous photo sequence in *Blow-Up*—another icon of the decade lost to Ford through Eileen's sharp tongue and willfulness.

Ford's greatest loss came in 1967, when amid popular commotion to rival the furor that had greeted the Beatles, Lesley Hornby, the androgynous and legendary Twiggy, landed in New York, with an engaging line in self-deprecating humor.

"Do you think your figure is the thing of the future?" shouted a journalist from the scrum of her arrival press conference.

"I suppose so, I dunno," giggled Twiggy in reply. "It's not really what you call a figure, is it?"

The honor and profit of representing 1967's most famous model on the planet was fought over by every agency in Manhattan, and Dorian Leigh, who already represented Twiggy in Paris, told Eileen that she would do her best to push the eighteen-year-old sensation, along with her boyfriend-manager, Justin de Villeneuve, in the direction of Ford. Yet after a reversed version of the "go-see" inspection, in which the model, for once, was able to subject the clients to a "beauty parade" and treat the rival agencies as meat, Twiggy opted, like Berenson and Veruschka, to go with Stewart rather than Ford.

Eileen later maintained that it was all a matter of money. It was Ford who rejected Twiggy, Eileen liked to claim, because Justin de Villeneuve asked for too much "mother" commission. "Justin tried to hold us to ransom," Eileen used to say.

But Twiggy herself maintained that her decision had nothing to do with Justin or with money, and everything to do with her reaction to Eileen's intimidating style when the two women met. "She scares me shitless," said Twiggy.

CHAPTER 23

RIVALRIES

You don't give people what they want. You give them what
they don't know that they want yet.

—*Diana Vreeland*

DISPATCHED TO PARIS BY EILEEN FORD WITH ORDERS TO SLIM
down her hips and lose twenty pounds, the twenty-one-year-
old Wilhelmina devised a regimen of hard work, black coffee, nonstop cigarettes, tomato soup on Wednesday, and one single, small
steak for lunch on Sunday—with no sauce. She was a disciplined
young woman, and since amphetamines were still available over the
counter in France, she helped her slimming along with a daily swal-
lowing of diet pills.

"I found myself walking along the Champs-Elysées with the cars
coming towards me," she later related, "but my body had no reaction
whatsoever . . . I was running on nervous energy."

The young woman who had come to Ford from Chicago was also
running on the determination to prove Eileen wrong in her prediction that she would never make a model. "I want Eileen Ford to eat
crow," she told Dorian Leigh—and she succeeded. When Wilhelmina
(born Gertrude Wilhelmina Behmenburg of Dutch and German
parentage) arrived back in New York from her Parisian "seasoning"
in the fall of 1961, "those hips" to which Eileen had objected twelve
months earlier had disappeared. Wilhelmina stood shapely and ready
at a lofty five foot ten (37-24-36) to conquer New York.

"Willy was so professional," remembers Wilhelmina's booker, Rusty Zeddis. "I think it was the German in her. She was born in Holland but raised in Germany till she was a teenager. If you saw her with no makeup, you wouldn't have given her a chance at all, but she was one of that generation of models who still carried their hairpieces around town in a bag and did all their own makeup as they went along. You knew that she would always arrive on time, looking like a million dollars. With so many of the girls, you could never be quite sure, even though you'd talked everything through with them on the telephone—you always had that worry. But Willy was a joy; you could count on her for everything."

The Ford head sheets from early 1962 onward document the profusion of bookings that the slimmed-down Wilhelmina won on her return from Paris—sixteen pages in *Vogue* in the month of April 1962 alone, plus five pages in *Mademoiselle* and two pages each in *Harper's Bazaar* and *Glamour*.

"We had Willy booked solid for months," remembered Eileen Ford. "With her beautiful cheekbones, she was the last of our 'couture' models of the 1950s. She was just perfect for all those early sixties Courrèges and Oleg Cassini clothes."

Nor did the Youthquake knock the last of the couture models off her perch. Wilhelmina could never be a Twiggy, but she could certainly match Jean Shrimpton. In 1964 the *New York Journal American* reported in "Private Lives of High Fashion Models" that Wilhelmina had climbed to the "tip of the heap of the 405 girls who work under contract to the city's top five agencies." Teaming up with Irving Penn at the end of 1965, she did a Christmas issue for *Vogue* that matched the work of any of her younger English competitors.

"Wilhelmina puts the Shrimp and Twiggy in the shade," the London *Daily Express* would pronounce in 1967.

By that date, however, Wilhelmina was no longer working for Ford—and not simply because she had jumped ship to sign with a rival agency. Having proved Eileen Ford wrong by becoming a top model, Wilhelmina was determined to prove that she could also become a top agent for models. On April 18, 1967, Wilhelmina Models was incorporated in the State of New York, and the agency opened its doors three months later on Madison Avenue. Eileen and Jerry Ford had serious competition.

WILHELMINA LATER DATED HER DECISION TO GO IT ALONE FROM A chance meeting with the photographer Irving Penn, who told her he had been trying to hire her for a job, but had been told by Ford that she was booked, when she was, in fact, available—the suggestion being that Eileen was giving Willy's work away to younger models.

"Ridiculous," snorted Eileen Ford at the suggestion. "Why should I try to force Penn to take some new girl he doesn't want, for a lower fee, if I have Willy waiting there, one of my proven best models, all ready to go?"

"It's a very familiar song," said Jerry Ford to Michael Gross thirty years later. "When a photographer uses a model a lot, and then doesn't—and then bumps into her, he doesn't say, 'You're too old.' He says, 'God, I've been trying to get you!' "

Booker Rusty Zeddis detected the hand of Wilhelmina's recently acquired husband, Bruce Cooper, in the breakaway. A producer on the *Tonight* show, Cooper acted as Johnny Carson's Svengali, writing his interview questions. He was a dark and controlling character—his past included a charge of attempted murder after he stabbed his second wife's first husband—and as "Mrs. Wilhelmina," he gloried in his control over his beautiful third wife.

"Bruce always had some sort of deal to push," Zeddis recalled. "Eileen used to call him 'the jewelry salesman.' He had these show business friends, like the singer Robert Goulet, who wanted to invest."

"Bruce was absolutely dreadful," remembered Wilhelmina's close friend Carmen Dell'Orefice, "a real creep, with yellow teeth and halitosis. Willy persuaded Dovima to come in to help develop the young models, and in no time Bruce was stuffing her—on the floor, in his office! Mrs. Wilhelmina? What a joke! He was so unfaithful. But no one told Willy what was going on. She was a lovely woman, and we all wanted to protect her from the monster."

The role that Bruce Cooper played in the breakaway creation of Wilhelmina Models seems the most likely reason why Eileen Ford reacted to the rebellion and rivalry of her top model with a surprising lack of bitterness—and even some acceptance. "Bruce was a brutal man," she used to say whenever the subject turned to Wilhelmina. "I always loved Willy. She looked after her girls. There was room in New York for both of us."

"Eileen had her own way of rationalizing things when she wanted to," remembered Rusty Zeddis. "She had such convoluted thoughts, and I reckon that she said to herself, 'It was *his* idea, not hers.' That was the way that she could live with it."

"Only liars like competition" was Jerry Ford's comment when asked about the new rival agency, and once they had become competitors, Eileen Ford and Wilhelmina Cooper effectively decided to lie, professing affection and respect for each other.

"When I graduated from high school, I went to see Eileen for advice about becoming a model," remembers Wilhelmina's daughter, Melissa. "She didn't think I was model material, and she said it straight out. That was always her way. But she was very warm and welcoming—with the same values as my mother. They struck me as very similar, modern women in wanting to be taken seriously for their work. So when it came to business, they took each other seriously, too, even though they were competitors."

As Bruce and Wilhelmina Cooper hung out their shingle in 1967, they made a point of trying to move their agency away from the tall, blonde Ford stereotype by hiring more brunettes, along with African American models. Playing to Bruce's show business strengths, Wilhelmina Models became the leading agency for film and television work, and by the early 1970s, after only four years of operation, its hundred or so male and female models were billing some three million dollars a year, as compared with Ford's five million. They were creditable runners-up in the big league, comfortably ahead of

Zoli, Stewart, and Plaza Five, from whose active management Natálie Nickerson Paine had retired in 1962.

The publicity for the successful new agency highlighted the teaming of the Coopers' marital talents, inviting comparison with Eileen and Jerry Ford: Wilhelmina was depicted as the talent scout and den mother, the partner with the "eye," while Bruce was presented as the brains of the outfit, the business and ideas man behind his wife. Yet Wilhelmina had brains enough of her own—and Bruce Cooper was no Jerry Ford.

"That was the key distinction between the two agencies," reflected Carmen Dell'Orefice. "Not so much the two women, but the caliber of the men. Jerry Ford was such a quality guy. He operated on a different moral basis from Bruce or anyone else in the business—and that's what made the difference."

As the years went by, Bruce Cooper's drinking grew worse, along with his increasingly flagrant infidelities. Wilhelmina kept looking the other way, working ever more furiously to recruit new talent, but like Plaza Five in the 1950s, Wilhelmina Models never managed to mount a sustained challenge to the preeminence of the Ford agency from which it had sprung.

"I just loved Willy, and I loved Eileen too," recalls Beverly Johnson, who joined the Ford agency in the early 1970s while still in her teens. "They were both hugely inspirational women to me."

As a young woman, Johnson had developed the ambition that would make her the first African American model to appear on the cover of American *Vogue*. "The *Vogue* cover was sacred ground," she says. "I now realize that I was not totally conscious, at the time, of exactly what I was aiming at, but I was definitely heading in that direction."

By the early 1970s, black models were making a major impact in U.S. fashion—American models had triumphed in France at the so-called Battle of Versailles in 1973, when a team of largely black U.S. models sensationally outclassed an all-white troupe of France's finest at a much-reported charity show. Yet U.S. *Vogue* remained a cor-

porate bastion of caution, cowed by what it imagined were the even
more conservative views of its advertisers and subscribers.

"There was a group of us together at [Richard] Avedon's studio one
day," recalls Johnson, "and Lauren [Hutton] became quite cross with
Dick. 'You shouldn't be getting ready to shoot yet another cover with
me,' she said. '*That's* who should be on the cover of *Vogue*'—pointing
at me. Dick said nothing, and there was an embarrassed silence as
everyone realized that he was not the person who made the decisions.
It came from some other people who were very, *very* high up."

Eileen Ford understood it completely. "The first time I told her
my ambition," remembers Johnson, "she just shook her head at me
sadly. She had this way of falling silent and pursing her lips when she
disagreed. 'I am sorry, dear,' she eventually said. 'But that is just not
going to happen anytime soon.'"

By the early 1970s, Eileen Ford, who had championed the cause
of China Machado a decade earlier, had quite a contingent of black
models on her books. With the development of ethnic hair and skin
products and the growth of magazines such as *Essence* and *Ebony*,
they generated good business.

"Eileen never seemed like a racist to me," says Johnson. "I felt very
close to her—I looked up to her in many ways as an almost parental
figure, a mother. And like a wise mother, she was very good at man-
aging expectations. 'Ninety percent of models end up broke,' she'd
say. 'Don't be one of them.'"

Eileen Ford, for her part, felt empathy for Johnson. She liked to
delve into the background of her models to find some detail that, to
her, explained them. "At school and college," Ford recalled, "Beverly
had been a champion swimmer. So she had developed this disciplined athletic mind-set; she thought just like Jerry, and I liked that.
She set her goals, and she was willing to sacrifice to achieve them.
But to my mind at that time, the cover of U.S. *Vogue* was a giant step
too far."

Wilhelmina, however, felt differently. She and her husband had
hired African American models from the start of her breakaway

from Ford and, seventeen years younger than Eileen, she had a sense that the times were changing.

"She was sitting in her office," recalls Johnson, "with her can of Coke and a cigarette—I can see her there now—and she just came out with it: 'I can get you on the cover of *Vogue*.' So I left Ford and I went to Wilhelmina. When I explained it to Eileen, she got it completely. She wished me luck."

For six months Wilhelmina did the lunching and the lobbying, and then telephoned Johnson early one morning in July 1974 with the news. Johnson had known the cover was in the air, but nothing had been promised, and that had made the anticipation keener. "Beverly. You've got it!" Wilhelmina told her. Pulling on her clothes so fast she forgot to put any cash in her pockets, the twenty-one-year-old ran down to her nearest newsstand at Lexington and Forty-Eighth Street. "This is me, this is me!" she exclaimed excitedly, pointing at the cover and promising to return with the money.

"Honey," replied the vendor, giving her an old-fashioned New York City look. "If that was really you, you'd be able to afford the magazine."

Six months later Johnson was back with Eileen Ford. "I was very grateful to Wilhelmina," she says. "She had worked hard, but it wasn't her alone that really made the cover happen. There was new thinking high up at *Vogue*—Alex Liberman and Grace Mirabella. They decided to try it out with the August issue, and as things turned out, we had been pushing at the right time. But when it came to getting classy work in overall modeling terms, Eileen was simply the best. Going back to her was the obvious business decision, and Willy understood."

Beverly Johnson was all business, going on to enjoy commercial success in ventures ranging from eyewear to black beauty products, and with movies, a music album, numerous TV appearances, her own memoir, and two beauty books. Forty years after her *Vogue* cover triumph, she is the busy working CEO of Beverly Johnson Enterprises.

"It was Eileen who taught me how to be a businesswoman," John-

son says today. "Not perhaps in the financial details, but in the principles that make for business success: set yourself clear goals, don't let
other people push you off course, never oversell things, never burn
your bridges. When I was not working in front of the camera, I loved
going into the office to spend time with her, to listen to her on the
phone, to see how she worked. She took me to business lunches. We
talked through things together, like the best way of raising my rates.
We fought a lot, but we always respected each other. I've never known
a woman of such personal power and energy. She just drove her way
through."

EILEEN NEEDED ALL THE POWER SHE COULD MUSTER IN FRANCE. BY
the late 1960s the Fords' partnership with Dorian Leigh in Paris had
been operating smoothly for nearly a decade, with the two agencies
shuttling models across the Atlantic to their mutual advantage. The
traffic would grow especially hectic in January and July, the months
of the biannual French couture and ready-to-wear collections, when
Eileen would send her office manager, Camilla Park, to France for a
month to help Dorian with the administrative workload. The Fords
also funded the legendary party that Dorian threw in her apartment
the night before the collections began.

"It was quite an event," Dorian proudly recalled in her memoirs,
describing how she did all the cooking herself—her kitchen skills
were as accomplished as her exploits in the bedroom. "I invited
everybody—friends, models, designers, editors, photographers, competitors, people I saw every day, and those I hadn't seen all year."

As Dorian's principal American partners, the Fords had always
been guests of honor at the gathering—until the party she organized
in January 1967. "When I got there," Eileen remembered, "I found
Dorian waiting for me at the door, standing beside Wilhelmina and
wobbling, loaded with all the martinis she had been drinking. 'What
are you doing here?' she demanded. 'Ger'out.'"

Dorian's own version of her payoff line was more elegant, but scarcely less menacing. "'Eileen,' I told her quietly, 'you can leave by the door or by the window. It's up to you.'"

The trouble between the two women stemmed, as so often with Dorian Leigh, from sex and money. In 1960 the Fords had lent Dorian sixteen thousand dollars to fund her new apartment and office in Paris, and she had failed to pay the debt, pleading embezzlement on the part of her latest and fifth husband, Iddo Ben Gurion. This attractive and athletic Israeli was half her age—twenty-three years old when they met, to her forty-six. According to Dorian, he would get up early every morning and pretend to go jogging in the park, when he was in fact jogging to her office before any of the staff arrived, to steal model check payments from the mail and divert them to his own numbered account in Germany.

When she heard the story, Eileen Ford laughed in disbelief. "I met Iddo," she later said. "He was a good guy, to my certain knowledge—and whatever the truth of Dorian's story, it was not because of him that she failed to pay us the sixteen thousand dollars she'd owed us for more than six years as our friend and business partner. The real problem was not Iddo but Dorian. She didn't care what she did to anyone, and she was totally dishonest about money."

A few weeks after the January 1967 party confrontation, the Fords filed suit against Dorian for their unpaid loan plus interest, a total of eighteen thousand dollars. When they won their judgment, they had no hesitation in enforcing the full payment, driving their former friend to a succession of other partnerships that ended with the closure of her agency in 1970. Raising still more money from various friends, Dorian Leigh left Paris in the summer 1971 for the town of Fontainebleau, where, at the age of fifty-four, she set up in business as a restaurateur, happy to put the modeling trade behind her.

So ended the twenty-year partnership between the two gifted women who had played mother and midwife to postwar modeling in America and beyond—with a catfight over money. Yet there was a wider and functional reason for their breakup. Dorian Leigh's original success in securing the right to operate as a model agent in France had led to the creation of rival agencies—she had at least half a dozen local imitators by the late 1960s—meaning that the Fords no longer needed to deal with Dorian alone when they came to Paris. It was in their interest, in fact, to develop business with more than one agency in order to harvest the best the city had to offer.

From the point of view of the multiplying French agents, however, this was exploitation. It seemed unfair that the Fords and other American agents could come to Paris and raid French talent without paying proper money for all the models they lured to New York. In 1966, Paris's modeling agencies formally combined to raise the money and fight their cause through a professional association that got as far as sending a delegation to New York—with no results.

Then, in 1969, a young Catalan American set up in business on Avenue George V, and soon found himself asking the same question that had inspired Wilhelmina and Bruce Cooper in New York two years earlier: why should Eileen and Jerry Ford go on ruling the world of modeling unchallenged?

CHAPTER 24

BREAKFAST AT
SEVENTY-EIGHTH STREET

*The dogs and cats in her house were all shelter animals.
And, in a sense, all of us models were strays.*

—Anette Stai, former Ford model, 2010

RENE RUSSO RECALLS BEING MET BY A BUTLER IN THE SUMMER OF 1972 on the doorstep of the Ford family's town house on East Seventy-Eighth Street. "He was not a butler," said Eileen. "He was Shelton, the driver. But maybe he looked that way to Rene."

Brought up in Burbank, California, by her divorced mother, a factory worker and barmaid, Russo had dropped out of high school in tenth grade and tried her hand at a variety of part-time jobs till she was spotted by a talent agent who took her to Nina Blanchard. Now she was in New York for the first time, age seventeen, passed on by Blanchard to the Ford agency, and met at the airport by a stretch limousine.

The "butler" was just the start of it. There was a cook, plus a housekeeper who showed her to the room that she was to share for the summer with two Swedish models, who were sitting gossiping to each other—stark naked.

"That's what Swedish girls do, I later discovered, when they relax," according to Russo. "After I got to know them, I learned how you can sit around the place naked, if you want to, as if you've actually got clothes on."

The girls were summoned to dinner at 7:30 prompt in the dining room, with individual silver salt and pepper shakers in front of each place, and an array of silver implements deployed on either side of the plate, as if laid out for a visiting surgeon. "Right on the outside there was this teeny-weeny, thin little fork I had never seen before," remembered Russo. "Turned out it was for extracting the meat from the claws of the lobster."

Other girls remember the mystery of the cream linen "handker-chief" in front of them that they were supposed to open and place on their lap, and the novelty of being expected to sit at a table and actually discuss the way of the world over supper instead of watching TV. "Eileen was always telling us," Russo remembers, "'Girls, you've got to educate yourselves. Now look at this artichoke . . .'"

Jerry Hall later said that her six months living with the Fords were "the most boring year of my life." When she met Eileen and Jerry in Paris in 1974, aged only eighteen, she was already hugely grown up and successful: working with Avedon, Penn, and Scavullo; her face on the cover of *Vogue* and every major French magazine; with lovers on tap and her own apartment in the *Septième*.

"Paris was wild," she remembers, "and very artistic."

Yet, eager to make it in New York, the young Texan accepted the Fords' invitation to stay at Seventy-Eighth Street while she got started—"and I came to feel, in a way, that perhaps I needed to be bored for a bit. Modeling in New York was such a demanding business compared to Paris. You had to get up early and arrive everywhere exactly on time. They didn't like you to chat. It was very hard work. They had all the dresses ready for you, no argument. At the start, the bookers had me rushing from job to job doing catalogue work to earn the money. So it was good just to get home at night to Eileen's, to kick off my shoes and be mothered."

Eileen took her mothering duties seriously. "When Mick Jagger started calling [for Hall], I didn't approve," she remembered. "I sent word that he must stay downstairs and wait for ten minutes. I called her mother on the phone in Texas, and we both agreed: Jerry Faye had to be home before midnight."

"Jerry Faye was just a delight," remembers Lacey Ford Williams, then fourteen, who shared her bedroom with the new arrival. "She was naturally a happy person, who made herself part of the family. 'Oh là, là, oui,' she'd cry. 'I've sure gotta pee!' She did yoga with Mother several mornings a week. I remember Mick Jagger's first present to her. It was a white tractor. After that it was a purple mink coat. We knew everything about the models and their boyfriends. We hung out in the bedrooms with them and just chatted, like sisters."

Eileen delighted in playing her Miss Jean Brodie role with her girls, especially at meal times. Elizabeth Peabody, a friend of the family, was amazed at the way in which Eileen micromanaged food consumption around the table: " 'Is that four string beans on your plate?' she'd ask. 'Make it three.' Then she'd turn to the next one: 'That looks like an awful lot of peas for you. Cut it by a third.' And she'd reach across the table to scoop the peas right off the plate."

"I was lucky," remembers Patricia van Ryckeghem, a Belgian model whose classic looks and short, dark hair became the face of Chanel makeup for many years. "I could eat just about anything and not gain weight—and Eileen knew that. 'You don't have to worry, Patricia,' she would say. But she knew exactly which girls were not so lucky as me, and she supervised their plates every mealtime, right down to the last slice of meat." Rene Russo remembers: "If she found an M&M's wrapper in the trash can, she would go absolutely berserk."

Eileen had devised her "Ford Model Diet" some twenty years earlier, first publishing the details in *Glamour* magazine in 1956, then reproducing variations in her advice columns and self-help books in the 1960s. Compared with the grapefruit diet and the other crash and deprivation crazes of the time, the Ford diet was positively healthy and sensible, advising slimmers to check the details with their doctor and to parcel out their food into five small meals a day of fruit, eggs, plain grilled meat or fish, and lots of vegetables—no sugar.

"Unless you eat, your body won't be able to burn off the extra fat . . . Don't drink for the duration—no wine, no beer, no gin-and-tonic, no sodas . . . Exercise as much as you like." A very Eileen touch, with some help from Betty Cashman, was: "*Think thin*. Pull your middle in, your rib cage up, and think how narrow and elegant you are becoming."

This was the regimen that Eileen followed for herself and organized for her family. "I eat it myself," she wrote, "and serve it to Jerry and our older children."

Eating with Eileen was always a healthy experience, with lean meat, fish, vegetables, and fruit—though she conspicuously failed to follow her own advice when it came to alcohol consumption. She bought up the entire wine cellar of a Manhattan restaurant that closed in the recession of the early eighties.

In 1970 she repeated the essence of her diet and dietary advice in her book *Secrets of the Model's World,* and she cheerfully turned up to promote the book on the popular *Dick Cavett Show* in January 1971—to be ambushed in front of a hostile studio audience by a panel featuring the novelist Gwen Davis, who declared that the function of the Ford agency was "similar to pimping," and Charlotte Curtis, women's editor of the *New York Times,* who argued that models were participating in a male plot to sell unnecessary goods to women through the sinister device of advertising.

"Advertising? What do you think keeps your paper in business?" was Eileen's brusque response to Curtis. Her defense of her Ford Model Diet was even more robust. "I never worry about fat people worrying about thin people, because slender people bury the dead."

Eileen Ford's *New York Times* obituary in July 2014 cited this statement as "infamous," because it appeared "to crystallize the perception of a fashion industry that was indifferent to complaints that it was promoting an unhealthy body ideal." Looking down from heaven, the ever-slender Eileen Ford must have smiled and shrugged her power shoulders to hear that. At the age of ninety-two, she had buried most of her contemporaries, including a good number of fat people, before it was her own time to go.

———

THE DAY STARTED EARLY AT SEVENTY-EIGHTH STREET, WITH THE models who were booked for morning sessions getting out of bed by six o'clock to start work on their makeup. "They put on their eyelashes one lash at a time," remembers William Forsythe, the only son of Eileen's elder half brother, Tom. "It was fascinating. They glued on each lash individually—like a nail salon, but with eyelashes instead. When I was staying in the house, I'd go in and talk to them as they glued and glued. They were very matter-of-fact, fixing their war paint for their first assignment."

Eileen and Jerry could be heard moving around in their bedroom on the floor below, with the television blaring out the *Today* show as they got ready for the day.

"I was lost in wonder at the ambition of some of those girls," remembers Forsythe, "and at their sheer professionalism. What they did was a form of art—performance art—that was unbelievably skilled, and I'm so glad that some people in the modern arts community have recently started to recognize models as significant artists. Those young women just had it, and you can't teach what they had. It's like being a great dancer."

Forsythe himself was on his way to being a great dancer, but in conflict with his father's wishes. "He wanted me to study business," he recalls. "But I started taking dance classes at college, and was offered the chance to go up to New York and study ballet at the Joffrey. My father was devastated, and I can understand why. It was an incredible honor for me, but you couldn't expect that to transfer to his world, the value of it."

Tom Forsythe was now over sixty and suffering from tremors that he called "nerves," later diagnosed as Parkinson's disease. He cut off his son without a penny.

"That was when Eileen stepped in," recalls William Forsythe. "I'd basically run out of options for living, and she said, 'You can come and live with us all at Seventy-Eighth Street—but you'll have to make me breakfast.' By which she was saying that I should not see it as some-thing for nothing. I had to basically take care of the house when they were away at weekends and traveling—which they did quite a lot."

There were two consequences to Eileen's gesture. In the long term, William Forsythe was able to embark on the career that would make him one of the world's leading modern dancers and choreographers. (He is particularly renowned for his innovative work with the Frank-furt and Stuttgart ballets.) In the short term, he was placed in charge, at the age of nineteen, of a houseful of teenage models.

"That's the side that Aunt Eileen didn't know," he recalls. "And I tried not to overdo it. She would call me 'Forsythe,' because Billy Ford was also in the house. I remember at one point I was sharing Billy's room when there weren't enough beds to go around, and an-other time I was sharing a bedroom with Miss Universe. It was really quite terrifying, because what young man usually lives in that kind of environment? You are nineteen years old, with way too many hor-mones. You're in a house filled with models. And some of them were very nice to me . . . But I did not want to incur the wrath of Eileen, and above all, I did not want to disappoint her. There was always this aura of excellence about Aunt Eileen. She gave of her best, and she expected the best. She was a model to us, so you felt that you had to give of your best as well."

Forsythe compares Eileen Ford to the character played by Mag-gie Smith in *Downton Abbey*—outwardly terrifying, but surprisingly softhearted within. "Aunt Eileen was the only adult in my entire fam-ily who actually supported me in my decisions," he says. "Without her it would have been very, very difficult—who knows?"

In later years, when Forsythe had risen to international stature, his only family supporter remained his aunt. He recalls: "When I had my first U.S. performance with the Stuttgart Ballet—I was at the fucking Met, for God sakes!—she was the only one who came. I don't think that modern dance was very much to her liking. She had pretty traditional tastes. But whether I was dancing, or whether I was cho-reographing, she would always come and see the work. Aunt Eileen had a fundamental core of loyalty about everything and everybody. She was a very powerful businessperson with a very high-powered career, but she always had time for me, and I bless her for that."

Eileen Ford's death in July 2014 evoked a flood of memories from ex-models who blessed her in a similar fashion. "Eileen Ford paid for my wedding," remembered Iris Bianchi (a gesture that several other models recall Eileen and Jerry making for them). "Later, when my son Ed was seven or eight, he got lost in Central Park, and I was desperate, ready to throw myself out of the window. I called Eileen and she dropped everything. She came straight around to my apartment and just held me until I was all right, and we found Ed again."

"Shortly after our daughters were born," remembered Jan Mc-Guire, a successful model in the late 1960s and '70s, "my husband, Sacha, was diagnosed with what turned out to be terminal cancer, and the first person I called after my own mother was Eileen. I will never forget our conversation from that pay phone in the hallway of Lenox Hill. She was so soft and so strong. And later, after Sacha died, she helped me make the contacts I needed with the foreign agencies to support my daughters."

Renée Toft Simonsen, one of the Ford stars of the 1980s, remembers the warmth and sympathy with which Eileen reacted to the anxiety attack that drove Simonsen out of modeling in 1988 and prompted her to work on a kibbutz in Israel, so she could "pick fruit, dress in ugly clothes, and grow hair under my arms."

"There was no reproach," she remembers, "only full-hearted love and support, though Jerry had just negotiated this fantastic Cover Girl contract for me, and my leaving must have cost them a lot of money. I never doubted that Eileen cared deeply for me. Whenever I traveled anywhere after I left New York, I would send one postcard to my mum, and another postcard to Eileen."

Simonsen identified the price tag for Eileen Ford's fierce loyalty to those she considered close. "Control was always a big issue in her life," she says. "She was never happy if she felt she was not in control."

Simonsen remembers coming back to Seventy-Eighth Street, after working late, to find Eileen and Jerry tucked up in bed. "I would go in to see them," she remembers, "and would lie down at the foot end of the bed, to tell Eileen about my day. She was fun and would laugh, but at the same time she never stopped trying to mother me, always telling me what to do, which irritated me a lot. I was seventeen, and she had all these ideas about how I should behave with which I did not agree."

If you were someone who was playing on Eileen's team and if you followed her rules, in other words, she would shower you with love. Yet if, for some reason, she ever felt that you were threatening her control of herself or a situation, she could react in a very different fashion.

CHAPTER 25

THE PANORAMA

The problem is that God gave man a brain and a penis, and only enough blood to run one at a time.

—Robin Williams

THE FIRST TIME EILEEN FORD MET JOHN CASABLANCAS IN THE late 1960s, she left the car running outside his office in Paris.

"I had just opened my very first agency," he recalled. "I was so proud. I'd found this wonderful space in the American Chamber of Commerce Building. When Eileen called and said she'd come by, everybody got dressed up and was standing to attention."

It was the summer of 1969 and John Casablancas, twenty-six years old, had joined the rush of start-up French agencies that had been created to fill the gap left by the decline of Dorian Leigh, shortly to shut up shop and head for her new career as a restaurant owner in Fontainebleau. Casablancas had named his agency Elysée 3, after his telephone number and as an echo of New York's defunct Plaza Five.

"I was totally shaking in my boots," he remembered of the day of her visit. "Eileen Ford was the Empress, Catherine the Great. So when she came in, said hello and good-bye, shook a few hands, and went straight back down to her car again, I was so happy and proud. I didn't realize until later that I had just been slapped in the face."

Casablancas soon discovered that this was Eileen's standard opening gambit. "She played divide-and-rule with all of us in Paris," he recalled in 2010, talking from Brazil, where he spent his final years. "The other agents told me her game. She went around the different agencies, cherry-picking the girls that she wanted to have in New York. And all we got in return, if we were lucky, were a few points of mother agency commission, plus some American beginners that she sent to us to be 'seasoned' in Paris."

Casablancas decided to try again. He had been mulling over an idea for a different sort of modeling agency, a successor to Elysée 3, that would not recruit large numbers of beginners and run-of-the-mill models, but would concentrate on just a dozen or so top-flight earners, the very best of the best, on whom the bookers and the marketing department would lavish all their attention. He would call it Elite.

"So on their next trip to Paris, I nailed Eileen and Jerry down for a proper meeting," he recalled. "I asked for an appointment where we could sit down and talk, and also have a drink."

The drink was Lillet, a dry, Martini-like aperitif that Casablancas had never tasted before. It was, he discovered, Jerry Ford's favorite tipple.

"Jerry and Eileen," he remembered, "were heavy drinkers. They really did drink a hell of a lot—Eileen especially. So after we'd had a few drinks, I explained my new idea, and when I'd finished, Eileen said to me straightaway, without a moment's reflection, 'You're a very nice young man, John, and I can tell that you are well educated. You come from a good family.' I think she was impressed that my sister had dated the Aga Khan for quite a time. 'But you really should find something else to do. You can't possibly know how all these things work. When it comes to modeling, you don't really fit into the panorama of what we do.'" Eileen was smiling warmly at Casablancas as she spoke.

"The Fords were a great double act," he recalled. "They gave off this aura together of 'This is how things should be.'"

But there was always something patronizing in Eileen's tone, he felt, as if she were brushing off an ingenue, would-be model.

"Being kind to the weak," he recalled, "was not one of Eileen's stronger qualities. Jerry had more charm about him, but he was really just as tough and ruthless as she was."

Eileen had a different recollection of the meeting. "Johnny knew nothing about models," she recalled, "except that he wanted to boff them. He was like all those spoiled little rich boys from Le Rosey—full of big ideas, and supported by Daddy's money."

EILEEN FORD MADE A MAJOR MISTAKE WHEN SHE UNDERESTIMATED the business acumen of John Casablancas. He certainly came from a rich family. His grandfather Ferran Casablancas invented a cotton-spinning machine, the Casablancas High Draft System, that was the making of the family fortune. "We lost our factories in Spain," Casablancas related, "because my father and grandfather were anti-Franco. But we still had cotton factories elsewhere in the world."

It was also true that Casablancas not only had attended the privileged Swiss boarding school Le Rosey, on Lake Geneva—it had its own skiing campus in Gstaad to which the entire school decamped in winter—but was expelled for seducing a kitchen maid. "My fatal attraction for beautiful women and easy challenges," he confessed in his memoir *Vida Modelo* (Model Life), "changed my life for the worse and forever."

Casablancas's expulsion on the eve of his applying to a string of top colleges sabotaged his higher education, and he muddled along for several years with lowly jobs at Merrill Lynch and in Barcelona property sales. Then his Le Rosey connections turned up trumps, sending him to Recife, in northeast Brazil, to help run the Coca-Cola franchise for the widowed mother of a schoolmate. For four years he worked as a soft drink distributor, confronting gun-toting underlings and countering anti-American protests against Coca-Cola by lending his trucks to the relief work of the popular archbishop of Recife, Dom Hélder Câmara, famous for his saying "When I give food to the poor, they call me a saint; when I ask why they are poor, they call me a

Communist." To launch Fanta as a "healthy" and fruit-filled new soft drink, Casablancas put dancing girls on trucks, atop piles of oranges, and drove them into country towns at dawn.

Back in Paris in the late 1960s, patching together a living in construction and import-export, he had the second amorous encounter that helped change his life, followed rapidly by a third. Both his later paramours were models—one of them a mannequin who worked for Paris Planning, an agency run by François Lano and Diane Gérald, a former assistant of Dorian Leigh; followed a few months later by a much longer-lasting partnership with Jeanette Christiansen, a former Miss Denmark, "an absolutely spectacular blonde; tall, with the deepest blue eyes, a miniskirt, and those thigh-high boots that were 'in' in the sixties and that you see today on streetwalkers."

Seeing his girlfriends go off to their bookings, professional model bags packed with makeup, hairpieces, and accessories, gave Casablancas his first direct contact with the world of the fashion model— and he was fascinated.

"Nothing had destined me for this profession," he later wrote. "I walked into it step by step, almost without noticing, as if guided by a subtle and powerful magnetic force. Some people call this destiny. I think that it was, above all, that I managed to convert my biggest faults into my biggest qualities—my weaknesses were transformed into the forces that pushed me ahead."

Modeling, in other words, got Casablancas's blood flowing to both the relevant parts of his body at once. Jeanette Christiansen had been staying in the same low-rent pension, the Hotel d'Argoult, where Casablancas was lodging, and he had assumed that her companion, Gunnar Larsen, a hippie-looking Danish photographer, was her lover. In fact, the relationship was platonic. Larsen made his living bringing Scandinavian models to Paris, and when he got to know Casablancas, he recognized a fellow scout.

"Larsen was the first person to say that I had been born to be a model agent," wrote Casablancas. "He put in a bit of money, along with my flatmate Alain Kittler, who was at Le Rosey with me. Elysée 3 was born through a combination of my ignorance about the business and Gunnar's insistence."

Casablancas's ignorance of the business rapidly became obvious. Elysée 3 folded within six months, and was saved only by an injection of funds from his father, Fernando Casablancas, who insisted that his son bring in a professional office manager, Tischka Nabi. Nabi was an experienced Corsican booker and scout who had done stints with Wilhelmina in New York and with Models International, the Paris agency run by Simone d'Aillencourt, the former model with whom the Fords had linked after their break from Dorian Leigh.

"Johnny was effectively bankrupt," remembers Nabi, "and it was his father who put him back in business—twice, in 1970 and again about a year later. He did not realize how long it can take in the modeling business for money to come trickling in, and the need to be careful until that has happened. John had a great eye for models— Jeanette Christiansen was a huge earner—and he had a real flair for promotion, but he did not have the business sense. He was like Eileen Ford without the Jerry."

Eileen and Jerry Ford themselves, meanwhile, felt that their skepticism about young Casablancas had been justified. "Johnny had all the talk and the charm," remembered Eileen. "But he did not know the nuts and bolts of the business. Jerry and I helped him out twice financially, through both of those early crashes. We didn't push him for the money that he owed us, and we kept on paying the 'mother' agency commission for the models that he had found for us. If we were really as cruel as he later complained, we could have chosen to put him out of business when he started. But we stuck with him—and he did not repay us kindly."

JOHN CASABLANCAS ANNOUNCED THE OPENING OF HIS NEW ELITE model agency in October 1972. His brother, Fernando, he explained in a letter to Eileen and Jerry Ford, would be taking over the running of Elysée 3, looking after its existing stable of beginner and mid-ranking models, "while I will be opening a completely separate agency in new offices." This new operation, Elite Model Management, would represent just "ten to twenty top models," catering to their special needs in an exclusive fashion.

Casablancas made much of the "new philosophy" that inspired Elite—top service for top models—but Tischka Nabi remembers the prosaic family politics that inspired the switch. "Fernando had lost his job at Time-Life," she recalls. "So their father told John to give him Elysée 3 to run, and to set up on his own again in a small way— and that was what became Elite."

In fact, Elite was never able to keep to its "elite" proposition. Casablancas soon found himself recruiting fresh talent that required development and promotion like any other beginner models, and as new recruits joined, he did not discard his original core of earners. So the agency spread and grew in numbers over the years like any other.

What made Elite different was the buzz that Casablancas managed to generate in Paris around his project, particularly among the new generation of French photographers, such as Patrick Demarchelier, and visiting young Americans: Mike Reinhardt, Alex Chatelain, and Arthur Elgort. Their talents attracted fresh faces, and it was the gift of the good-looking Casablancas to turn work into a great hubbub of excitement and fun. "Fun was my signature tune," he recalled. "So whenever I took the girls out to dinner, I made sure the press was there with their cameras."

This was precisely how Eileen and Jerry Ford had publicized their own young agency and models at the Stork Club twenty years earlier— but "fun" had a different meaning in the age of sex, drugs, and rock and roll. "My philosophy was simple," said Casablancas. "Women want to be sexy, and so do I. That's the different eye I brought to Elite. All the other agencies were run either by women or by gays. I was the first totally heterosexual agent in Paris."

"John introduced sex," said the photographic agent Jacques de Nointel, talking to Michael Gross about the impact that Casablancas made on the model trade in the early 1970s. "Don Juan, Casanova, their whole life put together is not equal to one year of John! John can look at a girl and in five minutes she takes off her underwear."

Casablancas's first marriage had already fallen victim to his numerous love affairs. "John was a seducer," recalls Tischka Nabi. "That was his style." Jeanette Christiansen, whom Casablancas would eventually marry, was a trusting and much-deceived partner. Her own modeling assignments in the early years gave Casablancas many opportunities for one-night stands, particularly with underage girls, of whom he grew particularly fond. His partners grew younger as he grew older. "John had very loose morals," says Tischka flatly. "I could not agree to how he behaved. I never heard any stories that he forced any of the girls, but many of them were very young."

Tischka had stayed with Elysée 3 to help Fernando Casablancas keep the agency afloat. "Fernando did not compare to John," she recalls. "He had none of his brother's flair—and whatever you say about John, you have to admit that he had some very bright ideas."

Casablancas laid much emphasis on design. He wanted an eye-catching emblem, so he devoted ten thousand dollars, a quarter of his total start-up capital, to commission the designer Malcolm Thompson to produce the notoriously suggestive Elite logo that remains the logo of the agency to this day. The brilliance of Thompson's design, with its three elongated central letters, *lit*, with the two round *e*'s on either side, was that the erotic "cock and balls" image was there only if you were looking for it. Otherwise, it looked like a clean, modern, easy-to-read label—curiously similar to the green logo of the Citer car rental agency, just a few doors away from Casablancas's office near the Arc de Triomphe.

Casablancas also enlisted the latest technique in model publicity: the printed "composite card," developed in the mid-sixties by English publisher and designer Peter Marlowe and much talked up by the head of Britain's Photographers' Association, Brian Duffy, who contended that photographers were the real clients of models. It was photographers or their assistants, Duffy pointed out, who actually picked up the phone to make the bulk of model bookings, but they were overwhelmed by the inconsistent publicity material sent out by the model agencies, ranging from cumbersome posters to scruffy photocopied head sheets of the type favored by the Fords. It would be a great help, he suggested, if all model photos and data could be standardized and stacked in neat desktop boxes, ideally along the lines of the color-coded index cards he had seen being used by detectives at New Scotland Yard—pink for swimwear, red for runway, blue for lingerie, and so on.

The fashion model as crime suspect? In practice, Duffy's color-coding proposal proved too complicated, but Peter Marlowe's simple and elegant A5 (5.8 by 8.3-inch) "comp cards" did catch on. They became the industry standard, and the publisher was soon producing thousands of them for successful models who wanted to promote their careers. Among them was Jeanette Christiansen, through whom Marlowe had met John Casablancas when he went to the Hotel d'Argoult in Paris to deliver her latest batch of publicity material.

"John came down to the lobby to collect the composite," he recalls, "and that was how I first met him. Here was this very good-looking guy with a very good-looking girl—I thought immediately that we would get along."

So it proved. Casablancas decided he would get new Elite-branded composite cards produced for all his models, and he started a collaboration with Marlowe that immediately outclassed every other agency in the slickness and professionalism of its promotion material.

"Ford didn't compel their models to do anything," remembers Marlowe. "But Elite models had to pay out three times a year for their promotional material. It cost them more money, but it meant that their composite cards were landing like confetti in photographers' studios everywhere—and that soon got them a lot of work."

As Elite took off in Paris, Casablancas started expanding to other cities in Europe—and particularly to Denmark and Sweden.

"I thought, 'Why the hell should Eileen have Scandinavia to herself?'" he remembered. "So I went to a business fair in Copenhagen one winter with Gunnar Larsen and came away with six lovely models who all worked for the Danish agency that supplied Eileen with talent. The agency went crazy and managed to claw the girls back from me. But I think that everyone in Scandinavia got the message."

Jerry Ford certainly took note of the unexpected rise of Elite. "Look, we did not think you would survive in this business," he confessed candidly to Casablancas at a meeting in Paris in the mid-1970s. Casablancas could not recall the precise date, but he did remember that, unlike their previous encounters, the meeting was called at Ford's request. "We have been working with all your competitors in Paris. But now we have got into a ridiculous situation. Our biggest models are saying they want to work with you when they come to Paris, so we must work out a modus vivendi."

The agreement, as Casablancas recalled it, was that Ford would work on Elite's behalf in America, with Elite representing Ford interests in Europe. So he was incensed when, a few months later, he heard that Eileen Ford had been on another of her scouting trips to Scandinavia.

"I went there soon afterward," he recalled, "and discovered that she had been bad-mouthing me to everyone, saying that I was a playboy, that I was selling my girls to Arabs, Jews, Lebanese, Iranians, God knows who. She said nasty things about me, and I can say the same about her—that Eileen Ford was a drunk and a racist. That woman was nothing less than a witch. Also, she was telling her contacts to send their girls to this new agency, Karins, that her friend Karin Mossberg had just opened in Paris."

Talking in 2011, Eileen Ford rejected Casablancas's accusations. "I never made any secret of what I thought of John's morals," she said. "He slept with his models, and that was unforgivable to me. We also discovered he was doing bad things in business: he was cutting commission in order to steal girls from other agencies, and he was paying his French photographer friends to choose only Elite models. Karin Mossberg was a very dear friend who had also been a very successful model of ours. But we never encouraged her to set herself up against John. He said all these things to excuse what he did next."

What John Casablancas did next, in the spring of 1977, was to take Elite Model Management to open a new headquarters—in Manhattan.

CHAPTER 26

MODEL WARS

Eileen Ford's game is crystal-clear. She wants my skin . . .
But I am a warrior. I will fight. I will never sleep with both
eyes closed as long as that woman is around.

—*John Casablancas*

Through the winter months of 1976 and 1977, John Casa-blancas conducted his invasion of Manhattan like a secret commando operation. "There was one trip," he recalled, "where I bumped into one of the Ford daughters outside Bloomingdales, right across from the new office space that we were already fitting out—the telephone system had gone in that day. I told her I was just passing through on my way to Venezuela."

The secrecy came to an end on April 29, 1977, with the dramatic double defection from Ford to Elite of booker Monique Pillard and financial controller Jo Zagami. The Casablancas invasion was out in the open, and Eileen Ford's dispatch of her marked-up "Judas Bibles" to the defectors laid down the style in which she, for one, was planning to react.

"She came out of her corner fighting," remembered William Forsythe, "clutching a Bible and quoting scriptures in a way that I would never have expected from her. I thought it was out of character. But she had had no natural predators for many years, so it came as a big shock to her."

"We reacted emotionally because we were hurt emotionally," explained Eileen. "We felt we had done so much for Johnny and for all the people that he stole from us—our own models, our own staff. And they left us for what? Thirty pieces of silver! There are things in life that matter more than money. We had helped John since he started, and we thought we were friends. That spring [of 1977] I'd done a big favor and pulled strings to get Jeanette into a very fashionable dermatologist. I later found out that on the very day she was at the beauty parlor I had arranged, John was applying for his license to operate in New York."

Jeanette Christiansen had moved to New York with Casablancas in the spring of 1977 and become pregnant later that year with their son, Julian, the future rock star. The couple got married in New York's City Hall the following year.

"Casablancas was basically unthankful to Eileen," said Soni Ekvall, the Swedish founder of the German agency Model Team, "and I think that is what hurt her. Business is business, but he could at least have rung her and said, 'I feel Paris is too small for me. I'm going to open in New York, and I'm not going to take girls from you.' That would have been ethical—instead of going secretly behind her back, then coming out all guns blazing."

"John Casablancas had a gorilla style of doing things," says Melissa Cooper, the daughter of Wilhelmina, "and I think that was what both Eileen and my mother had against him. There are ways and ways of stealing each other's models—my mother and Eileen had been doing it politely for years."

"He promised the girls fatter paychecks," remembered Janice Dickinson, with "reduced commissions and plenty of *fun*. He knew how to seduce women. Limos, dinner, roses, caviar, diamonds. He told each of them—me included—that she was *the best, my very favorite, destined for greatness* . . . There's not much loyalty in this business. In fact, betrayal is the norm."

If John Casablancas behaved like King Kong, however, the Fords' hiring of Roy Cohn as their attack dog attorney was hardly more subtle. Casablancas recalled in his memoirs how, early in May 1977, he had been working with Monique Pillard and Jo Zagami in his suite at the St. Moritz hotel, readying the plans for Elite's imminent opening on Fifty-Eighth Street, when they decided to go down to the hotel's restaurant, Rumplemeyer's, for some food.

"We were sitting there eating lunch," he wrote, "when I saw two sinister characters come in, Joe Hunter [Ford's vice president and head of the men's division] and the notorious Roy Cohn . . . Cohn and Hunter took a table nearby and sat facing us, staring threateningly. I thought that Monique and Jo would pass out."

Cohn's specialty was intimidation. "When I appeared in court," wrote Casablancas, "Roy Cohn shouted, pointed his finger in my face, and tried to browbeat me by every means possible."

Cohn's two lines of attack were a $7.5 million suit for betrayal of fiduciary trust, and an order seeking the deportation of Casablancas as an illegal alien. "Poor Eileen," laughed Casablancas later. "With a name like mine, she had to assume that I was an unsavory WOP. Well, maybe I was, but I was a WOP who was born in Queens. When I was born, in December 1942, my parents were living in Forest Hills—I was an American citizen from the day I appeared on this earth. The judge threw out the deportation suit without even hearing it."

The fiduciary trust suit, however, dragged on for years, alongside a parallel suit that the Fords brought against Monique Pillard. Casablancas countersued with allegations that the major New York agencies had conspired to fix prices and commissions—and Wilhelmina joined in with her own suit against Elite for four million dollars. Only the lawyers made money.

"It was a big mistake by Eileen and the others to launch all those lawsuits," said Casablancas later. "With all their bluster and hatred they simply betrayed their own fear."

The Fords' suit against Monique Pillard was finally dismissed in 1979, and after two years of toing-and-froing, both sides agreed to withdraw from the legal fray. All the pending suits were dropped—including Ford's original action for $7.5 million.

"The verdicts proved it," said John Casablancas. "We had done nothing at all illegal when I came to New York, except break the sacred commandment 'Thou shalt not compete with Eileen Ford.'"

"That lawsuit was the mistake of Eileen Ford's life," remarked Elite cofounder Alain Kittler to Michael Gross. "From one day to the other we were known. People thought we were rich and powerful when we were neither, because we were attacked for seven million dollars. So we made the breakthrough in two months."

Round one to Elite.

JOHN CASABLANCAS BROUGHT THE PUBLISHER PETER MARLOWE TO America to mastermind the graphic side of his campaign and to do something unheard of in 1977: to design and simultaneously launch every model's publicity material. "I wanted composite cards, posters, and a model book," Casablancas remembered, "a whole visual statement that clearly said, 'This is the best. Here is something stylish. Here is something new.'"

This had been Marlowe's idea, and he did not disappoint. The Englishman spent a month in New York on his hands and knees on the floor of the Elite offices, sorting out Polaroids, tear sheets, and color transparencies to mastermind a compendium of model images that he took back to London to be printed and shipped back across the Atlantic for mailing to every major U.S. client.

"There must have been ten tons of paper in that container," he recalls. "It was a model book like there had never been before—with all the images of the models that folded out."

Patty Sicular, later a model manager with Ford, Elite, and Trump, remembers the stir when the book arrived at the Manhattan advertising agency where she was working early in 1978. "People passed it around the office in wonder," she recalls. "It was a sensational book—a real, proper book, with beautiful girls, all beautifully laid out. It was such a contrast to the brown envelopes stuffed with clippings and head sheets that Ford and Wilhelmina had been sending out for years, with odd scribblings and arrows from the bookers—

'Look at this girl. This is the one we're talking about.' It took model promotion to a whole new level."

Wilhelmina, Zoli, and Ford phoned Marlowe immediately. "They all wanted me to do the same for them," the publisher recalled, "and I said that I was happy to, even though Elite was my primary client. Eileen took me to lunch and said that she would give me all of Ford's publishing business, provided that I stopped working for John Casablancas. I had to explain that that was impossible, that all my clients were competitors—at that stage I was working in twelve countries. It would be like the electricity company saying it would not supply one house when it was supplying all the others in the road."

"It was after lunch and over coffee," added Marlowe's wife, Gussy, recalling how Eileen made her move. "Jerry did not say anything. Peter tried to reassure Eileen about his discretion. But this was about something else—she was allowing her personal feelings to override business, and that's the nub of it."

Throughout the world of modeling, people were being forced to choose. When John Casablancas went to Rome in the summer of 1977 for the Italian collections, he provocatively booked himself into the Parco dei Principi hotel, where he knew the Fords always stayed, and received the response he expected.

"When I arrived," he remembered, "the manager came out to see me, full of apologies. 'I'm very sorry,' he said, 'but I can't give you a room. Mr. and Mrs. Ford have been staying with us for years.' 'That's all right,' I replied, and called up my friend Riccardo [Gay]. 'How many girls have you got staying in the Principi?' I asked him. 'Forty? OK—cancel all their rooms.' Riccardo called, I got my room, and when Eileen exploded, the manager told her he couldn't do anything, that I had a reservation."

Riccardo Gay was Italy's leading model agent, based in Milan. He had worked with the Fords from time to time, but was by now closer to Casablancas—and he had a mischievous streak. He traditionally presided over a grand dinner on the final night of the shows in Rome, and he decided to render the Model Wars in graphic form:

he arranged the seating for his guests in a huge horseshoe, where he would preside at the head of the table, with Casablancas and his allies ranged down one side of the room and the Fords facing them on the other.

"We were in a terrible dilemma," remembers April Ducksbury, the cofounder of London's Models 1 agency with José Fonseca. "José and I had been with the Fords most of the week. Eileen and Jerry gave these wonderful buffet lunches every day up on the roof of the Parco dei Principi, with their models and our models and all of the press. But Riccardo asked us if we would mind, for this evening, sitting on John's side of the room."

The trouble was that the Elite entourage was late for the dinner. It did not appear for half an hour, then an hour, then an hour and a half, and as the minutes ticked by, it became clear that John Casablancas was playing some kind of game.

"It was excruciating," remembers Ducksbury. "There was nothing to eat. Just wine and water and bread. It was so *rude* of John, and Eileen was getting furious. I wanted to leave. But Riccardo begged me to stay."

In the end, after what seemed to Ducksbury a full two hours, Casablancas made the entrance that he had clearly planned, with a party of laughing models and photographers who had been shooting at the *Vogue* studios, all of them spilling over the room and making a scene.

"I was livid," remembers Ducksbury. "I wanted to hit John with a bottle."

Still more livid was Eileen Ford, who realized the full extent of the insult offered her when Casablancas sat down beside Fonseca and Ducksbury. Taking her husband by the arm and ushering her models into a posse around her, she rose to her feet and swept out of the room.

The next day at lunchtime, Fonseca and Ducksbury went up shamefacedly to the roof terrace to offer their apologies—to be met by a grim-faced Jerry Ford. He was not interested in their explanations of being set up by the troublemaking Riccardo Gay. "We can't go on in this way," Ducksbury remembers him saying. "You've just got to choose."

THE PROBLEM FOR APRIL DUCKSBURY AND JOSÉ FONSECA, AS FOR other model agents around Europe, was that they did not want to choose. "We liked dealing with both Eileen *and* John," remembers Ducksbury. "We had worked so well with them both, and for about the same amount of time—in New York and Paris."

Models 1's small boutique of top earners—Ingrid Boulting, Marisa Berenson, Susan Murray, and Greta Norris—were not particularly eager to go all the way to New York. They much preferred traveling to Paris, where they enjoyed the risqué creativity of working with Helmut Newton, Hans Feurer, and Guy Bourdin, and with Demarchelier and the photographers gathered around Casablancas. Yet now Elite was drawing more of "the French crowd" to America, and Ducksbury decided that she would have to follow.

"I went to New York early in 1978," she recalled, "and I was really impressed by the Elite offices—a great big floor of a skyscraper, so swish. It put the old Ford building beside the bridge to shame. I loved Monique [Pillard], and Alain Kittler struck me as really efficient."

Kittler and Casablancas offered Ducksbury a generous commission deal on any models Elite took from Models 1, along with financial help to set up a New Faces department in London that would scout and nurture new talent. "It was all very professional," remembers Ducksbury, who had made an appointment to have lunch with Eileen Ford a few days later, hoping to negotiate some sort of compromise or perhaps get a comparable deal.

"When I arrived, I was met by Susan, her office manager, looking very embarrassed. 'Do you want lunch,' she said, 'before I tell you the bad news?' 'Tell me the bad news,' I said. 'Well,' she said, 'Eileen has gone away, and she's left you this message: "You're with us 100 percent, or not at all."' 'Perhaps we'd better not have lunch,' I said."

Ducksbury went back to London to discuss the New York situation with Fonseca, and the two women decided they had no choice. "Eileen had left us this ultimatum," she recalls. "What did she expect? We went full blast with John, and for ten years he delivered everything just as he promised. Our head of accounts loved working with Elite. They were extremely professional. We built up our New Faces department, which was John's idea, and he helped us find the finance to purchase flats in Chelsea for the models, which turned out to be excellent investments. He was always on the phone and gave us good advice every day. He was full of energy. Models 1 was already doing well, but in the late seventies and eighties we really took off because of John's input."

Seen from London in the early 1980s, Elite Model Management was the clear winner in the Model Wars.

CHAPTER 27

THE FORD EMPIRE STRIKES BACK

A model today has almost the same importance to an
advertiser or manufacturer as an actor or actress would
to a film producer. The models are the movie stars of
advertising.

—*Richard Talmadge,*
attorney to Eileen and Jerry Ford, 1980

AGE TWENTY-THREE IN 1977, THE RISING MODEL CHRISTIE
Brinkley found her loyalties painfully divided by the rivalry
between Ford and Elite. Like Models 1 owner April Ducksbury, Brinkley had operated very happily when the two agencies were working
together as a transatlantic team. "It was John who 'discovered' me
and got me started," she remembers. "But in those days he was Eileen's ally and representative in France."

All-American beauty though she was, Christie Brinkley, born
in Michigan and raised in California, had actually been discovered
in Paris, by a Casablancas talent scout, while living in a garret as a
young art student and enjoying a love affair with the rising French
political cartoonist Jean-François Allaux.

"The first time I went to see John," she remembers, "there were
these two photographers in the office, Mike Reinhardt and Patrick
Demarchelier, who jumped up all excited. 'Oh my God!' they said.
'We've got to ring Eileen Ford right now!' So from the very start I felt
I was part of a Ford-Casablancas team."

Brinkley met Eileen a year later, when she went home with Allaux, by now her husband, to see her parents in Los Angeles, and

discovered that Eileen and Jerry were holidaying in Palm Springs. "I couldn't wait to meet Christie," Eileen recalled. "I'd heard so much about her from John in Paris, and also from Nina Blanchard. So I invited her and her husband down for lunch. I asked her to bring her book."

By now Brinkley had built up quite a portfolio of work with French *Vogue* and other European magazines, and Eileen leafed through the pictures eagerly when the two women met, suggesting which images she should discard and which she might keep to use for future "go-sees."

"Eileen was wearing a bikini with a sarong," Brinkley remembers, "and as she was leaning over, leafing through the pages, one of her breasts fell out of her top. There it was, this breast just *there*, rather attractive actually, but she had no idea what had happened, and she went on flipping through the pages. Jean-François and I, two kids in our early twenties—we just didn't know where to look. And then we heard ice clinking as Jerry came down the corridor with the drinks. What were we going to say? Luckily, just at that moment, she leaned down a bit and everything fell back into place."

Brinkley and her husband were very happy in Paris, but Eileen prevailed on them to come to New York "just for a month."

"Of course," remembers Brinkley, "she had been lining things up for much more than a month's work—and it turned out Jean-François was very happy because he could work with his dream, the op-ed page of the *New York Times*. Eileen helped us find an apartment, so we ended up staying."

Like Jerry Hall before her, Brinkley discovered the difference between working in New York and working in Paris. "In Paris it was so casual," she recalls. "You might start with a long lunch, then hair and makeup for another hour, then shoot in the studio until ten at night. In New York, you would be booked for three sessions in a day, with just half an hour or so in between, starting early in the morning and going on till eight at night. It was hard work, but Eileen and Jerry and the bookers made it fun. I felt very happy at Ford."

Then, in the spring of 1977, John Casablancas arrived in New York and gave Brinkley a call. "John really did the loyalty number on me," she remembers, "reminding me that it was only thanks to him that I was with Ford. 'I was the one who discovered you,' he said. 'If it were not for me, no one would have heard of you. You are one of mine.' He kept on asking me, 'Are you loyal?' I hated hurting Eileen, but in the end I felt I had to be faithful—I had no choice but to go with John."

Eileen was not hurt, in fact—or if she was, she chose not to show it. "I can't say we were best pleased," she later said, "and we told Christie we thought she was making a big mistake—that we could do much more for her career. But we couldn't blame Christie. She was still very young, and she came to us very politely and sadly to explain why she felt she had to go. She was doing what she thought was the right thing—she was leaving for loyalty, not for money. So we gave her a kiss and told her she was welcome back anytime."

As with Bruce and Wilhelmina Cooper ten years earlier, Eileen focused on the role of the malignant man in the unhappy situation, which gave her the license to feel motherly sympathy for the other woman in the case.

"And anyway," she later recalled with a smile, "Christie came back to Ford after a year or so. None of the nice girls stuck with John for very long."

THE MERRY-GO-ROUND OF MODELS CIRCULATING BETWEEN FORD and Elite, and also into and out of the Wilhelmina agency in 1977 and the succeeding years, was bewildering. Brinkley and Janice Dickinson were the first departures from Ford to Elite, in the wake of the earliest defector of all, Maaret Halinen, who left Wilhelmina in May 1977. In the same few months, Barbara Minty, Lisa Cooper, and Beverly Johnson also left Ford for Elite. Cooper and Johnson later returned to Ford—but Johnson would then go back to Elite again.

Shelley Promisel, New York's leading freelance stylist in these years, remembers the models whispering in the changing room:

"Are you going to leave Ford? Do you know that so-and-so is going to Elite?" Aware of her proximity to the models, Johnny Casablancas phoned Promisel, suggesting that she might care to woo certain girls on Elite's behalf. "I told him," recalls the stylist, "that I could not ethically be any part of switching of agencies. I could pass on a phone number or a message. That was business—but I would not get involved in any more than that."

Promisel found that her own business was flourishing, as the rivalry between agencies grew hotter. "There's no doubt," she recalls, "that the Model Wars were good for the whole of the U.S. fashion business, and for New York in particular. The publicity brought such attention to U.S. photographers, makeup artists, stylists, and hairdressers—everyone involved. The rates paid to models went sky high. Girls that cost seven hundred fifty a day were charging fifteen hundred dollars a few years after Elite arrived, and that money knocked on down to the rest of us. I remember being flown over to London on [the] Concorde. I remember hot-air-ballooning over the South of France on a job for Christian Dior. I went on one trip to Paris for a few days and I came home with twenty thousand dollars."

"Everybody benefited," remembers Grace Mirabella, editor in chief of *Vogue* in these years. "Even the makeup artists got themselves agents."

The rival generals in the battle fascinated Felicia Milewicz, the models editor of *Mademoiselle*. "Johnny Casablancas and Eileen were like yin and yang," she recalled. "They were the opposing sides and styles of the business. Eileen made no secret about being traditional. As for Johnny, he never made a secret of his lifestyle."

Milewicz enjoyed the cozy parties that Eileen threw at her home in Seventy-Eighth Street. "It was so refreshing in those years," she recalls, "to go to a party where not everyone was stoned. Her young models would be there, all dressed up beautifully and behaving so well." Milewicz particularly enjoyed the way in which Eileen signaled to her guests that the party was over. "She would get out the Hoover and start running it over the carpet."

FORD'S GOLDEN GENERATION.
Eileen Ford poses for photographer Mark Shaw of *McCall's* magazine in April
1955, in front of eleven of her top models. *To the left of her*: Patsy Shally;
behind them, from left to right: Jean Patchett, Lillian Marcuson, Nan Rees, and
Leonie Vernet; *top row*: Dorian Leigh, Suzy Parker, Georgia Hamilton, Dolores
Hawkins, Kathy Dennis, and Mary Jane Russell.

FASHION WORLD ICONS. Richard Avedon in front of an exhibition print of his famous *Dovima with Elephants: Cirque d'Hiver, Paris, August, 1955.* Note the chain tethering the elephant's fo

Diana Vreeland, of *Harper's Bazaar* (1936–1962), later editor of US *Vogue* (1963–1971).

Ford model Dovima—Dorothy Virginia Margaret Juba—with Audrey Hepburn, 195

AUDREY **HEPBURN** FRED **ASTAIRE**

FUNNY FACE

co-starring **KAY THOMPSON** _with_ MICHEL AUCLAIR · ROBERT FLEMYNG

MUSIC AND LYRICS BY GEORGE AND IRA GERSHWIN
CHOREOGRAPHY BY EUGENE LORING AND FRED ASTAIRE · SONGS STAGED BY STANLEY DONEN
PRODUCED BY ROGER EDENS · DIRECTED BY STANLEY DONEN · WRITTEN BY LEONARD GERSHE

TECHNICOLOR®
VISTAVISION®

A PARAMOUNT PICTURE

FASHION ON FILM.
The movie inspired by Ford models and featuring Ford models—_Funny Face_, 1957, directed by Stanley Donen, with costume design by Edith Head and music by Roger Edens. Kay Thompson played Maggie Prescott, the character based on Diana Vreeland.

In Paris's Tuileries Garden, Dick Avedon, the movie's technical consultant, gives camera hints to Fred Astaire, playing the role of fashion photographer Dick Avery.

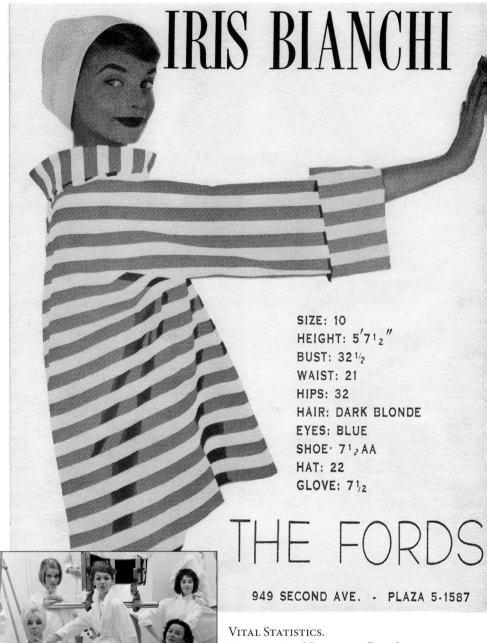

IRIS BIANCHI

SIZE: 10
HEIGHT: 5'7½"
BUST: 32½
WAIST: 21
HIPS: 32
HAIR: DARK BLONDE
EYES: BLUE
SHOE· 7½ AA
HAT: 22
GLOVE: 7½

THE FORDS

949 SECOND AVE. · PLAZA 5-1587

VITAL STATISTICS.
A promotional "composite" card photographed by Richard Avedon for Ford model Iris Bianchi, circa 1957. (*Photograph by Richard Avedon, © The Richard Avedon Foundation*)

Dorian Leigh with the models of her pioneering Paris modeling agency, July 1961.

LEARN TO BE BEAUTIFUL

A Complete Course in Beauty

LEARN BEAUTY THE MODEL'S WAY WITH A NEW METHOD OF BEAUTY STUDY THAT ENABLES YOU TO LEARN TO BE BEAUTIFUL QUICKLY & EASILY

THE ADVISOR TO THE WORLD'S FOREMOST MODELS TELLS YOU HOW TO APPLY MAKEUP, CORRECT BEAUTY PROBLEMS, LOOK SMART– LOOK BETTER– BE PRETTY

EILEEN FORD

Director of The Ford Model Agency

"EVERY WOMAN CAN BE HER OWN SORT OF BEAUTIFUL."
The front cover of Eileen Ford's 1961 LP: "The advisor to the world's foremost models tells you how to apply makeup, correct beauty problems, look smart—look better—be pretty."

REMAKING YOURSELF.
January 1959, Ford model Dolores Hawkins photographed for the cover of American *Vogue* by William Bell.

YOUTHQUAKE 1965.
Jean Shrimpton wears *Harper's Bazaar's* idea of a space helmet on the magazine's "winking eye" cover of April 1965; the holograms were applied by hand to the 100,000-issue print run. (*Photograph by Richard Avedon, © The Richard Avedon Foundation*)

Penelope Tree, longtime muse to British photographer David Bailey, who described her as "an Egyptian Jiminy Cricket."

k PAY SHEET.
d model Terry
o's pay sheet for
ruary 7, 1969
rtesy of Terry
o), with the
t five income
ries coming
n *Seventeen*
gazine, on whose
er she appeared
times in the
0s. On income
ling $4,865.91,
o paid an agency
mission of 10
cent ($486.59),
h a further 20
cent ($973.18)
ng to Jerry Ford's
serve Fund," to
er late payments.
full balance of
Reserve Fund,
o remembers,
ld usually
aid by Ford
hin three or four
nths.

THE FORD MODEL AGENCY
INCORPORATED
68689

CLIENT		INVOICE NUMBER	DATE MODELED			FIT-TINGS	HOURS		AMOUNT	PD. DIR.
			MO.	DAY	YR.		FROM	TO		
	SEVENTEEN	1850	12	06	68	1	230	300	12.50	
	SEVENTEEN	1851	01	21	69		900	500	125.00	
	SEVENTEEN	1852	12	26	68	1	300	330	12.50	
	SEVENTEEN	1853	12	26	68		1100	1200	25.00	
SCHIAVONE	SEVENTEEN	1854	01	20	69		100	600	125.00	
B LAMB	SIMPLICITY	1855	12	24	68	1	930	1000	25.00	
B LAMB	SIMPLICITY	1856	12	30	68		230	530	150.00	
B LAMB	SIMPLICITY	1857	01	10	69		200	500	150.00	
B LAMB	SIMPLICITY	1858	01	09	69		600	730	112.50	
B LAMB	SIMPLICITY	1859	01	07	69	1	130	200	25.00	
	VOGUE PATTERN B	1860	12	18	68	1	1130	1200	25.00	
	VOGUE PATTERN B	1861	12	27	68	1	1230	100	25.00	
J COWLEY	VOGUE PATTERN B	1862	12	20	68		200	300	50.00	
M MOORE	VOGUE PATTERN B	1863	01	06	69		200	330	-75.00	
ANGELA	VOGUE WRIGHT	1864	12	17	68		430	530	60.00	
	VOGUE WRIGHT	1865	12	13	68	1	500	530	30.00	
	VOGUE WRIGHT	1866	01	20	69		900	1030	90.00	
	VOGUE WRIGHT	1867	01	07	69		400	500	60.00	
									4,865.91 *	
			FEB	07	69		COMMISSION		486.59-	
			FEB	07	69		RESERVE FUND		973.18-	
TERRY RENO										

OUT OF TOWN.
On most summer weekends in the I
1960s and the 1970s, the Fords head
for their weekend home, in the sma
village of Quogue, Long Island, tak
with them their houseguests from
Seventy-Eighth Street.

Eileen in the garden at Quogue with her models. *Facing page*: Meanwhile, in London, Paris, and Manhattan, Ford's stars of the early 1970s secured their fair share of covers.

COVER GIRLS.

Jerry Hall
by Norman Parkinson,
British *Vogue,*
May 1975.

Ali MacGraw
by Alex Chatelain,
French *Vogue,* May 1971.

Rene Russo
by Arthur Elgort,
American *Vogue,* July 1976.

Beverly Johnson
by Francesco Scavullo,
American *Vogue,* August 1974.

MODELING GOES CORPORATE. Ford model Lauren Hutton had a girl-next-door look, said photographer Richard Avedon, that was "the link between the dream and the drugstore."

NOBODY
LOVES A
SMART
ASS

Lauren Hutton and Charles Revson celebrat[e] the signing of Revlon's record $200,000 'Ultim[a] II advertising contract in 1973, as negotiated b[y] Jerry Ford.

Sports Illustrated

JANUARY 27, 1975 · 75 CENTS

CANCÚN: MEXICO'S SPLASHY NEW RESORT

EYE SHADOW, COVER GIRL STYLE

COVER GIRL MOISTURIZED EYE SHADOW

Top Contract.
Cheryl Tiegs made her name sporting swimsuits, but she made her money with her multimillion-dollar Cover Girl contract, negotiated for her in 1979 by Jerry Ford.

MODEL WARS.
Hostilities began in New York's Model Wars in March 1977 with the arrival in America of Elite Model Management, headed by John Casablancas, "enjoying everything with one big roar of laughter."

Wilhelmina Cooper, CEO of Wilhelmina Models Inc., who buried her differences with Eileen Ford to tackle the interloper.

Maaret Halinen

Height 5'8½
Dress size 8-10 Am.
Bust 34B Waist 23½ Hips 35
Shoes 9 Med. Am.
Hair Blonde Eyes Blue

Hauteur 1.74
Confection 38-40
Poitrine 86 Taille 59 Hanches 89
Chaussures 40
Cheveux Blonds Yeux Bleus

elite
Elite Model Management Corporation
John Casablancas & Christine Lindgren
150 East 58th Street, New York 10022
Tel: 935-4500 T.V.: 935-4558
Telex: 62869UW Modelite

Elite Model Management
John Casablancas
7 Rue d'Artois, Paris 75008
Tel: 359 0396
Telex: 660076 Modelite

PETER MARLOWE COMPOSITE CARDS (LONDON) TEL: 01-584-8801

Janice Dickinson

Height 5'10
Dress size 7-8-10 Am.
Bust 34 Waist 23 Hips 34
Shoes 8½-9 Am.
Hair Brunette Eyes Brown

Hauteur 1.78
Confection 38-40
Poitrine 86 Taille 58 Hanches
Chaussures

Christie Brinkley

Height 5'8
Dress size 7-8-9 Am.
Bust 36 Waist 23½ Hips 35½
Shoes 7½-8 Am.
Hair Blonde Eyes Blue

Hauteur 1.73
Confection 38-40
Poitrine 91 Taille 59 Hanches 90
Chaussures 38½-39
Cheveux Blonds Yeux Bleus

elite
Elite Model Management Corporation
John Casablancas & Christine Lindgren
150 East 58th Street, New York 10022
Tel: 935-4500 T.V.: 935-4558
Telex: 62869UW Modelite

Elite Model Management
John Casablancas
7 Rue d'Artois, Paris 75008
Tel: 359 0396
Telex: 660076 Modelite

GLAMOUR
PAGE PULLOUT
SHAPE-UP
CALENDAR
FOR '78

RE BREAKUPS
RDER ON MEN
R WOMEN?

HE WILL TO WIN
OW TO GET
AND USE IT

7 GIFTS,
LOTHES &
ARTY IDEAS
O MAKE
OUR HOLIDAY
PIRITS SOAR

SPECIAL REPORT
ON A BRAND-NEW
CONTRACEPTIVE

PATRICE CASANOVA

ELITE RECRUITS.
These standardized model composite
cards were published early in 1978 by
Peter Marlowe to showcase Elite Model
Management's first and brightest
recruits raided by John Casablancas
from rival agencies—Maaret Halinen
(Wilhelmina), Janice Dickinson
(Ford), and Christie Brinkley (Ford).

Former Ford booker Monique
Pillard—"Judas" to Eileen Ford—with
Cindy Crawford, her highest-earning
model at Elite.

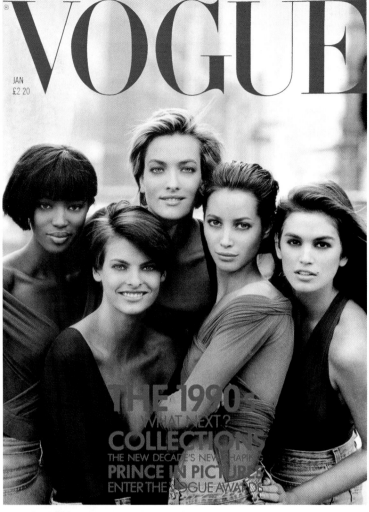

SUPERMODELS. British *Vogue,* January 1990—the cover by German photographer Peter Lindbergh that launched the "supermodels." *From left to right*: Naomi Campbell, Linda Evangelista, Tatjana Patitz, Christy Turlington, and Cindy Crawford.

1987: Eileen and Jerry Ford visit Red Square, Moscow, with (*left to right*) Christy Turlington, Monika Schnarre (winner of the Ford Supermodel of the World contest in 1986), and Renée Toft Simonsen (winner in 1982).

Social List of
Somerset Hills
2013

THE GOOD LIFE.
Eileen and Jerry Ford dance
up a storm at a family party
in the 1980s. *Below:* The Ford
mansion at "Hilltop Drive,"
Oldwick, in the Somerset Hills
region of Somerset County,
northern New Jersey.

At Ease.
Eileen Ford, age eighty-three, with her longest-serving model, Carmen Dell'Orefice, born in 1931, at New York's Women of Achievement dinner in March 2005.

The warrior at rest: Eileen Ford relaxes with her feet up in the library of her Oldwick, New Jersey, home.

John Casablancas, meanwhile, was entertaining his guests in a very different milieu—the disco and drug-soaked glamour of an extravagant new nightclub at 254 West Fifty-Fourth Street. It was unusual to find anyone there who was *not* stoned. Studio 54 had opened its doors in April 1977, the very month when the Model Wars began, and it became another of the battlefields on which the rival agencies tussled to establish their territory.

"It was a disgusting place," recalled Eileen, "truly disgusting. Every time we went there, Jerry and I would think back to the Stork Club, how elegant and sophisticated that had been. People dressed up for the Stork Club. For Studio 54 they dressed *down*. I will never forget the things I saw there—waiters in skimpy bikinis, and the things that were happening up in that balcony!" The balcony was the area that Studio 54 set aside for live sexual encounters—homosexual and heterosexual.

"Someone said," recalled Eileen, "that it was like the last days of the Roman Empire, and so it was. It was total degradation. But all the editors and all the photographers were there, and we felt that we had to go where the models went."

Rene Russo—who stayed loyal to Ford throughout the Model Wars—shared Eileen's opinion of Studio 54. "I went there just twice. I came from a neighborhood in Burbank where guys were getting drunk all the time. Studio 54 was an upscale version of that."

Eva Voorhees, another beautiful Californian, felt just the same. "I went there all of three times, and hated it. I thought, 'You've gotta be kidding me. People standing outside in a line to be rejected?' They chose you at the door for prettiness."

Yet for many Ford models, an expedition to West Fifty-Fourth Street became the ideal way to round off a hectic day. "'Studio' was sort of our club," recalls Renée Simonsen, who modeled with Ford, and Ford alone, through most of the 1980s. "The problem was going home afterward to Seventy-Eighth Street. You had to get past the creak at the top of the stairs."

"The creak" was a legendary hazard for the generations of young

Ford models who stayed at East Seventy-Eighth Street. It was a step in the staircase right outside the Fords' bedroom, and tradition had it that Eileen had had the "creak" installed at that particular spot so she could check on nighttime latecomers.

"I don't know if that's true and whether she really did install it," says Anne Anka, one of the earliest "creepers-in" to be caught during her stay in the early sixties. "But she sure as hell never got it fixed."

Eileen herself would chuckle with delight at the ingenious devices her protégées devised to defeat her curfew rules, awarding the garland to the young Christy Turlington when she became a lodger in the late 1980s. "Christy would take her clothes downstairs before dinner," Eileen loved to relate, "and would hide them, all neatly folded, inside the washing machine in the laundry room. Then, after dinner, she'd appear in her pajamas and say very casually, 'I'm just going downstairs to do some laundry.' She'd be out the door in a flash in her glad rags—and we thought that she was still downstairs or up in her room."

THE MODEL WARS CAME TO AN ABRUPT PAUSE IN THE SPRING OF 1980. Wilhelmina died on March 1, at the age of forty, victim to her many years of chain-smoking. "She had developed a cough the previous fall," recalls her daughter, Melissa. "But she went on working, out on the road, promoting the book she had just written, and going out to sell the agency. She never saw herself as the priority. She only got the diagnosis early in February—inoperable lung cancer. Three weeks later she was dead."

The Fords stood alongside John Casablancas and his wife at the memorial service. Scores of models packed Riverside Chapel, surrounding a devastated Bruce Cooper, who, in the months that followed, drank more heavily than ever. In July he sold the agency to his wife's assistants, Fran Rothschild and Bill Weinberg, who had worked for a time at Ford, and retired to a farm in Cooperstown, New York, where he died from a heart attack in 1989.

"It was a media event," wrote the wayward Janice Dickinson, describing Wilhelmina's funeral. "All those people looking so chic in black." Wilhelmina had taken on Dickinson in her early years and had nurtured her career. "I couldn't believe Willy was dead," Dickinson wrote. "She was the one who had validated me when I was starting out. Now she was gone . . . I needed some drugs. They weren't hard to find in that crowd."

By a sad irony, Wilhelmina had made the last of her 350 cover appearances only months before, on the cover of *Fortune* magazine for December 3, 1979, headlining an article by Gwen Kinkead on the Model Wars: "Ugly Competition for Pretty Faces: The Price of Beauty Is Getting Beyond Compare."

"God makes models, and He doesn't make many of them," Kinkead began, quoting a saying much favored by Jerry Ford. "So the faces that launch a thousand products cost twice as much to hire as they did just two years ago."

In a well-researched analysis of the Manhattan modeling business, Kinkead offered the cold economic reason behind the rivalry that was promoting such heated emotions: the burgeoning American consumer economy and its accompanying explosion of print advertising that put models at a premium. "The true competitors aren't the models at all," wrote Kinkead, "but the advertisers, who are bidding ever more generously for a limited supply of talent."

Eileen and Jerry Ford, in other words, might resent the intrusion of John Casablancas, but his arrival was a simple reflection of the marketplace. There was more than enough room in New York for another modeling agency, along with several hundred new models—indeed, Elite's competition had pushed up model rates, previously underpriced, to a proper market level. Ford might have lost market share to Elite in the three years since 1977, but its billings, like those of the industry as a whole, had increased 10 percent per year.

"The Ford success," wrote Kinkead, "has transformed modeling from an amateur pastime for idle society debs of the Twenties, who frequently forgot to bill their clients, into a highly paid, profitable and disciplined profession, governed by canny agents."

Shaking hard revenue figures out of all the leading agencies, including fourth-placed Zoli, Kinkead showed how Elite, in third place, had managed to build up annual billings of $6.6 million in the previous three years, a creditable effort, but still well behind the $11 million annual billings of Wilhelmina, who sat in second place to Ford's $11.8 million. With 93 male and 259 female models, Ford comfortably remained "the largest stable in the industry."

With its emphasis on money and figures, the article featured Jerry Ford more prominently than his wife, but Eileen did manage to have her say on what mattered to her.

"'When I took my sixteen-year-olds to Rome to work,' she declared proudly, 'they not only saw the Pope, they heard the Vatican choir and learned by heart every figure on the Sistine Chapel . . . They weren't out at Jackie O's with fast crowds, like girls from other agencies. Who's to teach these children values if we don't?'"

A few months after the *Fortune* piece appeared, both *Time* and *People* magazines revisited the theme of the Model Wars and reconfirmed the Fords' ongoing primacy. "Ford is still the world's dominant agency," declared *People* on the basis of the figures it researched, "three times as big as its nearest competitors, Elite and Wilhelmina Inc."

The best news of the summer, however, for both Eileen and Jerry was that, in June 1980, Christie Brinkley left Elite and became a Ford model again.

CHAPTER 28

COVER GIRLS

That face, that face, that Cover Girl face!

—*Noxzema Cover Girl commercial, 1982*

I T WAS IN THE SUMMER OF 1980," EILEEN FORD REMEMBERED, "NOT long after Memorial Day, when I picked up the phone and it was Christie. 'You were quite right,' she said. 'I want to come back.' I was so happy, I cried."

Christie Brinkley is rueful about her years with Elite. "John Casablancas never made a pass at me," she recalls. "In fact, he was always most correct with me personally. But I remember that I once got a call from the office saying they had this really fabulous job for me in the South of France—on a yacht. 'You're going to meet some very important people in the industry,' they told me. 'So you go down there and be very, *very* nice to them, and it will help your career.' I told them to get lost."

Brinkley had more important concerns about the Casablancas commercial style. "I started hearing," she says, "that some of the models were getting special deals—less commission, even zero commission. Or that Elite was giving them their publicity for free. So I asked John if he could give me free publicity, and he said, 'We can't give you anything that we don't give to anybody else.'"

In saying this, Casablancas was certainly lying. Janice Dickinson and other models have made no secret of the special deals Elite offered to get them on board—from reduced commission to exemption from charges for model cards. The final straw for Brinkley came when she shot a poster with Mike Reinhardt that neither she nor Reinhardt liked, but which Casablancas published anyway. Both model and photographer sued Elite—"We actually won the case," she recalls, "somewhat to my surprise"—and Brinkley went back to Ford.

"It was like being home again," she remembers. "Eileen was so warm, and Jerry, well, he was such a lovely, great big Cary Grant type, with his carnation always in his buttonhole. They were both so delighted to have me back—and I was so glad to *be* back."

As well they might be. With the lost sheep back in the fold, Ford once again represented the three top-earning models of the late 1970s and early '80s: Christie Brinkley, Lauren Hutton, and Cheryl Tiegs— the three top-earning models anywhere in the world.

LAUREN HUTTON—THE MOST ENDEARING OF FUNNY FACES, WITH her crossed eyes, her lopsided features, and the gap between her teeth—had been with Eileen Ford since early in 1966, when she went to the Ford office, having been rejected by Plaza Five, Frances Gill, and the Stewart agency, which were, at that date, the leading agencies after Ford in New York. Eileen Ford was in the process of rejecting her, too—"She had a funny eye," she later recalled, "that traveled around in circles"—but then took a second look when Hutton revealed, almost on her way out the door, that she had attended H. Sophie Newcomb College in New Orleans.

"Sophie Newcomb," explained Eileen, "was the Barnard College of the South. They were famous for their thinking women. They had the first-ever women's basketball team to wear bloomers. I must confess that I did not like Lauren's wandering eye, nor the gap in her front teeth. I thought that those things were definite problems, and I actually told her that she should get her teeth fixed. But I came to realize that there was something different about Lauren. She *was* a thinking woman—with very independent ideas. It seemed to me that a fresh image might be created."

Seven months later, Diana Vreeland came to the same conclusion and sent the twenty-three-year-old to Richard Avedon. The first of Lauren Hutton's twenty-five-plus *Vogue* covers appeared soon afterward, on November 15, 1966, and it was, of course, the gap between her front teeth that made her one of the faces of her generation. Hutton's quirky facial features made her look both ordinary and extraordinary—"the link," as Richard Avedon put it, "between the dream and the drugstore."

Hutton and Ford had a prickly relationship. "I was embarrassed," confessed Hutton, "that I'd caught Eileen's attention by being pushy about where I went to college. I never told her I paid my way through Sophie Newcomb by waiting tables on Bourbon Street."

Hutton did not like visiting the Ford office—"I did most of my business on the phone with Rusty [Zeddis]"—and she insisted on her right to take lengthy vacations. "After smiling at the camera for two months nonstop," she explains, "I needed to heal myself."

Hutton's healing took place in wild and remote corners of the world, trying to save endangered elephants in Kenya or chomping termites with Pygmies in the jungles of the Congo. In the twenty-first century there is not a self-respecting supermodel who does not venture into the wild to hug a tree or save the planet—UNICEF has a special department that matches celebrities with worthy causes and avoids philanthropic duplication. Yet in the late 1960s, such behavior was regarded as distinctly weird—and also dangerous for a model's career.

"Once," Hutton recalls, "when I came back from a month away, a model sniffed at me, 'What are you doing here? You committed suicide.' The wisdom was you wouldn't get work again if you stayed away too long."

Hutton flouted the wisdom, and Eileen Ford supported her, despite her own misgivings. When a newspaper ran a scare story about the unconventional model "going missing," Eileen jumped in sharply.

"She's not 'missing,'" she retorted. "She's swinging from a vine. She marches to her own drummer. She's like Holly Golightly, but with her head screwed on."

Hutton today recalls Eileen Ford as "a cloak to us. She threw a huge cloak of safety over the girls in her care—and that made her, in my book, a great changer for the sake of women."

Working for Ford, Mary Laurence "Lauren" Hutton would enjoy one of modeling's longest and most distinguished careers—two careers, in fact, after she came back as a "mature," or "classic," model in her late forties. She also enjoyed no little success as an actress, notably in *American Gigolo*, with Richard Gere, in 1980. Yet it was in 1973, when Jerry Ford negotiated her two-hundred-thousand-dollar contract to advertise Revlon's Ultima II, that she made modeling history. Revlon turned Lauren Hutton into the highest-paid model of her generation—with the possible exception of Cheryl Tiegs and her Cover Girl contracts.

THE IRONY OF COVER GIRL'S EVER MORE LUCRATIVE PAYMENTS TO Ford models and others from 1961 to the present day is that the brand originated with a modeling agency. The connection with Harry Conover was terminated with the implosion of his company in 1958, but in 1961 Noxzema initiated a new television advertising campaign that was based explicitly on the appeal of the modeling business. A cover from that month's *Vogue* or *Harper's Bazaar* or *Mademoiselle* magazine would be displayed in the TV studio on an easel, and the real-life model from the cover would then walk onto the set to stand alongside the easel and answer a few questions, explaining how Cover Girl products had helped her create and maintain her personal confidence and beauty.

The advertisements enjoyed incredible success. From 1962 to 1967, Cover Girl rose to number one in unit sales among all liquid makeups in North America, and through the rest of the 1960s and '70s, the campaign continued to achieve an annual growth rate "in the double digits," according to *Advertising Age*, putting the company consistently ahead of both Revlon and Maybelline in the mass-market cosmetics sector.

Charles Revson, the creative and very hands-on owner of Revlon, was furious. As Cover Girl products started to crowd out his Revlon lines from their once dominant positions in the drugstores, he issued an ultimatum to Condé Nast, Hearst, and the other publishers of glossy magazines. He would withdraw all Revlon advertising from their magazines, he threatened, unless they ceased lending their prestige to the Cover Girl advertisements, which, in his opinion, gave an unfair and unpaid-for advantage to his principal rival. The magazines, he said, could no longer allow their covers and mastheads to be used to endorse Cover Girl products.

Cover Girl hit back. After an unsatisfactory year or two in which the brand was reduced to featuring the homier covers of *Good Housekeeping* or *Better Homes and Gardens* in its ads, it developed a strategy that placed still more emphasis on the models. Its advertisements now featured an imaginary magazine, *Cover Girl*, complete with a mocked-up cover, and it interviewed the cover model as before, talking about her personal reliance on the products.

"It worked just as well," remembers Cover Girl account executive F. Stone Roberts of SSC&B (Sullivan, Stauffer, Colwell and Bayles) Advertising, now chief executive of Roberts and Langer DDB. "In the early advertisements we would pay an extra fee of a few hundred dollars to the young woman for her words and for her personal appearance—the day rate, or double. But once the focus was on the model, Jerry Ford made sure that his girls got more than that."

Bonnie Trompeter, Colleen Corby, Dorothea McGowan, Iris Bianchi, Anne de Zogheb, Karin Mossberg, Terry Reno, Evelyn Kuhn—at least twenty Ford models appeared in Cover Girl advertisements in the 1960s and early '70s, but none matched the selling power of Cheryl Tiegs, the long-haired, blonde, California surfer girl who was working in those years for Stewart Models. Then Stewart faltered in 1976, and Tiegs switched to Ford.

"I already knew both Eileen and Jerry quite well," Tiegs remem-bers, "and part of me felt that I really belonged at Ford. I always used to write JerryandEileen as just one word. They both gave me such a very warm welcome. In no time at all I felt as if I had always been a Ford model—and Jerry got me some magnificent new contracts."

Working with Lauren Hutton at Revlon, Jerry Ford had been de-veloping a new concept of "usage" in the payment of Ford models for advertising work. Dorian Leigh had done her famous Revlon "Fire and Ice" advertisements in the 1950s and '60s for the standard day rate of $250, but when Ford tried to get more than that for her sister Suzy Parker, Charles Revson refused. "He thought I should be work-ing for the sheer joy of working for Revlon," Parker later recalled sar-castically.

"Jerry told Revlon they couldn't have Suzy unless they paid her properly," recalled Eileen, "and there was a standoff. Revson refused to budge. I guess he had time to think about it and thought rather differently by the time Lauren came along."

Lauren Hutton secured a huge two-hundred-thousand-dollar contract from Revlon in 1973—and later gave credit for it to Cat-fish Hunter, the free-agent baseball pitcher, who was holding out for an unprecedented three-million-dollar contract with the New York Yankees in the early seventies.

"The second I told Avedon that I should have my own contract like Catfish Hunter, he got it. 'Make it exclusive,' he said. So I went home and told my old man." Hutton's "old man" was her mentor and boyfriend Bob Williamson, a Pygmalion figure she laughingly called "Bob God," who masterminded her career and investments. After his death in 1997, it was discovered that Williamson had mis-managed and squandered thirty million dollars of Hutton's fortune, but Hutton nonetheless credits him with being the key to the Revlon contract.

"After Dick took the pictures that snagged [Charles] Revson's in-terest," she says, "it was Bob who told Jerry Ford the terms we wanted for the contract—just twenty days' work a year, no morals clause [which meant Revlon could not cancel the contract for "bad behavior"], etcetera, etcetera. They talked on the phone for hours. There was a phone booth in the street outside the Revlon offices, and Jerry would call to check everything with Bob before he went in, and then again when he came out."

Hutton's booker, Rusty Zeddis, does not dispute Williamson's role in the story—"Those two pretty well knew where the path was." But Eileen Ford denied it fiercely, pointing out that Jerry had no choice but to report to Williamson, since he did all the talking for Hutton. "Who else should he talk to?" she asked. "It was Jerry who proposed and negotiated that whole deal with Charles Revson personally— every single dollar of it. He worked on it for four months. We never liked Bob Williamson, who was always pretending to be so clever and was clearly manipulating Lauren. We weren't a bit surprised when we heard he ran off with her money."

Revlon insiders doubt that Jerry Ford negotiated much of the deal with Charles Revson personally—the tycoon delegated contract details to Bill Mandel, his executive vice president. But early in 1973 the contract got signed, and Rusty Zeddis remembers the day Jerry Ford sent her to the forty-ninth floor of the General Motors Building to collect it. "He told me to leave work and go and sit outside Charles Revson's office till he signed it. It was a big day for Ford when that piece of paper finally came back to the office."

The Hutton-Revlon contract of 1973 gave shape to Jerry Ford's concept of "usage." He had been studying the economics of the perfume and makeup business, whereby, in contemporary values, the 3.5 ounces of scented liquid in a hundred-dollar bottle of perfume cost no more than two dollars to produce. The glass container is more expensive, at six dollars or so, with packaging taking the unit cost up to twelve dollars at the most. The entire remaining balance, nearly 90 percent of the price paid by the consumer, is then parceled out among the distributor, the retailer, and the advertising agency, along with the mysteriously named area "research and development."

"Even the girl behind the counter in Bloomingdales would get several dollars in sales commission," recalled Eileen. "So Jerry reckoned that our girls should be getting cut in on the whole thing as well."

Eva Voorhees recalls how "usage," as negotiated by Jerry Ford, worked out with one of her own, quite modest Revlon commercials in the early 1980s. "I got paid fifty thousand dollars for the one day's shoot," she says, "with extra payments depending on how they used it, whether on the packet or as a counter card. I remember seeing my image once on a counter card and a little flyer. So Ford phoned the advertising agency, and that was another nine thousand dollars. If commercials got shown abroad, then Jerry chased for the royalties on that."

Jerry Ford went on developing these principles in the ground-breaking contracts he negotiated for Cheryl Tiegs from 1976 onward, culminating, in 1979, in the largest cosmetics contract ever to that date—$1.5 million for a five-year exclusive contract with Cover Girl.

"In one sense," recalls F. Stone Roberts, "the deal was much less than it sounded. The million and a half was not guaranteed. We only committed and paid for one year at a time—two hundred fifty thousand or so. But we had to agree on the price of the future option years at the beginning so we could hang on to Cheryl if she got the results—and she certainly did. She had the ideal brand personality that we wanted: clean, fresh, and wholesome, the All-American girl next door. The problem with so many models is that they look snooty and intimidating. But Cheryl looked the sort of gal you could share a secret with. And Christie [Brinkley] delivered the same when we signed her up later."

Jerry Ford negotiated all these contracts with F. Stone Roberts. "He was always trying to squeeze out just that little bit more," recalls Roberts, "for the model and also for the agency—guaranteed expenses or an extra service fee. Jerry could be very ingenious and *very* charming. But he had this gift of stopping the bidding just at the point when you were starting to think that the price was getting extortionate. 'Pigs get fat, and hogs get slaughtered,' he used to say. We had a lot of laughs over that."

"He was an absolute gentleman, straight as an arrow," remembers

George Feld, who dealt with Jerry Ford at Revlon. "His word was 'it.' There was never any question of changing the terms later."

By the early 1980s, Jerry Ford was king of New York's long-term makeup contracts. As well as Christie Brinkley and Cheryl Tiegs at Cover Girl, and Lauren Hutton with Revlon, Ford also had Karen Graham with Estée Lauder, Sunny Griffin with Avon, and Patricia van Ryckeghem with Chanel—all on contracts worth hundreds of thousands of dollars. John Casablancas could match Eileen Ford's eye for talent and even surpass her promotional flair, but he was no match for the solid, multimillion-dollar negotiating talents of her husband. Jerry Ford was Ford's secret weapon in the Model Wars.

THEN THERE WAS FORD'S MEN'S DIVISION. NOT SURPRISINGLY, PER-haps, John Casablancas devoted his principal energies to the female side of his business. Elite did not regard its male models as standout performers, while Jerry Ford, on the contrary, saw his men's division as a particular jewel in his crown. He had inherited his men's team in good condition from Huntington Hartford, and he took pride in developing it even further. "Eileen's girls may earn more for the moment," he liked to say. "But my boys go on longer"—this last line delivered with a definite sense of double entendre.

The success of Ford Men owed much to its vice president, Joey Hunter, a former male model with a touch of the Godfather about him. "Joey always seemed to have a black Town Car idling outside," remembers Ken Steckla, a model manager who worked for Nina Blanchard in Los Angeles, "waiting to whisk him off to an Italian restaurant somewhere."

"There was no one more brilliant in the day-to-day operations of the agency than Joe," remembers Patty Sicular, now with Trump Model Management, "so clients, photographers, the best models—they would all want to come back for more. In every booking that I do to this day, I try to insert a little bit of Joey. He was also great at handling Eileen when she got heated. He was so diplomatic. My former boss in advertising used to say that Joe Hunter could tell you to

'Fuck off,' and he'd be so charming about it that you would walk away saying, 'Thank you.'"

Joe Hunter was also the eagle-eyed catcher of the Ford softball team—one of the best amateur teams in Manhattan. "Every year we made it to the New York semis or finals," remembers Jack Scalia, who, like many male models, was a professional actor, working in such series as *Dallas*, *Remington Steele*, and *All My Children*. "I remember one year we made it to the final against the New York FBI—and we beat them! We absolutely should have, of course, with the most beautiful women in the world sitting in the bleachers and cheering us on. You pitch pretty well, let me tell you, when you are getting waved at by Christie Brinkley. That night we all went to Studio 54 wearing our softball uniforms. There we were rubbing shoulders with Andy Warhol, Mick Jagger, and Truman Capote! It was surreal."

Scalia was intrigued by Jerry Ford's regular Tuesday morning disappearance from the office to play squash at the University Club on Fifth Avenue, and asked one day if he could tag along, since he was an athlete who worked out quite regularly. His eye for the ball had won Scalia a third-place draft with the Montreal Expos as a pitcher, and though injury had forced him to forfeit his baseball dreams, he reckoned he could put up a credible showing against an amiable old buffer who was twenty-five years his senior.

After two games, Scalia had not won a point. His shirt was soaked in sweat, and the score stood at 15–0, 15–0 in Jerry Ford's favor.

"I reckon he felt pity and gave me the four points that I managed to take off him in the third game," remembers Scalia. "I had bounced off every wall of the court, as this guy, a quarter of a century older than me, for Christ's sake, stands calmly in the middle, flicking the ball here and there, cool as a cucumber, while I ran myself ragged around him. 'Perhaps we can meet up again,' I said afterward, as we stood in the shower. I tried to summon up a smile. 'Do you really want to go through all that again?' asked Jerry."

For all his urbanity and charm, Jerry Ford operated on a basis of unsentimental realism—as his Swiss friend Roland Schucht discovered in the late 1980s. "Jerry got Christie Brinkley a million-dollar, four-day job with Procter and Gamble," Schucht recalled. "She had to pose and model clothes, then smile at the camera and say, 'Such and such a face cream is so-o-o smooth.' All the filming went fine, but something went wrong with the recording equipment, there was some glitch, so the advertising agency phoned to ask if she could drop by the studio, just to record that single sentence again.

"'That will be no problem at all,' said Jerry. 'Christie can come into town next week from Long Island just about any time—choose your day. And we will bill you another two hundred fifty thousand dollars.'"

CHAPTER 29

SEX AND DRUGS AND SUPERMODELS

It's very embarrassing when you meet, like, a Russian
prostitute, and she says she's a supermodel. And you're
like, "Hey, me too!"

—*Stephanie Seymour*

CHERYL TIEGS WAS THE FACE OF COVER GIRL FOR A FULL TWENTY
years, and Jerry Ford gleefully renegotiated her fee upward on
a regular basis. "Every year the sales figures showed that Cheryl sold
the product brilliantly," remembers the Cover Girl advertising account manager, F. Stone Roberts. "But we were doing focus groups all
the time, and they showed that no one seemed to believe that Cheryl,
in her private life, actually *used* the product that she advertised. They
assumed she bought herself something more expensive, but *they*
happily bought Cover Girl on her say-so—which shows you how the
whole business of beauty is fundamentally irrational: an art, not a
science.

"When people buy a beauty product, whether it's perfume or pimple cream, they are making an emotional decision. They are buying a
little piece of the dream. And there are other sorts of wishful thinking. Women will say that they only wear Chanel or Estée Lauder. Then
you dump open their purse, and out falls Maybelline or Cover Girl."

Fashion's fundamental disconnect between dream and reality was
fortunate for both Cover Girl and Cheryl Tiegs. In 1979 her husband,
Stan Dragoti, a movie producer, was arrested at Frankfurt airport

with twenty-five grams of cocaine wrapped in foil, taped to his back, and another thirty grams of the drug in his suitcase. Dragoti claimed he had only recently become a coke sniffer, when he discovered that his wife had started an affair with the photographer Peter Beard while on assignment in Africa. He was very depressed, he explained to the court, and needed something "to kill the pain."

The German judge was sufficiently sympathetic to send Dragoti back to the United States with a suspended jail sentence and a fine of fifty-five thousand dollars, while the court of public opinion was even more forgiving to his wife—whom he divorced the following year. Cocaine and adultery made no evident impact on Tiegs's image as the wholesome All-American girl next door with whom you would like to share a secret—possibly because she evidently had secrets that she might like to share with you.

Drugs became rife in modeling in the late seventies and early eighties. "Sometimes in New York, the models would arrive in the morning straight from Studio [54], totally wasted," remembers the stylist Shelley Promisel. "Then I'd phone the agency and ask for replacements straightaway. Elite was always quite casual about that sort of thing, but if Eileen ever heard about it, she took it very seriously. It defamed her name.

"I remember getting to one photographer's studio, and there was Janice Dickinson, stark naked up on a rafter, stoned out of her mind and left over from the previous session. We just left her up there and got on with it."

Quite apart from its "high," cocaine made models thin. "You could *see* the girls who were using," recalls Promisel. "As the weeks went by their faces got thinner. They looked really great—you couldn't honestly say otherwise. Cocaine was the greatest appetite suppressor of all.

"When you're in the changing rooms with the girls and they are naked, you become their confidant, their shrink, and their love adviser. They would tell you about their drugs. How they would take cocaine on a Friday and Saturday night. It was a fast, speedy high that made them feel powerful. But then they would be too hyper to have sex. So they would take quaaludes (methaqualone, a barbiturate substitute) to bring them down and make them horny."

Gia Carangi, the Wilhelmina model who died of drugs and AIDS-related causes in 1986 at the age of twenty-six, became the subject of the 1998 movie *Gia*, starring Angelina Jolie (with Wilhelmina played by Faye Dunaway).

"Gia was two hours late once when I was on a trip for *Ladies' Home Journal*," said Promisel. "It is always the stylist's job to wake up everyone on the shoot. So there I was, knock, knock, knocking at her door. She was on the bed completely out of it. She had OD'd on heroin. The editor and the photographer dealt with the medics. I had to call up Willy and get her to send another girl down straightaway."

After the death of Wilhelmina, who had fostered Gia, as she had also mentored Janice Dickinson, Richard Avedon phoned Jerry Ford.

"He said, 'I promise that I will book Gia if you will represent her,'" remembered Eileen. "Well, that was very thoughtful of Dick. He was trying to help the poor girl. He thought that our 'family style' might help her with her problems. But she only lasted about twenty-five minutes. She failed to show for the very first booking we got her. We sent a limousine to make sure she got there on time and she used it to give her dogs a ride around Manhattan."

Bookers often had to pick up the pieces as the drug culture invaded the fashion business. "When you're a booker, you have to be a parent, a psychologist, and a doctor," remembers Ken Steckla. "We were the ones who'd have to call Betty Ford or Hazelden and put them into rehab—and you had to place your own feelings on hold: if you get angry, there's nowhere to put it. A photographer rings you furious, asking, 'Where is the bitch?' So then you phone the model, all sweetness and light—'Hi, honey. What happened to you? Are you feeling all right?' I lost count of the times I had to fall back on the old excuse: there were some girls who seemed to have their period twenty-eight days a month."

"I found out why Eileen was so dictatorial," says Shelley Promisel. "You needed to be in that business, with so many egos and defective characters to deal with, and the drugs all around, making everything worse. I was the same—like Gestapo in the dressing room. My energy kept everyone on time, so we finished on time—that's how I earned my money. No one wanted it to go over the hour. It was a tough business where a lot of lying went on."

Eileen herself maintained her hard-boiled exterior when discussing the excesses of the 1970s and '80s. "Look," she would say, "the girls who went under were lost souls. No one could have helped them; and the girls who got through it had that inner strength which you're either blessed with or you're not. There's only so much you can do to help anyone on this earth."

The survivors of the era, however, remember more warmth than that. "I always felt protected by Eileen," says Renée Simonsen, "in big ways and small. When I was in Paris once, I said, 'You know, Eileen, I'd like to do some photographs with that Helmut Newton.' And she said, 'No, Renée, he does nude pictures—and he doesn't pay much anyway.' That was fine with me—I never wanted to get my breasts out, and I was in the business to make money and pay my way through university, which I did. When I had my anxiety attack and thought I was going crazy, she and Jerry were both so supportive to me."

In the early 1980s, elite model management took over from Wilhelmina as the number two agency in New York. John Casablancas was challenging Ford more strongly than ever by the middle of the decade. Yet Jerry Ford's trinity of top advertising earners—Hutton, Tiegs, and Brinkley—kept the older agency solidly at number one, with new talent also coming in regularly, thanks to an initiative dreamed up by the Fords' youngest daughter, Lacey.

Lacey Ford, twenty-three years old in 1980, and her elder brother, Bill, twenty-eight, had started work at the agency around the outbreak of the Model Wars. Their elder sister Jamie, thirty-three, never wanted any involvement with the family business, while Katie, twenty-five, the second daughter and third-born child, had headed for TV syndication, then management consultancy, before joining the agency later in the 1980s.

Lacey's idea sprang from the ancient tradition of the TV beauty contest that went back to the Miss Rheingold commercials of the 1940s and '50s. Stewart Models had enjoyed brief success in the late 1960s with its Model of the Year contest—Cybill Shepherd was its discovery of 1968—but had run into copyright problems over the concept. Lacey's idea was for an international pageant, Ford's Face of the Eighties, involving entrants from Ford's partner agencies around the world, with a guaranteed modeling contract going to the winner. The first two contests came up with a pair of winners who both became instant '80s faces: Norway's Anette Stai in 1981, and Denmark's Renée Simonsen the following year. The two young women went to live on Seventy-Eighth Street, and were featured in *Vogue* (Simonsen on the cover) within months of arriving in New York.

Elite's Look of the Year pageant was John Casablancas's tribute and riposte to Lacey Ford's bright idea. The Elite talent contest was a direct imitation, and it came two years behind Ford's, but it soon got its own results. Two of Elite's teenage finalists in 1984 were Stephanie Seymour and Cindy Crawford. A new generation was appearing, and it was Ford who suggested a new title for these models. In 1986, with the eighties more than halfway out the door, the Face of the Eighties talent search was given a new name: Ford Supermodel of the World.

SUPERMODEL IS A MUCH MISUSED WORD. JOURNALISTS, AND EVEN fashion historians who should know better look back to the era of Dorian Leigh, Suzy Parker, Jean Shrimpton, Twiggy, and Penelope Tree and describe these women as "supermodels." They were not. They may have been superstars, but they were not supermodels in the sense of the term as it developed in the late 1980s. Lauren Hutton, Cheryl Tiegs, and Christie Brinkley do not technically qualify, either. They were certainly super-successful, but they were, in fact, the precursors who prepared the way for the generation of young women who rose after them on the ultra-lucrative advertising contracts pioneered by Jerry Ford. The supermodels, a small and select group, mingled catwalk excitement with music videos and the growth of celebrity journalism to create a new sort of fashion category. They were also unusual in that, while coming from different agencies and countries, they operated together as a pack—a sort of club. In a profession with more than its fair share of cattiness, they were friends.

Cindy Crawford and Stephanie Seymour got together under the Elite umbrella. At Ford it was Christy Turlington and Naomi Campbell who bonded, thanks to the Empress of Seventy-Eighth Street. Turlington arrived at the Ford house in the summer of 1985, a sixteen-year-old sophomore with the Latin looks of her El Salvadorean mother, taking a break from high school to test the waters of New York fashion.

"Christy was always a quiet, sweet girl," remembered Eileen. "She fitted right in. Of course, she only told me later about the trick she'd worked out with the laundry—hiding her clothes in the washing machine, then sneaking out of the house without us knowing."

During the hot and humid New York summer days, the sixteen-year-old dutifully trudged through the rounds of go-sees that Eileen had arranged for her—with Eileen ringing in from time to time to check that everything was going according to plan. When the Fords were invited, in the spirit of glasnost, to take three of their brightest new models to Moscow in 1987, on the eve of the breakup of the Soviet Union, they took Turlington, along with Renée Simonsen and Monika Schnarre, the latest winner of their Supermodel of the World contest. Back in New York, Eileen even did some personal deal making on Turlington's behalf.

"It was the only advertising deal that I ever made," she recalled with pride—and a little surprise. "It was a Good Friday, so Jerry and I were at home, and I answered the phone. It was Calvin Klein. He said he was considering Christy to advertise his Eternity fragrance—she was just starting to take off but was not really known—and asked me how much she would cost. Jerry wasn't around, so I just said the first figure that came off the top of my head—seven hundred fifty thousand." Calvin sounded a bit surprised and went silent for a moment. Then he said, 'All right.' I felt very pleased with myself—seven hundred fifty thousand to Christy for just twelve days' work!"

The Fords' relationship with Naomi Campbell was more challenging. "Naomi came across from London to live with us for the first time when she was sixteen," remembered Eileen. "That would have been about the time when she met up with Christy. But she left soon afterward because I wouldn't let her smoke in the house. I always tell people that Naomi Campbell worked for us four times—and always left for the same reason. The fifth time I said, 'Naomi's coming back.' But Jerry said, 'Oh, no she isn't.' I always had a soft spot for Naomi. She was a rascal, but she had that spark, that self-belief and view of herself that meant she was always going to succeed—with us or without us."

It takes a diva to know a diva. Naomi Campbell was the ultimate example of the sort of woman described by Martin Amis in his 1989 novel *London Fields*. There are glamour girls, he wrote, whose looks proclaim that you can do what you like with them, and then there is the woman who proclaims that "*she* could do what she liked with you."

John Casablancas was only too happy to sign up the high-earning young model who had parted company with Ford, but several years later he faxed out an unprecedented letter on Elite Model Management notepaper—"To Whom It May Concern: Please be informed that we do not wish to represent Naomi Campbell any longer." The letter was cosigned by Monique Pillard.

"Poor John," commented Eileen on the subject of this much-publicized resignation, opening her eyes wide and shaking her head in mock sympathy. "I guess he finally discovered that taking good care of supermodels is rather more difficult than boffing them. And he even got Judas to sign it!"

———

IN JANUARY 1990, BRITISH *VOGUE* DECIDED TO PREDICT THE HOT new faces of the coming decade, and the magazine lighted on the young Americans Christy Turlington and Cindy Crawford; Linda Evangelista, from Canada; and the German model Tatjana Patitz. Naomi Campbell was the British face of the future, and the five were photographed together by the German fashion photographer Peter Lindbergh in a striking black-and-white image that showcased the separate beauty of each young woman, while also capturing their curious unity as a group.

When the singer George Michael saw the *Vogue* cover, he instantly knew these were the faces he wanted for the music video of his latest song, "Freedom '90." That fall the five models appeared on MTV sensuously lip-synching the rambling lyrics to the melody in an extended seven-minute film that helped the song rise to No. 8 on the *Billboard* Hot 100.

Yet it was what happened next that lifted the supermodels into a new dimension. Donatella Versace saw the music video and persuaded her brother, Gianni, to hire Turlington, Campbell, Crawford, and Evangelista to walk the runway of their October 1991 collection in Milan, and to lip-synch "Freedom '90" again while wearing Versace's famous clothes in "happy black"—with George Michael, naturally, invited to sit in the front row.

Runway models had traditionally been considered specialists, a skinny and athletic breed apart, not necessarily very pretty or glamorous, but highly professional at displaying the intricacies of haute couture garments—they were living, walking fashion dolls. Print models were considered too voluptuous and individual for the catwalk. Their day rates were far too expensive, especially by the early 1990s, and their increasingly recognizable popular identities were considered a distraction from the serious business of setting out the details and range of an expensive dress collection—designers were scared of the print models' fame.

Yet "Fame on fame means *more* fame!" argued Donatella Versace to her brother, and so it proved. Gianni Versace laid out the hundred thousand dollars or so needed to bring Campbell, Evangelista, Crawford, and Turlington to Milan—plus luxury hotel suites and transatlantic tickets on the Concorde—and the result was a sensation. Some overlap of runway and print had already started in the late 1980s, but with the Versace show of October 1991, the transformation was complete.

"Naomi! Linda! Cindy! Christy!" The flashguns popped, photographers crowded the end of the runway calling out the girls' names, George Michael beamed from his seat among a roll call of other celebrities, and a new type of mass media marketing event had been created. Fashion hyperbole reached new heights, with descriptions of the Versace happening ranging from "orgasmic" to "biblical." "It was such a 'Wow!' moment," recalls the fashion commentator Tim Blanks of Style.com. "It symbolized the whole era."

The supermodel concept became inescapable, and the high-octane fashion runway show took the place that it occupies to this day alongside the "red carpet" of Oscar night and movie galas as a platform for modern celebrity.

The successors of the fashion doll had come a long way from the days of models being anonymous wage slaves. "We have this saying, Christy and I," declared Linda Evangelista in October 1990. "We don't wake up for less than $10,000 a day." The young woman's notorious boast had been made possible by the advertising contracts negotiated in the previous two decades by Jerry Ford. Yet a roll call of the supermodels named by British *Vogue* in January 1990 as the faces of the future revealed that only one of them, Christy Turlington, was represented at that moment by the Ford Modeling Agency. All the others—Naomi Campbell, Linda Evangelista, Tatjana Patitz, and Cindy Crawford—were on the books of John Casablancas, at Elite.

CHAPTER 30

HOPPING LIKE BEDBUGS

You're product, baby. That's all you are . . . Fashion seems
so glamorous, but it's just advertising.

—*Hairstylist Ara Gallant to Janice Dickinson*

IT WAS QUITE EARLY IN 1990 THAT CHRISTY TURLINGTON, JUST
twenty-one but already a multimillionaire after her years on the
Ford books, got herself a lawyer and went to see Jerry Ford. "Christy
told Jerry that she did not want to pay us any more commission,"
remembered Eileen. "She had been talking to some of the other girls
about the special deals that they were getting from their agencies, and
she thought that she should have the same. Jerry said he was sorry,
but he couldn't let her off her commission. He'd have to do the same
for the whole agency, and then, why would he have an agency? So
Christy said good-bye to us."

For the time being, at least. Not long afterward, Christy Turlington was to be found back in the Ford fold (at a reduced rate of commission), along with Naomi Campbell, when, in March 1991, Ford
decided after forty years, on the initiative of Iris Minier and Katie
Ford, to abandon the hazards of operating through local French
agents and to open its own office in Paris. Ford Paris even picked up
some extra supermodels for a while—Elle Macpherson, a trophy who
was already a big name, along with Shalom Harlow, Amber Valletta,
and Minier's Manchester discovery, Karen Elson. All stayed with

Ford Paris for a year or so, but not much longer than that. Loyalties were fickle in the age of the supermodel.

"By the early 1990s the models were hopping from agency to agency like bed bugs," recalled Michael Gross, who was just starting to research his book *Model*, the first attempt at a full-scale study of the industry. "The system did not operate 'top down' anymore—and 'top down' had always been Eileen Ford's style." Jerry Ford had helped hand models the power of money, and in doing so he had helped to disempower the modeling agencies.

"Times were changing," recalled Felicia Milewicz, models editor of *Mademoiselle*, "and Eileen did not like it. I remember how *Mademoiselle* had brought over a young avant-garde photographer from France, who shot the girls in some unusual settings—and he shot one of Eileen's girls sitting on top of a toilet. The lid was down and the girl was fully dressed. It was hardly pornographic or 'heroin chic,' but Eileen was furious. I'll never forget. I was at a party a few days later and Eileen came in. The moment she saw me, she literally ran across the room and started screaming, 'How dare you make one of my girls look like a hooker? This whole industry is going downhill! I thought you were better than that!'

"She was beside herself with rage and I had to leave the party. I felt unfairly attacked and very upset, but deep inside I felt that she was right. I loved Eileen for being herself. She knew who she was."

In March 1992, Eileen reached her seventieth birthday, which happened to be the fifteenth anniversary of the start of the Model Wars. In the decade and a half of slugging it out, Ford had just about maintained its mastery in the arena that mattered to Eileen, the New York fashion scene, while Elite had diversified into other U.S. cities and into charm and model schools run by John Casablancas's brother, Fernando.

"Morally and emotionally, Jerry and I certainly won," Eileen liked to say, choosing to concentrate on the personal side of the battle. "Christie Brinkley came back to us, and so did the others who mattered."

In cold money terms, however, the Elite network had actually overtaken Ford by the early 1990s, with a turnover that, at around thirty-five million dollars, was some ten million dollars larger than Ford's. Yet both sides could pick out figures to claim victory based on their own definition of what mattered, and by 1992 the two adversaries were tiring of the endless campaign. They were ready for a settlement, so long as it did not involve one of them having to admit defeat by selling out to the other.

Enter Horst-Dieter Esch, a flamboyant German entrepreneur who had recently bought control of Wilhelmina Model Management and who, at the end of 1992, ambitiously proposed an amalgamation of New York's top three agencies to create a juggernaut that could conquer the world.

"It was a brilliant idea," remembered Roland Schucht, the Swiss financier who handled the negotiations on behalf of Ford, "because no one lost face. The idea was to yoke Elite and Ford together, harnessed by Wilhelmina, with Esch running the whole conglomerate from above."

A basic condition of the deal was that the entire Ford family step out of the picture. "Jerry and I were quite ready for that," recalled Eileen. "Katie wanted to stay involved. But the offering price was no small potatoes. There was fifteen or twenty million dollars on the table, Jerry told me, if we walked away."

Fifteen to twenty million dollars was far beyond any normal valuation of Ford's assets as a fluctuating service company that could demonstrate no long-term assets, especially in an age when the top models came and went as they willed. Roland Schucht urged Jerry to take the money and run.

"We sat down to negotiate seriously," Schucht recalled, "and it looked as if the Model Wars were going to end with Ford and Elite getting joined together, with Wilhelmina in charge of them both. We had Swiss companies set up, investors, everything. Then we discovered that Esch had been sentenced to six and a half years in jail back in the early eighties for fraud, negligence, false declarations, and goodness knows what. I don't know how or why we hadn't found that out earlier. Our jaws dropped when we heard it—and he stayed so relaxed. He said he'd made no secret of it. He said he thought everybody knew. Anyway, the deal was dead at that moment from our point of view."

Also dead was Jerry Ford's appetite, at the age of sixty-eight, for continuing to go into the office to do deals and run the complex finances of a multimillion-dollar modeling agency on an everyday basis.

"Jerry and Eileen had bought this wonderful plot of land on top of a hill in New Jersey horse country to build their retirement mansion," recalled Schucht. "It was their dream. I climbed up a tree with Jerry to see what the view would be like from their bedroom window. We could just see a lake in the distance, and I remember thinking as we hung on there together, up in the branches, 'He's never going to want to come down from this.'"

EILEEN FORD WAS FEELING THE SAME. THE EVER-RISING PROFILE OF the fashion business, and of models in particular, had attracted the attention of investigative journalists, and in 1988 a pair of television exposés, *American Models in Paris*, produced by *60 Minutes* in two episodes, had revealed some of Ford's French operatives and partners in a deplorable light. The scandals involved the problems that were now almost routine in the model world—drugs and sexual pressure, particularly on underage girls—and there was no suggestion that Eileen herself knew what was going on. Yet that was the problem.

Diane Sawyer set her victim up perfectly. She asked Eileen on camera how she would react if Jean-Luc Brunel, the owner of the Karins agency with whom Ford was then doing the most business in Paris, were to be accused of drugging and pressuring underage girls—or any girls—to go to bed with him and important clients. Eileen said she would not believe it, and then had to watch the *60 Minutes* tape rolling as model after model, many of them fresh-faced, young American girls, testified to Brunel's doing just that.

It was a moment of utter humiliation, on prime-time television, for the über-mother who had always boasted that she knew how to protect her most vulnerable charges. Eileen's transparent horror at Brunel's behavior was both genuine and pitiful—as one viewer put it, she looked "as if she'd seen a ghost"—and Ford later severed all links with Brunel. Yet at the age of sixty-six, Eileen Ford no longer looked like a woman who was on top of her game. "I trusted Jean-Luc," was all she would say in later years about the incident. "And he let me down. These things happen, and you have to move on."

As she progressed through her sixties, Eileen's heavy drinking became a concern for some of her friends. "Whenever I came back from Denmark," remembered Renée Simonsen, "I would bring her a carton of Danish cured salmon, which she adored, and several bottles of Danish aquavit, which she adored even more."

The consumption of the clear, high-octane aquavit in a chilled triangular glass became Eileen's four o'clock ritual—"Much more healthy than tea," she used to say with a twinkle—to be repeated at regular intervals into the evening. "As she became tipsy," recalls one of her friends, "she would become just like a little girl—giggly and flirtatious and definitely rather fun. So Jerry would become her father when that happened—and also her rehab. 'Eileen!' he would say quite sharply, raising his eyebrow and looking meaningfully at the glass. 'Yessir,' she would say with a smirk. 'You are my lord and master!' And she would put down the glass till next day. I think she was lucky to be blessed with a very hard head."

Eileen Ford was also blessed with the overarching primacy of self-control that had driven her since childhood. She might have drunk heavily—being tipsy clearly provided her with welcome relief from her unrelenting public face—but there was always that parental voice of reproof and warning inside her. The pride of the Ottensosers never allowed her to topple totally over the edge.

At the age of seventy, the "Matriarch of Modeling" delivered her verdict on the fast-changing world of fashion to *American Photo* magazine, starting with a welcome to the supermodels. She very much liked these young women, she said, because "they have much more of a sense of self"—and she also welcomed the general loosening of the business. "Once it was a strict rule," she said, "that a Ford model would not pose nude. Now, yes. The world changes."

She even hinted at a change in her own attitude toward the question of models and sex. "Let's not call it sex," she said. "Let's call it chemistry . . . Models are young people by definition. Their genes are jumping around. So it happens. And frankly, you want chemistry between a photographer and a model. That has to be part of the relationship. You just hope the chemistry doesn't run rampant."

Back at the office, however, the matriarch remained indomitable in many of her strongly held prejudices. High-end editorial was still the only modeling that really counted in Eileen's eyes as "true" and "serious." She paid reluctant lip service to the "plus size" divisions that developed in the late 1970s to cater to larger women—"But she just wasn't 'into' Plus Sizes," remembers Ford booker Patty Sicular, "no matter how much money they made."

Ford model Ann Harper had been in the vanguard of the "fuller-figure revolution" in the 1980s, publishing the bestselling *Big Beauty Book: Glamour for the Fuller-Figure Woman*, and bringing revenues to her agency that outdid those of many a high-fashion model. Yet her boss remained somehow uneasy at the profit. "Ann did wonderfully for us," the eternally slender Eileen used to say. "But I'm sorry, as I see it, fat is just not fashionable."

Her feelings were very much the same about the older, "classic" model divisions that also proliferated in these years, aimed at editorial and advertising with the "more mature" woman in mind. "Older people don't want to look at older models," she'd say. "It reminds them of themselves."

By the 1980s and '90s "classic" modeling campaigns for Revlon and Estée Lauder "anti-aging" products were providing lucrative second careers for older Ford stars such as Lauren Hutton and Karen Graham, but Eileen knew just what she thought about aging women. "I look at myself in the mirror," she remarked to journalist Judy

Bachrach, "and all I see is an old trout. I know that I don't want to look at that."

Eileen's solid gold egotism, interpreting everything in the world as it appeared to her own eyes, provided a clue to her success. In one sense she remained forever the eighteen-year-old wannabe who went to Harry Conover on the eve of World War II, dreaming of *Vogue* but ending up in the advertisements of the *Mademoiselle* college issue. Could it be that for the best part of half a century Eileen Ford had built up her modeling agency to make her own personal dream come true vicariously—through the success of her "girls"?

The full and proper development of Ford's plus size and classic modeling divisions, along with a number of other Ford modernizations, had to wait for the arrival of daughter Katie, aged thirty-seven in 1993, who finally took full control of the agency at the beginning of May in that year, working in partnership with the long-serving Ford executives Joey Hunter and Marion Smith. Eileen and Jerry decided that the time had come to hand over the reins, six weeks after Eileen's seventy-first birthday, and just over forty-six years since Jerry Ford first picked up the phone to help out his wife with her recently established model-booking business.

On the eve of her retirement, Eileen gave an interview to business management expert Lloyd E. Shefsky. "Don't wait for success to come from the tooth fairy," she told him, "because there is no tooth fairy. To be really successful, you have to work your heart out . . . I always knew I would work, because my mother told me I would work. When I grew up, you believed your mother. She went to work when she was thirteen."

Shefsky featured Eileen's thoughts in his international bestseller *Entrepreneurs Are Made Not Born*, based on conversations with more than two hundred successful tycoons. He asked each of them to define the opposite of work, and he awarded Eileen the garland for the "ultimate" answer.

"The opposite of work," she said, "is death."

CHAPTER 31

FULL CIRCLE

And quiet sleep and a sweet dream when the long trick's over.

—*John Masefield, "Sea Fever"*

E ILEEN AND JERRY FORD'S LIFE AS RETIREES DID NOT GET OFF TO a good start. In March 1993, the Fords' custom-built dream house on the hill at Oldwick, near Tewkesbury, New Jersey, caught fire and burned to the ground. No fewer than twenty fire companies battled the blaze, according to the *Philadelphia Inquirer*; the fire could be seen from miles away.

"It was our third country house," remembered Eileen. "When they raised the taxes on Long Island, we sold Quogue and moved to Connecticut—it was easier for people to get out there from the city. Then we based our Oldwick plans on the Connecticut design."

"Jerry was especially embarrassed," remembered Roland Schucht. "Only two weeks before the fire, he'd had the whole place inventoried with a camera crew for insurance purposes. I told him that a professional arsonist would have let a little more time than two weeks elapse! Files and files of the company records in the basement got burned—and Eileen's beloved wine cellar was ruined by the heat."

"What upset me most," recalled Eileen, "was losing all the family silver that my mother gave me. It got melted down. But things are just things. We built a new house and we started again."

There was a small private road leading along the top of the hill from the main drive to the garage, and Eileen had a special street sign made for it, "Hilltop Drive," the same name as the street on which she grew up in Great Neck.

"There's just one thing you need to know," said Jerry Ford to the chauffeur the couple hired to drive their Volvo whenever they wanted to travel into Manhattan, an hour and a half away on a day of light traffic. "It's all about her."

"There's just one thing you need to know," Eileen said to the same driver a few days later when she got into the car to be taken on her first trip. "I am very, very difficult."

Her separation from the agency was not total and immediate. She was close to her daughter Katie, as to all her children, so both she and Jerry offered advice when it was requested. "As I saw it from the outside," says Katie's elder sister, Jamie, "it looked like strands of DNA separating to replicate cells, reaching for each other even as they move apart. Katie and Mom had a wonderful ability to talk business together."

By the mid-1990s all four Ford children were married and starting a brood of offspring that became a focus of intense interest to their doting grandparents, who would happily board planes and travel for hours to attend school grandparents' days. Eileen's present-giving propensity went into top gear. With the help of mail-order catalogues and frequent visits to F.A.O. Schwarz, she filled a whole room at Oldwick with lavish presents that she would dispatch to her eight grandchildren and five great-grandchildren on Christmases and birthdays—and unlike her father, she did *not* require the recipients to give half the gifts to charity.

For several years the highlight of every spring was a huge family skiing holiday in Colorado. Jamie Craft remembers one evening when all the grandchildren spilled out into the sparkling, moonlit darkness of a snowy evening, running ahead of the grown-ups to dinner, while Jerry Ford put his arm round his wife.

"It doesn't get much better than this," he said.

They had an old-fashioned marriage. Eileen's domain was the house and the children—she loved combing the local farm stands and markets for fresh produce to be prepared by Marlene, her housekeeper and cook. Jerry did the typically male things—anything that required assembly, repair, or driving a tractor. And almost every day, to Eileen's enduring annoyance, he insisted on playing a game of tennis or squash.

Shortly before one of the couple's wedding anniversaries, Jerry commissioned photographer Jimmy Moore to shoot a photograph of the couple walking in their Oldwick woods, and he showed it proudly to his children. "The old girl still looks pretty good, doesn't she?" he said.

Eileen's days as a diva were not quite over. There were interviews and galas, and every spring, she presided in glory over Ford's Supermodel of the World competition, traveling with Jerry to the exotic corners of the world where the contest was staged, visiting old friends along the way. One year, they dropped in on Inger Malmros and Torgny Vikbladh of Sweden Models in Malmö, who noticed how Jerry's tastes had gone quite wild with retirement. "He would dress in big checks," remembers Torgny, "with bright Irish green socks and corduroys that had little dogs printed on them."

As the years went by, though, the friends grew fewer. Felicia Milewicz remembers attending the funeral of photographer Francesco Scavullo in 2004, at St. Jean Baptiste, a Catholic church on Lexington Avenue. "He was such a wonderful photographer," remembers Milewicz, "who made so many stars. Yet on the day of his funeral, the church was virtually empty. I can remember only two models who bothered to come.

"The whole family of the Fords was on parade in the church, though—Eileen and Jerry, with Jamie, Billy, Katie, and Lacey all standing beside them. That's another thing about Eileen," Milewicz added; "she raised her children to be four such exceptionally well-mannered human beings, so loving and loyal. They were a credit to her—and to Jerry as well."

Later that year, in November 2004, the Fords were back in church again—in the grand surroundings of St. Thomas, on Fifth Avenue, where Eileen and Jerry had decided to celebrate the sixtieth anniversary of their runaway wedding in special style. "We never got married in church," Eileen remembered, "so we decided that our sixtieth anniversary was a good moment to do it. I remember Jerry telling the children, 'The time has come to make you little bastards legitimate.'"

"It was a tender and very moving occasion," recalled their daughter Jamie, "with all of the family in a side chapel at St. Thomas. But it was bittersweet for us, because that was when we first realized that my father was sick. He had difficulty standing up during the ceremony, and at the reception he had to stay sitting down to deliver his speech. He and Mom had just got back from Copenhagen, and we thought it was the jet lag. But it was a month before he recovered."

Jerry Ford had an infection that had damaged two valves in his heart, and an operation to replace them came nowhere close to restoring his squash-playing fitness. After two months in the hospital he had lost fifty pounds. "He became like an old man within a year," remembered Roland Schucht. "He had been skiing up until his eightieth birthday and he could beat the shit out of me at tennis. Then suddenly he was pale and gaunt, and his clothes flapped off his body like a scarecrow."

The Fords decided on a last grand tour of Europe, revisiting the scenes of their former triumphs. Their scouting trips to London, Paris, and Scandinavia had been the glory of their agency's expansion in the fifties and sixties—the blend of business and the high life that was the hallmark of their style. Forty years later they finished their trip with a visit to the castellated grandeur of Crom Castle, on the shore of Lake Erne in County Fermanagh, Northern Ireland, the stately home of their former model turned countess Anna Karin Bjorck, then flew back home with Eileen's usual stash of caviar and gourmet contraband in their suitcases—not forgetting the bottles of aquavit.

The double heart valve replacement bought Jerry another four years of life, but in the summer of 2008 he was in and out of the hospital again. Brother Allen and his wife, Nancy, were shocked when Jerry came down to Washington for a visit. "He was just skin and bone," Allen remembers. "Nancy went to hug him, and she couldn't believe how thin he was. I think Jerry knew that he did not have long, but he did not act sad. He was dressed as beautifully as ever."

Jerry Ford died of pulmonary fibrosis on August 24, 2008, age eighty-three. Models flew from around the world to his memorial service later that fall at St. Thomas Episcopal Church, the scene of the renewal of his and Eileen's vows four years earlier, on Fifth Avenue, just south of the University Club where he used to play squash every Tuesday. Katie Ford made a moving speech. Lacey Ford made a funny one.

Afterward, the models all trooped up Fifth Avenue to mingle for lunch at the club—an extraordinary array of two hundred or more elegant and leggy women, some young, some perhaps a little faded, but all holding themselves magnificently, beauty on wheels, many dabbing their eyes as they walked. "I would swear," Eileen liked to remember, "that the traffic on Fifth Avenue paused in wonder for a moment to let the procession pass."

The pastor of St. Thomas joined the gathering afterward, dressed in the elaborate robes that he had worn for the funeral service, and Eileen felt she should make some comment on his colorful outfit. "I must say that I have never seen vestments quite like that," she remarked.

"Thank you," replied the pastor, looking around the roomful of beautiful women in a bemused, yet happy fashion. "And I must say that *I* have never seen a congregation quite like this."

THE BOTTOM-LINE TRIBUTE TO JERRY FORD HAD COME AT THE END of 2007, nine months before his death, when Katie Ford succeeded in selling the family business to Altpoint Capital Partners, a New York–based private equity firm with Russian management and backing. The sum involved has never been disclosed, but it was in the tens of millions of dollars, and it was certainly far more than the modeling agency was worth a year later, after the economic crash of October 2008.

"Jerry was so proud of Katie," commented her mother with pride. "He was getting pretty sick by then, but he reckoned she had done a wonderful piece of business. There'd been somebody else before the Russians, who'd agreed on a deal, then tried to cut down the price on the closing day. Katie said that the Ford family did not behave in that fashion. She kept her nerve, and in the end she got the price that she wanted—at the top of the market."

Eileen herself had been sick at the time of her husband's funeral, suffering from meningioma, a benign variety of brain tumor that ran visibly in a line from front to rear, along the top of her skull. A six-hour operation at Sloan Kettering had removed most of the tissue, but the tumor kept returning, restricting her ability to walk as she grew older, but never her spirit. "I'm very lucky," she liked to say. "God gave me my memory but took away my hearing. There are lots of things, I find, that I don't want to hear these days."

After Jerry's death the Oldwick gift room grew fuller and busier than ever, with the wrapping and dispatching masterminded by Helen, a Filipino assistant whom Eileen would bring in the day after Christmas to start preparing the gifts for next year. Eileen also worked assiduously at her Christmas and birthday card list, corresponding with former models around the world, along with total strangers she encountered and made into friends.

The tributes flowed thick at the celebration of her ninetieth birthday in March 2012, a lunch party organized by her children and her ex-son-in-law, André Balazs, Katie Ford's former husband, at his Standard Hotel in the Meatpacking District. The toasts proliferated and the champagne flowed as famous model after famous model rose to her feet to share her memories of Eileen. Now reliant on a walker, Eileen could no longer rise or sit down unaided, but she had an answer for each of them—and she looked immaculate in one of her specially tailored Escada blazers in navy blue with pink trim on the lapels. "*Not* the Escada," she was careful to point out afterward, "that you see in the window of the shops."

Shopping on Fifth Avenue with Eileen Ford in her final years was like going walkabout with a less nimble version of the Queen. Everyone was delighted to see her, and she would stop for a gracious word with each, from the doorman at the University Club to the receptionist at Louis Licari, her destination every Wednesday morning for her weekly styling and tint. She also kept up her Botox injections at regular intervals. "What else can you do," she liked to ask, borrowing an adage of her well-preserved friend Carmen Dell'Orefice, "when the ceiling of your living room is falling in? Don't you call the plasterer?"

In the heyday of the agency, Eileen had patronized Norman Orentreich, the pioneer of hair transplants and a number of other cosmetic techniques that he performed on Ford models at his Fifth Avenue clinic. As a worker at the coal face of the beauty business, Eileen declined to get bothered about women (or men) who turned to plastic surgery if they felt they needed to "get help." She acknowledged that she herself had indulged in "a couple of procedures," whose details she would not specify. On a bad day her skin bore unmistakable signs of having been stretched up around the ears, while her eyes were open with a gaze of rather-too-startled surprise.

From the hairdresser, she was off to lunch with an old friend or former model at her favorite restaurant, Le Cirque, before driving back to the country. And woe betide the driver who did not get Mrs. Ford home in time to see Judge Judy rapping her gavel at four o'clock—a slice of American life Eileen liked to enjoy while sipping her first chilled glass of aquavit.

She wore her peculiarities as a badge of honor, particularly the hours she spent on the weekend watching televised football games, along with her breakfast dependence on the rabidly tabloid reports of the *New York Post*.

"'Shut the Truck Up!'" she would chuckle over her cup of Earl Grey, reading out the headline of a report on the Teamsters Union and its attempts to muzzle one of its members. "These days," she liked to say, "my knowledge of the world comes almost totally from the *Post*—with just a little help from Fox."

Yet her sentiments were more liberal than her deliberately contrarian opinions might suggest. When London Fashion Week came around, she would search the trade papers avidly for news of Erin O'Connor, the beanpole-like Anglo-Irish model who had been one of the last guests to stay in her home in New York. Alarmed by the hazards surrounding the flocks of unchaperoned models arriving for Fashion Week's razzamatazz without help or supervision, O'Connor had founded the "Model Sanctuary," a calm haven where they could relax with nutritious food and healthy drink, along with in-house mentoring and counseling—"a non judgmental listening ear," as O'Connor put it, "with all that was good for the mind, body and soul."

Eileen liked to feel that O'Connor, the first model to be appointed vice chair of the British Fashion Council, was upholding and advancing some of the safe haven principles she had established at Seventy-Eighth Street. "Erin told me that she always felt so supported and *protected* when she was in our home," Eileen would relate. "From everything I hear about modeling today, it's even more of a jungle out there than ever."

Her grandchildren continued to delight her. She was very proud of her much-tattooed grandson Gerard Ford Craft, who moved to St. Louis to open Niche and a mini-chain of other award-winning restaurants specializing in local farm produce. The copy of *Food and Wine* magazine naming Craft one of the ten best new chefs in America occupied a prominent place on her Oldwick coffee table.

She also derived particular pleasure from the activities of her second daughter, Katie, who used her wealth and leisure from her share in the sale of the agency to set up a foundation, Freedom for All, to campaign against modern-day slavery, and against the trafficking of women in particular. Michelle Obama expressed surprise, on meeting Katie in June 2014, that she had previously been running the legendary Ford Modeling Agency—"And you went into *that*?"

"Isn't the plight of exploited women a strange cause to adopt," asked a journalist making a similar point in 2010, "after you've been running a model agency for a dozen years?"

"On the contrary," replied Katie. "I consider that I am directly carrying on my mother's work. Freedom for All is about fighting for the protection of women against largely male abuse, while giving them the empowerment to build up their own lives. That's exactly what my mother and father fought for in the world of modeling. Ford stood for style and class and beauty—the very best. But I am proud to say that it also stood for care and protection, and for the most important human values."

THROUGHOUT HER WIDOWHOOD, WHEN SHE RETIRED TO HER ROOM for the night, Eileen Ford would take a leather-framed photograph of her husband to bed. It showed the football hero in his prime, with his wide shoulders and smiling eyes, and before she switched off the light, she would plant a broad kiss on Jerry's lips. Then she would lay the picture down on the pillow on her husband's side of the bed, close her eyes, and go to sleep beside him.

"Jerry was always her anchor," said Roland Schucht, "and she was never quite the same after he was gone. He was always so calm and organized—strong, handsome, and charming, and always utterly happy to do things her way. Jerry never wanted the limelight. He was a totally secure guy, contained within himself. So he was always happy to let Eileen take the credit for whatever she wanted—and that suited her perfectly, of course."

Eileen talked about Jerry in the final months of her life when she met up with Christie Brinkley, her onetime protégée, now sixty years old, after her starring performance as Roxie Hart in the long-running Broadway hit production of *Chicago*.

"She came backstage," remembers Brinkley, "coiffed and elegant, which almost concealed how frail she was. She was paper-thin and clearly very ill, but she still had that power she always radiated when entering a room. Her eyes were sparkling, and when we started talking about the old days, it was as if the years had never been. 'I'm so proud of you,' she kept saying, and there were tears in her eyes. 'I always told you,' she said, 'that you can do anything you want.' It was such a full-circle moment for me. Eileen defined a whole era, along with a huge part of my life. I got where I got because I knew that Eileen Ford believed in me, and I am certain that was true for so many of her 'girls.'"

Eileen Ford was admitted to Morristown Memorial Hospital near her Oldwick home early in July 2014, after she fell following an outing to the ballet. It was the same hospital where her husband, Jerry, had spent his final days, and she died there of complications from meningioma and osteoporosis on July 9, 2014.

Shortly before her death she had celebrated her ninety-second birthday at Le Cirque with her children, F. Stone Roberts, Carmen Dell'Orefice, and a group of other friends. "She was looking magnificent," remembers Carmen—"happy and laughing, and as Escada-ed as ever. The way she was carrying on, she looked good to me for another fifty years."

"Feel my bump!" Eileen said cheerily, inviting people to feel the tumor that was growing up through the top of her skull like a little egg. In the last few months the doctors had prescribed steroid pills, which helped relieve her symptoms, but at the cost of significantly increasing her rage levels. The idea of Eileen Ford taking a pill every day to make herself angry struck those in her Oldwick household as highly comical—including the lady herself. "Oops, I'm so sorry," she would say, after firing off some verbal missile of particular venom or viciousness. "It must be the steroids!"

Back at her pied-à-terre on Sixty-Sixth Street, she met up with Iris Bianchi, who had had her own home in the same building for many years. "I saw a lot of her in those last few weeks," recalled Bianchi. "She came down to my apartment every day, looking beautiful, being funny, and we had so much fun together. Whatever her ailments may have been, her brain was operating one hundred percent. She was witty as ever, and she had so many plans—and so many jokes."

As the years rolled back, Eileen of the eleven fiancés made a surprising final appearance. "She told me, as we said good-bye for what turned out to be the last time, that she had one last project to complete—she was going to find herself a rich boyfriend for her final years. She didn't mind how old and fat he was, she said, so long as he had a nice private jet."

BEAUTY BUSINESS

LISA SIMPSON: Good looks don't really matter.

MISS HOOVER (second-grade teacher, Springfield
Elementary School): Nonsense, that's just something
ugly people tell their children.

—The Simpsons

IN NOVEMBER 2007, AS KATIE FORD WAS NEGOTIATING THE SALE OF her parents' modeling agency for a reputed fifty million dollars, a group of researchers from Harvard Medical School and the Massachusetts Institute of Technology arrived at a fresh take on Edward Thorndike's theory of the "halo effect" that helped explain the growth and prosperity of modeling agencies in the previous eighty-five years. What are the mental processes involved in the so-called "beauty bias," asked this group of psychologists and media experts—"the predictable preference and pursuit of physically attractive individuals"— and do men and women view facial beauty in different ways?

The team raided newspapers and magazines for a selection of faces that the culture viewed as either "average" or "beautiful," and then presented these to a group of heterosexual men and women— with an intriguing twist. As the sequence of faces passed across their computer screen, the guinea pigs were told they could suspend the sequence at any time if they wished to dwell on the attractions of any particular face. They simply had to press alternately on the M and N keys at the bottom of their keyboard, thus controlling their viewing time.

The performance of the group of male study participants was predictable. The men allowed the male images to cross their screen without significant intervention, then toggled between the *M* and *N* keys vigorously to retain contact with the images of women they fancied—what a nonscientist might crudely identify as the "loins effect." When it came to the female participants, however, they fingered-and-thumbed *both* groups. The women worked hard on the keyboard to retain the images of good-looking men—and then expended just as much energy to look at the female faces they found attractive. The loins did not rule. Beauty for these women clearly involved more complex factors than just being "turned on" by the opposite sex.

One experiment elaborately confirmed what can be observed in any hair salon: that women can devote hours to leafing through glossy magazine pictures of other women—along with the basic truth of which Eileen Ford never lost sight: a model may or may not be considered "sexy," but if she wants to be commercially successful, she must appeal to women, not to men.

Researchers have yet to fix on any solid explanation for this. Is the world of fashion based on some fundamental, tooth-and-nail competitiveness among women in pursuit of a mate? Or, quite to the contrary, can we see sisterly cooperation at work in the sharing of style and beauty strategies? Whatever the reason, *Forbes* magazine's register of supermodel earnings demonstrates the money to be made by having the right kind of face. On August 18, 2014, one month after Eileen Ford's death, *Forbes* reported that the combined annual earnings of the world's twenty-one highest-paid models added up to $142 million. So a quarter of a century after Linda Evangelista made her famous remark about not waking up for less than $10,000 a day, the average supermodel was waking up for a daily $18,525. The figure was $26,000 per day, in fact, if calculated on the basis of working a five-day week.

Forbes research revealed that most of the wealth of these attractive young multimillionaires, living proof of the "beauty bias" in modern culture, derived from their clothing and beauty contracts, with the models taking their cut on the "usage" basis originally identified and negotiated by Jerry Ford. Some did not deign even to belong to model agencies; they could comfortably afford their own personal managers. And when it came to agencies, by far the largest number of the top twenty-one faces belonged to IMG Models, a division of the International Management Group founded by Mark McCormack to handle the media careers of sports figures and celebrities.

Gisele Bündchen, the highest-paid model in the world for eight years in a row, is now thirty-four and has been on the books of IMG for over a decade. *Forbes* estimated her income, before fees and taxes, at $47 million in the twelve months to August 2014. In addition to having lucrative contracts with H&M, Chanel No. 5, and Carolina Herrera, Bündchen is a brand name in her native Brazil, where she is the face of Pantene and Oral-B, and has her own line of lingerie, Gisele Bündchen Intimates, and her own line of jelly sandals. Originally discovered in an Elite talent contest and promoted by John Casablancas, Bündchen forsook Elite in 2000, taking her bookers with her, a desertion that Casablancas described as "the biggest disappointment in my life."

Casablancas sold out his share in Elite shortly after Bündchen's departure and announced his retirement from the business in a bitter interview with France's VSD magazine in which he spared no recrimination. He described Heidi Klum as a "talentless German sausage," but he reserved his greatest venom for Gisele Bündchen—"my most hated enemy . . . a monster of selfishness." Overall, Casablancas complained, models and supermodels were "spoilt, unbearable troublemakers . . . I'm leaving a business I detest. I'm leaving stars who are unprepared for success and surrounded by idiots and leeches."

When Casablancas died at age seventy in July 2013 after a prolonged bout with jaw cancer, the fashion business was parsimonious in its mourning. His warmest tributes came from Elite's successful young Brazilian models, Ana Beatriz Barros, Alessandra Ambrosio, and Adriana Lima, as well as from Amber Valletta and Linda Evangelista. Yet when it came to the impressive array of the biggest names whose careers Casablancas had advanced in the previous century—Claudia and Cindy, Christie B. and Christy T., Elle and Eva, not to mention Gisele, Heidi, Iman, Janice, Naomi, and Stephanie—there was nothing. Silence.

Eileen ford derived no evident pleasure from the travails of John Casablancas in his declining years. At any mention of the man who had once been her own "most hated enemy," she would purse her lips meaningfully and open her wide eyes balefully to deliver her famous "Eileen stare."

The tributes on her own death one year later, almost to the day, were both plentiful and profuse. Some people may have felt afraid of the "Dragon Lady," as her model Barbara Summers once described her, but it turned out that, in the end, everyone really loved Eileen, starting with her very topmost of top models: "RIP Eileen Ford," tweeted Rachel Hunter. "Strong loving industry pioneer!" "[The Fords] protected what were basically like kittens, beautiful kittens," Lauren Hutton told the *New York Times*, referring to the legendary house on Seventy-Eighth Street. To which Christy Turlington, who had lived in the house, added: "She kept an eye out for me, and because she did, I think other male agents and photographers were more careful around me, more respectful. Every young model should have such protection."

Among the less predictable tributes was a letter posted, out of the blue, by someone her family had never heard of. James Picerno, vice president of a San Francisco bank, had, apparently, met Mrs. Ford nearly a decade before, when he was stacking shelves in a local supermarket. "I credit many of my successes," wrote Picerno, "to the conversations we had during her regular trips to Kings Food Market in Whitehouse [near Oldwick, New Jersey], where I was a stock clerk. I will always remember the frank, direct and tough advice that she gave me years ago to strive for more and better for myself. Although I may not achieve her very ambitious wish for me to become the governor of California (a wish that she often referenced in the Christmas cards I received from her over the years), I will always know that I am better for having known her."

Such recollections of the unknown Eileen featured prominently among the six hundred fifty guests who gathered for her memorial service on October 18, 2014, at St. Thomas, Fifth Avenue, the scene of Jerry's memorial service six years earlier. As in 2008, the array of gracefully aging models lit up Fifth Avenue on an already sunny fall morning, and Bill Cunningham of the *New York Times* was on hand to record the participants with his camera for a photographic essay, "Paying Respects," on the proper attire to be worn at a funeral or memorial service. There was only one hat on display with a mourning veil (worn by an English visitor), and the photographer's verdict was that the most successful outfits were those worn by Carmen Dell'Orefice and Christie Brinkley, each of whom had enlivened her black suit with a long, brightly colored silk scarf wound loosely around her neck. The vivid splash of color, said Cunningham, showed "celebration amidst the mourning."

Celebration was the theme of the service. Katie Ford had a bottle of champagne opened with a pop as she started her address in the large and elaborate cathedral-like church, where a posse of gorgeously robed High Anglican gentlemen had been assembled for the passing of the Jewish-Quaker debt collector's daughter. Monkish plainsong echoed off the rafters.

"My mother had a plan for everyone," recalled Ford's second daughter. "Ask, and she would tell you. Don't ask, and she would still tell you."

Speaking from the lectern, Katie's daughter Isabel Balazs described the misadventures of the Stone Roberts family, who had labored for days to load their Christmas tree with ornaments and precious family heirlooms, only for it to topple to the floor minutes before the arrival of Eileen (known as Gong to her grandchildren). The tree had barely been hoisted up again, with a small fraction of its ornaments surviving, when Gong swept in through the door.

"I have to tell you," she pronounced, "that your tree looks terrible."

The following year, Eileen's arrival at the Robertses' home was preceded by her chauffeur bearing a mountain of boxes filled with glittering ornaments she had purchased on her travels in the previous twelve months.

"I knew you needed help with your tree," she explained.

Afterward, in the University Club farther up Fifth Avenue, as the crowd toasted her memory, there would be much talk of never seeing the likes of her again, and a sense of loss—the loss of a person, obviously, but also a loss of direction. The world of fashion relies on its female popes and dragon ladies, its Edna Woolman Chases, Diana Vreelands, and Eileen Fords, to create the illusion that its merry-go-round of built-in obsolescence is actually going somewhere meaningful—that it might even stand for values beyond pleasure and profit. How can you believe in your heart that hems *have* to be long or short this season without someone bossy to insist that they must be so?

Eileen Ford never pretended, in fact, to tackle the fundamental fault lines of the fashion industry. In this respect she was as obsessed by appearances as the next woman; appearances were her business, after all. On April 24, 2013, a month less a day following her ninety-first birthday, the tragedy of the Rana Plaza collapse and fire in Greater Dhaka killed 1,130 Bangladeshi workers who were cutting and stitching for such Western fashion retailers as Benetton, Bonmarché, the Children's Place, Joe Fresh, Mango, Matalan, Monsoon Accessorize, Primark, and Walmart. This followed the deaths of more than a hundred workers the previous year in a fire at the nearby Tazreen factory where, as in New York City's infamous Triangle Shirtwaist Factory fire of 1911, some of the emergency exits were found to have been chained shut.

A century of progress had shifted the scandal to the other side of the world, but slavery remained slavery, with the Main Street shopping of Western women now dependent on the cut-price labor of Asian workers, many of them women. Thirty seconds of reflection makes clear that a pair of jeans retailing for $9.99 in Des Moines or

Biloxi could not possibly have been stitched together for a decent living wage anywhere in the world. Yet that is the economic underpinning of a consumer culture in which the purchase and parading of underpriced clothes has become a primary leisure activity.

When challenged with questions about the basics of her business, Eileen would purse her lips and say nothing. It was not her department—a problem she posted away in her mental "Way of the World" folder, like the challenge of getting Beverly Johnson on the cover of *Vogue* in the 1970s. Eileen left her daughter Katie to campaign to free the modern-day slaves. On her own account, she felt no conflict.

Eileen Ford knew all the things she had set out to achieve, and she knew that, by and large, she had accomplished them. She had taken care of her models. She had fought for them, had protected and enriched them, and had helped, in partnership with her husband, to turn their once lowly profession into an industry in which women got paid spectacularly more money than men. In this respect alone she had helped empower the cause of women, even if some who spoke for that cause disagreed. She had also cared for and raised her own family, enriching them not a little in the process.

"She championed the values that were important," declared the canon of St. Thomas from the pulpit at her memorial service. "Truth. Commitment. Hard work. Responsibility. Respect." The canon based his tribute to Eileen on Christ's famous words from John's Gospel: "I am the good shepherd: the good shepherd layeth down his life for the sheep."

If it struck some as strange that Eileen Ford should be equated with the Son of God, even by analogy, this was, after all, a woman who had once compared those who betrayed her to Judas.

"Before we part," the canon intoned, "let us bid farewell to our sister . . . One day, we will greet her again in a place where Christ wipes away all tears."

The possibility of meeting up in heaven with Eileen Ford offered a bracing prospect on a Saturday morning. "It gives a whole new dimension," remarked one worshipper, "to the promise of eternal life."

Meeting Eileen Ford

oh these English girls, so unprofessional,
no sweater bra, no waist cinch. FAT! FAT! FAT!
...and off with those eyebrows

"Meeting Eileen Ford" as depicted by 1960s model Grace Coddington,
today the Creative Director of US *Vogue*.
(Drawing by Grace Coddington © 2012)

APPENDIX: TOP FORD MODELS

It is not possible to make a precise inventory of all the models who worked for Eileen Ford, but surviving records suggest that more than a thousand models, male and female, were listed on her books from 1947, when the Ford agency was founded, until its sale in 2007. Some had been scouted and developed by Eileen Ford. Others started, continued, or concluded their careers with rival agencies or, in the case of European models, worked for Ford by arrangement with their mother agencies. Listed here is a partial, and by its nature imperfect, roster of two hundred men and women who bore the title "Ford model" at different times, as selected by Neal Hamil, Joe Hunter, Iris Minier, and Patty Sicular, four colleagues of Eileen Ford over the years.

1940s–1950s

Marilyn Ambrose, Betty Cornell, Simone D'Aillencourt, Elise Daniels, Lorraine Davies, Carmen Dell'Orefice, Kouka Denis, Dovima, Pat Geoghegan, Anne Gunning, Georgia Hamilton, Sunny Harnett, Dolores Hawkins, Tippi Hedren, Lucinda Hollingsworth, Bettie Johnson, Dorian Leigh, Sophie Malgat, Lillian Marcuson, Elsa Martinelli, Barbara Mullen, Sandra Nelson, Ruth Neumann, Natálie Nickerson, Suzy Parker, Jean Patchett, Joan Pedersen, Millie Perkins, Nan Rees, Mary Jane Russell, Helen Ryan, Anne Saint Marie, Carolyn Scott.

1960s–1970s

Maud Adams, Ulla Andersson, Barbara Bach, Kim Basinger, Candice Bergen, Iris Bianchi, Anna Karin Bjorck, Jane Blackburn, Susan Blakey, Susan Brainard, Christie Brinkley, Kate Capshaw, Monique Chevalier, Barbara Clement, Colleen Corby, Cathee Dahmen, Agneta Darin, Anne de Zogheb, Janice Dickinson, Faye Dunaway, Maggi Eckhardt, Cristina Ferrare, Jane Fonda, Agneta Frieberg, Karen Graham, Erin Gray, Sunny Griffin, Melanie Griffith, Shelley Hack, Dayle Haddon, Julie Hagerty, Jerry Hall, Veronica Hamel, Alana Hamilton, Ann Harper, Lois Heyl, Anjelica Huston, Lauren Hutton, Beverly Johnson, Jolie Jones, Hellevi Keko, Evelyn

Kuhn, Donyale Luna, China Machado, Dorothea McGowan, Ali Mac-Graw, Peggy Moffitt, Linda Morand, Karin Mossberg, Jennifer O'Neill, Sandra Paul, Sondra Peterson, Wanakee Pugh, Terry Reno, Chris Royer, Rene Russo, Brooke Shields, Jean Shrimpton, Naomi Sims, Martha Stewart, Micaela Sundholm, Lisa Taylor, Cheryl Tiegs, Penelope Tree, Susan Van Wyck, Rosie Vela, Vera von Lehndorff (later Veruschka), Nena von Schlebrügge, Hilke Wendorff, Wilhelmina.

1980s Onward

Carol Alt, Emme Aronson, Shari Belafonte, Marisa Berenson, Karen Bjornson, Naomi Campbell, Kim Charlton, Sophia Coppola, Dianne de-Witt, Kirsten Dunst, Karen Elson, Carol Gramm, Maaret Halinen, Bridget Hall, Shalom Harlow, Kristy Hinze, Rachel Hunter, Chanel Iman, Milla Jovovich, Twiggy Lawson, Kelly LeBrock, Martha Longley, Rosemary Mc-Grotha, Kristen McMenamy, Elle Macpherson, Bridget Moynahan, Carolyn Murphy, Erin O'Connor, Catherine Oxenberg, Jade Parfitt, Gabrielle Reece, Crystal Renn, Maggie Rizer, Isabella Rossellini, Ines Sastre, Monika Schnarre, Stephanie Seymour, Renée Simonsen, Anette Stai, Sharon Stone, Christy Turlington, Amber Valletta, Frederique van der Wal, Patricia van Ryckeghem, Patricia Velásquez, Vendela, Eva Voorhees, Veronica Webb, Alek Wek.

Ford Men

Jeff Aquilon, Gene Barakat, Bruce Bauer, Ryan Burns, Bill Clune, Chad Cole, Bill Curry, Ted Dawson, Nacho Figueras, Keith Gog, Matt Gontier, Joe Hunter, Barry Kaufman, Boris Kodjoe, Brad Kroenig, Fabio Lanzoni, Ryan Locke, Bill Loock, Ted McGinley, Jim McMullen, Bob Menna, Kevin Rice, Patrick Saint Clair, Jack Scalia, Stephen Shellen, Steve Shortridge, Tony Spinelli, Oren Stevens, Andy Warhol, Scott Webster.

ACKNOWLEDGMENTS

All I ask is a merry yarn from a laughing fellow-rover.

—*John Masefield, "Sea Fever," 1902*

I N THE SUMMER OF 2010, A FEW MONTHS AFTER I STARTED WORK on this book, I drove with Eileen Ford, eighty-eight years old in March of that year, to revisit the scenes of her youth. We had been introduced by friends, Les and Judy Gurren, who lived near the Ford home in the woods of Oldwick, New Jersey, and it was Les who drove us along Route 78 to the New Jersey Turnpike, bypassing Manhattan on our left to locate Long Island and the no-man's-land memorably described in *The Great Gatsby* as "the Valley of Ashes"—today the hardscrabble row houses of Queens.

Reaching Great Neck, we drove down Northern Boulevard, past the angular metal rides of the Adventurers Inn amusement park. "This was all just countryside and swamp when we lived here," remembered Eileen. "And there were no Orientals." We were passing a row of Chinese and Korean take-out restaurants, and the old Ford dealership now offered Honda Infinitis. Yet the elegant copper spire of St. Paul's Episcopal Church was still standing on Grace Avenue, one of the main streets.

"That's where I used to teach Sunday school—and I think I knew people who lived *there*." She pointed at Tuscany Court, a faded filmset development of Spanish Colonial cottages, balconies, and court-yard walkways from the days when Great Neck was the Beverly Hills of the East.

Now we were driving uphill through the leafy and lake-y streets of Great Neck Estates, but we were lost for words when we arrived at 2 Hilltop Drive, for the long, half-timbered Tudor, Eileen's child-hood home, was derelict. Where there once were roses, now there were dandelions. The Ottensosers' former residence stood brown and funereal, the pitched eaves shabby for lack of paint.

"I can't believe it's fallen apart," said Eileen, looking out through the car window, crestfallen.

If the house had been alive, she might have made the effort to get out of the car, but she was walking with difficulty those days—and why disembark to look at a corpse? She turned her back rather firmly, consigning what she had just seen to the past, and looking down the road at the neighboring houses.

"That's where the Devondorfs lived," she said. "And that was the house of Captain Rospini, who was the head of the Italian Line. It was all more open than this—all these trees must have grown. We used to play softball in the street."

There was nothing more to stay for, so we drove back toward town, past the bucolically named suburban boulevards: Clover Drive, Nirvana Avenue, Flower Lane, Lilac Lane, and a whimsical touch of Dickens—Pickwick Road.

"This is the way that Daddy would have been driven to the station."

She clenched her jaw as we passed an apartment building called the Kenwood. "That's where I went to the dentist—he didn't believe in Novocain."

Back on Grace Avenue, we turned left and headed down toward the waterside and Louie's Oyster Bar and Grill, "Famous Since 1905" for its seafood. Monday night was Lobster Night (two juicy Maine lobsters for the price of one) and also Frank Sinatra Night. This was in homage to the almost-local resident who, according to cherished legend, liked to relax on the deck of Louie's in the 1940s and '50s with his infamous Rat Pack, savoring his *vongole* as the sun went down. So we sat out where Frank and his friends must have sat, chewing contentedly on our lobsters—Eileen did enjoy her food—while the crooning of a passable Sinatra sound-alike wafted out of the bar.

As we left, shuffling our way through the tables of families and young courting couples, Eileen, who was wearing her very brightest red raincoat, suddenly stopped, and we turned with her to look at the table of an attractive young brunette of eighteen or nineteen, evidently out for the night with her boyfriend.

"Have you ever thought of being a model?" Eileen asked without preamble, putting down her card in front of the surprised-looking girl, who clearly did not know what to say.

"This is Eileen Ford, of the Ford Modeling Agency," I interjected. During the meal, I had caught sight of the young woman over Eileen's shoulder and thought that she had quite a pretty face. But now, since Eileen has spoken, I could see cheekbones. . . .

The young woman was looking down at Eileen's card, but the name "Ford" clearly meant nothing to her—nor did the prospect of becoming a model with Ford or any other agency. She smiled and mumbled politely, and we passed on.

As we looked across the darkening waters of Manhasset Bay, we spied a single green light flickering at the end of a boat dock, small and far away, prompting speculative talk about the light that Jay Gatsby might have gazed at across the bay, trying to pick out the boat dock of Daisy Buchanan, his unrequited love.

"Never read the book," said Eileen.

I WOULD LIKE TO THANK MY FRIENDS LES AND JUDY GURREN FOR introducing me to Eileen Ford, their neighbor in Oldwick, New Jersey, and for the idea that grew into the writing of this book. I spent many happy weeks in their company and especially hers, enjoying the hospitality of Eileen and of her family—Jamie Ford Craft and her husband, Robert Craft; Katie Ford; Lacey Ford Williams and her husband, John Williams; and Billy Ford—all of whom I must place at the head of my gratitude list. This is neither an official nor an authorized biography. Members of the Ford family have read and commented on certain sections of the text, but they have been gracious in their detachment. They have exerted no pressure on me to present a particular view of their parents; nor would I have accepted any pressure. This is my own personal take on an extraordinary woman and on the extraordinary industry she helped to shape with her husband Jerry. In researching Jerry, I am grateful for the counsel and memories of his younger brother, Allen Ford. William Forsythe's insights as the son of Eileen's half brother, Tom, were a revelation.

Interviewing some of the world's most alluring women has been no penance, and I would like to express my thanks to the Ford models and their family members whom I was lucky enough to have interviewed in person, on the telephone, or through the good offices of Skype: Maud Adams, Emme Aronson, Iris Bianchi, Anna Karin Bjorck, Janey Blackburn, Susan Brainard, Christie Brinkley, Bill Clune, Joan Pedersen Coleman and Kernan Coleman, Melissa Cooper, Agneta Darin, Carmen Dell'Orefice, Kouka Denis, Andrea Derujinsky, Dianne deWitt, Betsy Fadem, Nyna Giles, Keith Gog, Barbara Clement Gould, Karen Graham, Jerry Hall, Dolores Hawkins, Tippi Hedren, Joe Hunter, Lauren Hutton, Lois Hyl Jewell, Beverly Johnson, Ulla Andersson Jones, Dinah Dillman Kaufman, Lorraine Davies Knopf, Monique Knowlton, Martha Longley, Ali MacGraw, Jan McGuire, Jim McMullen, Linda Morand, Barbara Mullen, Bettie Johnson Murray, Catherine Oxenberg, Wingate Paine II, Daniel Patchett, Sandra Paul, Millie Perkins, Terry Reno, Hilke Richards, Rene Russo, Helen Ryan, Jack Scalia, Renée Toft Simonsen, Eva Sinnerstad, Micaela Sundholm, Cheryl Tiegs, Penelope Tree, Patricia van Ryckeghem, Patricia Velásquez, Eva Voorhees, Jennifer Paine Welwood, Anne de Zogheb (who became Mrs. Anne Anka), and Amy Auer, the daughter of Jean Patchett.

Some of these interviews were recorded by the filmmaker Jeth Weinrich for the documentary he is shooting on the life and work of Eileen Ford. I am grateful to him for his good cheer and companionship when we worked together in Los Angeles, and for allowing me to view the footage he shot of interviews with John Caplan, Soni Ekvall, Arthur Elgort, Michael Gross, Rachel Hunter, Brad Kroenig, Erin O'Connor, F. Stone Roberts, Jerry Schatzberg, Anette Stai, and Lisa Taylor.

Scouts, bookers, and assistants know the inside story of the modeling industry, so I owe much to the secrets shared by Bridget Burke, Jane Hallaren, Neal Hamil, Joe Hunter, Iris Minier, Tischka Nabi, Monique Pillard, Cathy Quinn, Patty Sicular of IconicFocus, Dottie Franco Solomon, and Rusty Donovan Zeddis. On the photographic side, my thanks to Chris Duffy, Bill Helburn, Lois and Robert Lilly, Mark Maryanovich, Mike Reinhardt, Dick Richards, and Melvin Sokolsky, and to Takouhy Wise of Staley-Wise Gallery. Also to Jim Caccione, Robert Donnelly, David Downton, Suzanne Hodgart, Susan Pedersen of Chester Camera and to Roy and Zoë Snell for their help with the design and pictures inside this book.

Elsebeth Mouritzen was my mentor in Scandinavia as I followed the trail blazed in Denmark and Sweden by Eileen, modeling's first international scout. I must also thank, for their guidance and hospitality, Erik Brandt, Inger Malmros and Torgny Vikbladh of Sweden Models, and Sandra Foss, as well as Elsebeth's husband, Bent.

In England, I am grateful for the knowledgeable help of my friends Greta Norris, Diana Melly, and Edina Ronay, and for the special insights of José Fonseca and April Ducksbury Fawcett of Models 1, who worked both with Eileen and with John Casablancas, and stayed friends with both. Thank you also to Sarah Doukas, to Jonathan Phang, and to Peter Marlowe, Mr. Composite Card, who generously put at my disposal the resources of his historic archive: modelscomposites.com. Nigel Rees offered his usual expert insight into obscure quotations. Edda Tasiemka provided her invaluable newspaper clippings, as she has now for more than forty years. Dr. John Stephens was my standby on medical matters. Humphrey Burton provided a good story about his friend Leonard Bernstein "of

Boston." Thank you to Annabelle Halsor, Jane Turner, and particularly Lesley Baker in my wife's office for their secretarial backup.

In the United States, I am grateful for the many people to whom Eileen introduced me, all of them helping me to understand her better: Kay Bourland, Christopher and Bea Daggett, Polly Ferguson, Evelyn Kuhn, Louis Licari, John Louise, Felicia Milewicz, Grace Mirabella, Dr. Catherine Orentreich, Nancy Pyne, F. Stone Roberts, John and Paula Runnells, Roland Schucht, Stanley Sokolsky, Mark Stankus, Martin and Norma Stevens.

My thanks, too, to Judy Bachrach, Eve Claxton, Charlie and Peggy Davies, George Feld, Lonson MacCargar, Shelley Promisel, and Sumner Putnam, Tom Youngblood—and to Lorraine Caggiano, who helped arrange my long and fascinating interview in 2012 with John Casablancas. On opposite sides of Florida, the American friends I owe to Saudi Arabia, Ben Dyal and Tom Fillion, brought their impeccable literary taste to the critiquing of my drafts, while my longtime editor and mentor, Bill Phillips, kept me up to the mark from Block Island.

My British research assistant, Moyra Ashford, would like to thank Jane Thoner at New Jersey's Plainfield Public Library for clinching evidence on Justice Hand, who officiated over the runaway marriage of Eileen's mother; Patty Edmonson at Cleveland Museum of Art for Nat Ottensoser's link to early-twentieth-century design; journalists Jan Rocha in São Paulo, Brazil, and Rasheed Abou-Alsamh in Brasília, for material on John Casablancas; Gussy Marlowe for her hospitality and long memory; and two guardians of family history who belong in the special category of sharing long-hidden family secrets: Stephen Sheppard in Pensacola, Florida, for the cuttings at the bottom of his father's sock drawer about Shep's "secret" marriage to Eileen, and Los Angeles artist Hilda Wagner for the album left by her uncle, John Hamilton Wagner, "Ham," one of the most remarkable characters to cross Eileen's path. Moyra also extends her thanks to Ipek Halil for her help compiling and checking the bibliography, and to David Sherwood, James Brooker, and Tamas Kappeter of Flamble

Ltd. for computer setup—and occasional rescue. Last, but not least, thanks to Ancestry.com and the online archives of the *New York Times*, the Library of Congress, and the Leo Baeck Institute, New York.

My American research assistant, Susan Link Camp, would like to thank Sidney Achee, Eileen's high school classmate; Euva Anderson, for her interview assistance; Verna Tamborelle Beaver, a Barnard College classmate of Eileen's; Dr. Bruce Becker, teacher of a student who made contact with Eileen in 1993, eliciting an illuminating response from her; Priscilla Bodnar, who provided the rare issues of *Paris Match* and of an Italian magazine about Suzy Parker's 1958 car crash; Joanna Sedlmayr Bridges, daughter of Jean Compo, the model and Barnard College classmate of Eileen's; Dr. Bruce Camp for his help with biblical references; Judith Caplan, genealogist from New York; Cliff Cheng, the photographer who introduced us to Wilhelmina's daughter, Melissa Cooper; Craig Colley, owner of Pix & Dubs in Laguna Niguel, California, for the transfer of video to DVD and of LPs to CDs; Rosetta DeBernardinis, who made notes for a biography of Eileen in the mid-1980s; Ann Doxsey, webmaster for Alpha Theta Beta sorority at Hofstra University; Helen Mueller, former model and friend of Eileen's; Dr. John Hattendorf, director of the Naval War College Museum, Newport, Rhode Island; Andy Howick of mptv Images; Albert Kallis, illustrator; Trudy Kallis, illustrator's model; Jim Kelly, historian of the USS *William R. Rush*, Shep Sheppard's ship in World War II; Jeff Kenney, archivist at Culver Military Academy; Sidney Monroe, Monroe Gallery of Photography in Santa Fe, New Mexico; Betsy Norfleet, daughter of Betty Hanf Norfleet, model and Barnard College classmate of Eileen's; Maureen O'Connell, county clerk, Nassau County, New York; Dr. King Odell at Moses Brown School, Providence, Rhode Island; Kevin Proffitt, senior archivist for research and collections at the American Jewish Archives; Scott Schmitt, owner of San Juan Photo and Digital in San Juan Capistrano, California; Eva Tekien, IconicFocus partner; Suzan Tell, Records and Research Department, New York City Surrogate's Court; Virginia Villa, digital photography and organization; and Dr. Yvonne M. Ward, honorary research associate at La Trobe University, Bundoora, Australia.

My own debt is immense, to both Moyra and Susan, veritable Nancy Drews in their sleuthing. It was their resourceful digging that unearthed the secrets Eileen spent her adult life trying to hide—her Jewish heritage, her hasty and hidden marriage to "Shep" Sheppard, and the deliberately concealed role played by Natálie Nickerson in the early success of the agency—and they have provided the same precision and freshness in their approach to every other chapter. Moyra brought her command of Portuguese and her knowledge of Brazil to her translation of John Casablancas's 2008 memoir *Vida Modelo*— not published in English—but the responsibility for its use is all mine. Susan's specialist knowledge in the history of modern fashion modeling has helped secure many of the original images in the picture section, and on the cover.

My editor, Jennifer Barth, has been a model of wise judgment and support as I have missed deadline after deadline—my thanks to her and to her editorial support team at HarperCollins, New York: Jenna Dolan, Fritz Metsch, Joanne O'Neill, Beth Silfin, David Watson, and Erin Wicks. Also to my agents, Gráinne Fox in New York and Jonathan Pegg in London.

On top of recently presenting me with a beautiful granddaughter, my daughter Scarlett has, from the start of this project, provided me with guidance that is the more appreciated in coming from a very skillful and successful professional writer. And as for my darling wife, Jane, who has had to go to sleep on too many nights recently with the MacBook tap-tap-tapping beside her—she is quite simply, as I say on the dedication page, my own fun-filled, loving, and inspiring Model Woman.

Robert Lacey
London
January 2015

PHOTOGRAPHIC SOURCES

Picture research by Susan Camp and Suzanne Hodgart.
With special thanks to Terry Reno and Patty Sicular.

PHOTOGRAPH SECTION 1, FOLLOWING PAGE 150

Loretta and Eileen Ottensoser (courtesy of the Ford family).

Nat Ottensoser and his FAPA advertisements (Moyra Ashford Private Collection and Susan Camp Private Collection).

Nat Ottensoser with Eileen, also with her brother Bobby (courtesy of the Ford family).

Eileen Otte, "Bo" Meyer, and Great Neck High School exterior from the Great Neck High School *Arista* yearbooks (Susan Camp Private Collection).

Eileen Otte senior photograph, and Junior Prom Committee photograph from the Barnard College *Mortarboard* yearbook (Susan Camp Private Collection).

John Robert Powers (© Bettmann/Corbis).

Harry Conover (George Karger/Pix Inc., The LIFE Images Collection/Getty Images).

Walter Thornton (Estate of Mitchell Jason).

Eileen Otte modeling for Macy's and Saks At 34th advertisements in *Mademoiselle*, 1941, and on the cover of *Campus Classics for Knitters* (Susan Camp Private Collection).

Eileen on the cover of *Liberty* magazine (cover © 2015 GLT Liberty Management Company. All rights reserved. Photograph by Mead-Maddick, © 1997 Kiki Mead-Maddick Haynes, © 2015 GLT Liberty Management Company. All Rights Reserved).

Eileen and Charles Sheppard wedding (*Charleston Evening Post*, February 2, 1943, page 5; courtesy of Stephen Sheppard).

J. Hamilton "Ham" Wagner (courtesy of Hilda Wagner).

Eileen Otte with Jerry Ford (courtesy of the Ford family).

Carmel Snow and Alexey Brodovitch (Walter Sanders/The LIFE Picture Collection/Getty Images).

Eileen Ford and Natálie Nickerson's 1947 partnership agreement (courtesy of Wingate Paine II and Jennifer Paine Welwood).

Natálie Nickerson, *Harper's Bazaar*, January 1947 (© Hearst Publications. Photograph by Richard Avedon, © The Richard Avedon Foundation).

Barbara Mullen photographed by John Rawlings for *Vogue* (© Condé Nast Archive/Corbis).

Jerry and Eileen Ford with Mr. and Mrs. A. J. Powers (courtesy of the Ford family).

Huntington Hartford in Palm Beach (photograph by Bert & Richard Morgan/Hulton Archive/Getty Images).

Carmen Dell'Orefice, *Vogue*, October 15, 1947 (Erwin Blumenfeld, © Condé Nast Publications).

Eileen and Jerry Ford in their Second Avenue office, also with Joan Pedersen and Jamie Ford, and Barbara Mullen (all photographs by Nina Leen/The LIFE Picture Collection/Getty Images).

Suzy Parker (photograph by Sharland/The LIFE Images Collection/Getty Images).

Jean Patchett (photograph by Irving Penn, © Condé Nast Publications).

PHOTOGRAPH SECTION 2, FOLLOWING PAGE 214

Eileen Ford with eleven models in *McCall's* magazine, April 1955 (© Mark Shaw/mptvimages.com; colorization by Roy Snell and Zoë Snell, © roysnell@mac.com).

Richard Avedon and *Dovima with Elephants: Cirque d'Hiver, Paris, August, 1955* (Sara Krulwich/New York Times Co./Getty Images).

Diana Vreeland (© Thomas Hoepker/Magnum Photos).

Dovima with Audrey Hepburn (Paramount/The Kobal Collection at Art Resource, NY).

Funny Face poster (Paramount/The Kobal Collection at Art Resource, NY).

Richard Avedon with Fred Astaire (© David Seymour/Magnum Photos).

Iris Bianchi composite card (courtesy of Iris Bianchi; photograph by Richard Avedon, © The Richard Avedon Foundation).

Dorian Leigh and models (photograph by François Pages/Paris Match via Getty Images).

Learn to Be Beautiful, cover of Eileen Ford's 1961 LP (courtesy of the Ford family).

Dolores Hawkins, *Vogue*, January 15, 1959 (William Bell, © Condé Nast Publications).

Jean Shrimpton on *Harper's Bazaar* cover, April 1965 (courtesy of Nicholas Haslam © Hearst Publications. Photograph by Richard Avedon, © The Richard Avedon Foundation).

Penelope Tree photographed by Arnaud De Rosnay (© Condé Nast Archive/ Corbis).

Terry Reno on *Seventeen* cover, April 1967 (© Hearst Publications).

Terry Reno's 1969 Ford Model Agency account statement (courtesy of Terry Reno).

The Fords' Quogue weekend home letterhead illustration (courtesy of the Ford family).

Eileen Ford at Quogue with models (Co Rentmeester/The LIFE Picture Collection/Getty Images).

Jerry Hall, British *Vogue*, May 1975 (Norman Parkinson/Vogue © The Condé Nast Publications LTD).

Ali MacGraw, French *Vogue*, May 1971 (Alex Chatelain © Condé Nast Publications).

Rene Russo, American *Vogue*, July 1976 (Arthur Elgort © Condé Nast Publications).

Beverly Johnson, American *Vogue*, August 1974 (Francesco Scavullo © Condé Nast Publications).

Lauren Hutton, 1974 (Archive Photos/Getty Images).

Lauren Hutton and Charles Revson, June 1973 (Pierre Scherman/*Women's Wear Daily*, © Condé Nast Publications).

Cheryl Tiegs poses for *Sports Illustrated* Swimsuit Issue 1975 (Walter Iooss Jr./*Sports Illustrated*/Contour by Getty Images).

Cheryl Tiegs for Cover Girl, 1979 (© Cover Girl/Procter & Gamble).

Jerry Ford, 1989 (© Deborah Feingold/Corbis).

John Casablancas and Elite Models, 1978 (photograph by Marco Glaviano © 2014).

Wilhelmina Cooper (AP/Press Association Images).

Elite Model Management composite cards (courtesy of the Peter Marlowe model composite archives at www.modelscomposites.com. Maaret Halinen photograph by John Stember ©; Janice Dickinson photograph by Mike Reinhardt ©; Christie Brinkley, *Glamour* December 1977 © Condé Nast Publications).

Monique Pillard with Cindy Crawford (Ron Galella Ltd./WireImage/Getty Images).

British *Vogue* January 1990 (Peter Lindbergh/Vogue, © The Condé Nast Publications LTD).

Jerry and Eileen Ford with models in Moscow (© Jean-Loup Debionne, 1987).

Eileen and Jerry Ford dancing at a family party (courtesy of the Ford family).

Social List of Somerset Hills 2013 (courtesy of Patricia Lurker © iStock.com/ rhyman007).

"Hilltop Drive," Oldwick, New Jersey (Roger-Viollet/TopFoto).

Eileen Ford with Carmen Dell'Orefice (WireImage/Getty Images).
Eileen Ford in her Oldwick study (Roger-Viollet/TopFoto).

LINE DRAWING, PAGE 264

Excerpt and line drawing from *Grace: A Memoir* by Grace Coddington, copyright © 2012 by Grace Coddington. Used by permission of Random House, an imprint and division of Penguin Random House LLC. All rights reserved. Any third party use of this material, outside of this publication, is prohibited. Interested parties must apply directly to Penguin Random House LLC for permission.

COVER IMAGES

Front cover photographs (top left to right):
  Christy Turlington Burns (© Peter Lindbergh).
  Jean Shrimpton (© Duffy Archive).
  Jerry Hall (© Brian Aris).
  Naomi Campbell (© Timothy Greenfield-Sanders).
  Christie Brinkley (Michael Thompson © Cover Girl/Procter & Gamble).
Bottom: Eileen Ford at her agency desk in 1948: © Nina Leen/Getty Images.

Author photograph by Mark Maryanovich.

Digital preproduction of image files on cover and also in picture inserts by Roy Snell (roysnell@mac.com) and Zoë Snell (zoe167@me.com).

NOTES

Many of the records of the Ford Modeling Agency were destroyed in March 1993 by the fire that gutted the home of Eileen and Jerry Ford at Oldwick, New Jersey. The narrative of this book has therefore relied heavily on the recollections of models and employees, along with members of the Ford family—and on lengthy interviews with Eileen Ford herself in the final four years of her life, recorded by the author in twelve Mead Composition notebooks labeled A–L, a total of 2,400 numbered pages. These interviews and observations are identified in the source notes that follow as Ford Notebooks, followed by the page number. Other interviews are identified on the first occasion they are cited by the date of the interview.

Prologue: Supermodels for Breakfast

2 "Good morning, Johnny": John Casablancas and Ana Maria Baiana, *Vida Modelo* (Rio de Janeiro: Agir Editora, 2008), p. 217.

2 "saluted each other like royalty": Interview with Sarah Doukas, Models 1, London, March 23, 2011.

3 "I liked that style": Ford Notebooks, E79.

3 "Come back and see me": Anthony Haden-Guest, "Model Wars," *New York*, July 25, 1977, p. 31.

3 "not one girl in two hundred ": Ford Notebooks, E80.

4 Jerry Ford took care of the business: James Mills, "The Godmother," *Life*, November 13, 1970, p. 51.

4 her happiest hunting grounds: Ibid.

4 Ford's revenue from that was roughly twenty thousand dollars: Gwen Kinkead, "The Price of Beauty Is Getting Beyond Compare," *Fortune*, December 3, 1979, p. 60.

4 In 1970 the agency raked in: Mills, "The Godmother," p. 51.

4 the "godmother" of modeling: Ibid.

4 "Johnny's problem": Ford Notebooks, E81.

4 "She really could be ferocious": Interview with Rusty Donovan Zeddis, July 17, 2014.

5 "I remember Dick quite losing his cool": Off the record.

5 "radically contrasting philosophies": Interview with John Casablancas, November 28, 2012.

5 the Elite masthead logo: Casablancas, *Vida Modelo*, pp. 166, 167.

6 "I was the playboy": Interview with John Casablancas, November 28, 2012.

7 "Jerry and I were not happy": Ford Notebooks, F53.

7 "pointed her long fingernails at me": Casablancas, *Vida Modelo*, p. 217.

7 "Willy and Bruce were furious": Ford Notebooks, A83.

7 "a torrent of accusations": Casablancas, *Vida Modelo*, p. 217.

8 "We cannot even recruit": Ibid.

8 varying dates: *Vida Modelo* sets the confrontation in the fall of 1976; Eileen Ford recalled it happening in the spring of 1977.

8 "So many lies!": Casablanca's interview, November 28, 2012.

8 "his beautiful Swedish girlfriend": Ibid., p. 224.

8 "doing a great job": Michael Gross, *Model* (New York; William Morrow, 1995), p. 309.

8 Halinen gave two weeks' notice: Haden-Guest, "Model Wars," p. 32.

9 "much too ethnic": Janice Dickinson, *No Lifeguard on Duty* (New York: HarperCollins, 2002), p. 44.

9 "I'm sorry, dear": Ibid.

9 kiss-and-tell memoir: Dickinson, *No Life Guard on Duty*.

9 the penis size of her famous lovers: *The Jonathan Ross Show*, posted August 16, 2008. Part 1: https://ww16th.youtube.com/watch?v=tXujjl8563I. Part 2: http://www.youtube.com/watch?v=w6jpRKPS_g4.

9 "to punish Eileen": Mark S. Malkin, "Janice Dickinson: Her Lips Aren't Sealed," *New York*, May 27, 2002.

9 "She was in my life": Ibid.

10 "sitting at the guillotine": Interview with Tischka Nabi, August 13, 2014.

10 "I'll always be grateful": Interview with Monique Pillard, New York, February 22, 2011.

11 "And I would do it again": Ford Notebooks, D3.

11 "It was only a paperback": Interview with Monique Pillard, New York, February 22, 2011.

Chapter 1: Nothing to Do But Look Pretty

12 "I'd LOVE to be a model": *Millie the Model*, Marvel Comics, Issue 113, March 1962.

12 "for the benefit of the ladies": Antonia Fraser, *Dolls* (London: Weiden-feld and Nicolson, 1963), p. 41. In 1731 Prévost wrote his novel *Manon Lescaut (L'Histoire du Chevalier des Grieux et de Manon Lescaut)*, which inspired operas and ballets by Massenet, Puccini, and others.

12 "if you send for it": Fraser, *Dolls*, p. 43.

12 "has just come from England": Ibid.

13 "clap her new clothes . . . it was considered vulgar": Edith Wharton, *The Age of Innocence* (Ware, Hertfordshire, UK: Wordsworth Edi-tions, 1994), p. 163.

13 To dress fashionably: Ben Dyal, e-mail to author, December 30, 2013.

14 "It was not seemly": Pierre Balmain in his memoir *My Years and Sea-sons*, quoted in Elizabeth Ewing, revised by Alice Mackrell, *History of 20th Century Fashion* (London: Batsford, 2008), p. 13.

14 up-and-coming magazine magnate: Caroline Seebohm, *The Man Who Was* Vogue: *The Life and Times of Condé Nast* (New York: Viking Press, 1982), p. 95.

14 the world's first-ever salaried fashion photographer: Harriet Worsley, *100 Ideas That Changed Fashion* (London: Lawrence King Publishing, 2011), p. 25.

14 "smote me in the face": Gross, *Model*, p. 32.

15 "ro-to-gra-vure": Irving Berlin, "Easter Parade," as sung by Judy Gar-land and Fred Astaire in *Easter Parade* (MGM, 1948).

15 By the height of the 1920s: Geoffrey Jones, *Beauty Imagined: A History of the Global Beauty Industry* (New York: Oxford University Press, 2010), p. 60.

16 In his seminal paper: Edward L. Thorndike, "A Constant Error in Psychological Ratings," *Journal of Applied Psychology* 4, no. 1 (March 1920): 25.

16 called this phenomenon the halo effect: For two recent collections of surveys on the modern beauty culture and business, one by a male author, one by a female (with their respective assumptions already ev-ident in their titles), see Daniel S. Hammermesh, *Beauty Pays: Why Attractive People Are More Successful* (Princeton, NJ: Princeton Uni-versity Press, 2011), and Deborah L. Rhode, *The Beauty Bias: The In-justice of Appearance in Life and Law* (New York: Oxford University Press, 2010).

16 "Beauty is a greater force": Earnest Elmo Calkins, "Beauty the New Business Tool," *Atlantic*, August 1, 1927.

17 changing the sensibilities of Americans: Ibid.

17 "behind all these changes": Ibid.

17 Retail sales of cosmetics: Jones, *Beauty Imagined*, p. 108.

18 cosmetics sales as a whole fell: Ibid., p. 109.

18 "It's up to the women": Loring Schuler, "It's Up to the Women," *Ladies' Home Journal*, February 1932.

18 all got their start: David E. Sumner, *The Magazine Century: American Magazines Since 1900* (New York: Peter Lang Publishing, 2010), pp. 75–76.

18 "wash your blond child's hair": Penelope Rowlands, *A Dash of Daring: Carmel Snow and Her Life in Fashion, Art and Letters* (New York: Atria Books, 2005), pp. 243, 528.

18 nearly doubled its circulation: From 104,910 in 1932 to 191,333 in 1938. This compared with *Vogue*'s sales of 313,000 spread over its three editions (French, English, and American) in 1937. "Reporting Paris Styles Is a Business," *Life*, September 6, 1937, p. 33.

19 "A sixteen-year-old heart": Eileen Ford, *Secrets of the Model's World* (New York: Trident Press, 1970), pp. 164, 165.

19 "then promptly forgot": Ford Notebooks, J187.

Chapter 2: Origins

20 "People are like a cat": Will Rogers, Foreword, "Warning," in Eddie Cantor with David Freeman, *My Life Is in Your Hands* (1928; repr., New York: Cooper Square Press, 2000), p. xvi.

20 "my Finnish grandfather": Ford Notebooks, B6.

20 "He didn't get rich": Ford Notebooks, B39. Also phone interview, October 28, 2013; and interview with Eileen Ford, Oldwick, NJ, February 13, 2010.

21 "could afford a warm coat": Interview with Eileen Ford, Oldwick, NJ, February 13, 2010.

22 "knew about shopping and fashion": Ibid.

22 Loretta used to relate: Ibid.

23 Out of his overalls: World War I U.S., Draft Registration Cards, 1917–1918, obtained through www.ancestry.com.

23 "married while you wait": "Marriage Made Easy," (Plainfield, NJ) *Daily Press*, Friday, May 28, 1909.

23 legally too young to marry: Certificate and Record of Marriage, 693, June 27, 1909, State of New Jersey.

23 gave birth to twins: William Forsythe interview, Frankfurt, June 9, 2012.

23 "committed a great wrong": "Deserted Her to Marry Another," *Mathews* (VA) *Journal*, July 4, 1912, p. 3.

24 Caroline G. Higgins had been working: "Last 'Divorce Wednesday,'" *New York Times*, June 20, 1912, p. 6.

24 "My mother was very, very pretty": Ford Notebooks, D6.

24 Scottish Rite, Thirty-Third Degree: Obituary, "Died: Ottensoser, Louis," *New York Times*, April 17, 1923.

25 "Blondes are vain": "Are Blondes 'Trouble Makers'?" *Washington Post*, January 18, 1914, p. 48.

25 listed Loretta Forsythe: Certificate of Incorporation of the Fifth Avenue Protective Association from the State of New York, Office of the Secretary of State, September 25, 1914.

25 "I learned from my parents": Interview with Eileen Ford, Oldwick, NJ, February 13, 2010.

Chapter 3: The Most Talented Child Ever Born

27 he changed his given name to Louis: Engagement announcement, "Betrothed: Ottensoser–Lesser," *American Israelite*, May 20, 1887.

27 met with varying success: *New York Times*, November 13 and 14, and December 5, 1907.

27 Louis and his wife repaid: "Rights of Depositors," *Yale Law Journal* 42, no. 6 (April 1933).

27 Louis paid off his obligations: *New York Times*, April 13, 1913.

28 The dunning agency listed: Certificate of Incorporation of the Fifth Avenue Protective Association from the State of New York, Office of the Secretary of State, September 25, 1914.

28 less prosperous Finnish Irish family: George J. Kneeland, *Commercialized Prostitution in New York City*, Publications of the Bureau of Social Hygiene, June 24, 2011.

29 Fannie had a fondness: Jamie Ford Craft, e-mail to author, November 28, 2013.

29 When Nat and Loretta got married: St. Matthew's German Evangelical Lutheran Church, Jersey City, NJ. The couple were married by the Reverend F. Arnold Bavendam on the evening of March 12, 1916.

29 "My parents doted on me": Ford Notebooks, F27 and F29. Also interview with Eileen Ford, Oldwick, NJ, February 13, 2010.

29 how she came by her name: Jamie Ford Craft, e-mail to author, November 28, 2013.

30 "kind of seedy": Interview with Eileen Ford, Oldwick, NJ, February 13, 2010.

Chapter 4: Great Neck

31 "It was a matter of chance": F. Scott Fitzgerald, *The Great Gatsby* (Ware, Hertfordshire, UK: Wordsworth Editions, 1993), p. 5.

31 "two unusual formations of land": Ibid.

31 "as just a little town": Ford Notebooks, D68.

32 Eileen had no knowledge of this: The Fitzgeralds lived at 6 Gateway Drive, Great Neck, from October 1922 to April 1924, the year before the publication of *The Great Gatsby*. Mary Jo Murphy, "Viewing the Unreal Estate of Gatsby Esq.," *New York Times*, September 30, 2010.

32 "Beyond our garden wall": Ford Notebooks, D68.

32 "members of the Caucasian race": House deeds in the famous postwar suburb of Levittown contained such limitations, and the author recalls reading "restriction" clauses in the title deeds of houses in Grosse Pointe, Michigan, when he lived there in the early 1980s.

32 The number of these clubs exploded: Kenneth T. Jackson, *Crabgrass Frontier: The Suburbanization of the United States* (New York: Oxford University Press, 1985), p. 99, cited in Judith Goldstein, *Inventing Great Neck: Jewish Identity and the American Dream* (New Brunswick, NJ: Rutgers University Press, 2006), p. 45. I am most grateful to Ms. Goldstein for her book and for her elucidation of Great Neck's particular identity in the years when the Ottensoser family lived there.

33 "the Sanhedrin of the successful": *The New Yorker*, January 27, 1927, p. 23. Cited in Goldstein, *Inventing Great Neck*.

33 "is for every race and creed": *Great Neck News*, September 22, 1928, p. 15, cited in Goldstein, *Inventing Great Neck*, p. 40.

33 chose *not* to chronicle: Goldstein, *Inventing Great Neck*, p. 38.

34 "Mrs. Alexander's pale-blue chiffon dress": Ford Notebooks, B37 and B40.

34 "The many folk of the stage": *Great Neck News*, April 5, 1925, p. 10, cited in Goldstein, *Inventing Great Neck*, p. 36.

34 "WEST EGG NOT US!": *Great Neck News*, March 13, 1926, p. 18, cited in Goldstein, *Inventing Great Neck*, p. 39.

35 "raised Tom like another son": Ford Notebooks, B39.

35 "My father was so young": Interview with William Forsythe, Frankfurt, June 9, 2012.

36 He discovered the truth: Interview with Eileen Ford, Oldwick, NJ, February 13, 2010.

36 "we listened to *Amos 'n' Andy*": Ford Notebooks, B79. The first radio

program to be distributed by syndication in the United States, *Amos 'n' Andy* ran as a nightly radio show from 1928 to 1943; http://en.wikipedia.org/wiki/Amos_'n'_Andy.

36 "harmonize commercial activity": Art in Trades Club Mission Statement, 1926. Patricia K. Edmonson, "The Tension Between Art and Industry: The Art-in-Trades Club of New York, 1906–1935," thesis, University of Delaware, 2008.

37 "Great Neck was a classy community": Ford Notebooks, B54.

37 "most of us come from Poland or Italy": Cited in *Alistair Cooke's America* (London: British Broadcasting Corporation, 1973), p. 273.

37 a yacht club and polo club: Goldstein, *Inventing Great Neck*, p. 46.

37 "this unprecedented 'place'": Fitzgerald, *The Great Gatsby*, p. 113.

Chapter 5: The Bobbsey Twins

38 "Books were my treasure": Ford Notebooks, B79.

38 "I read every volume": Ibid., B80.

38 "on a fashionable street": Laura Lee Hope, *The Bobbsey Twins at Home* (Marston Gate, UK: Amazon reprint edition, no date), p. 4.

38 "Well, I declar' to gracious": Ibid., p. 6.

39 "As I look back": Ford Notebooks, A188.

39 "Bobby and I were very close": Ibid., A189.

40 "My mother had such dress sense": Ibid., A71.

40 "Both my parents were very social": Ibid.

41 "We are going to the poorhouse": Ibid., A73.

41 "I cried and cried": Ibid., F38.

41 teachers wore long black gowns: Ibid., A191, D68, and F38.

42 Financial disaster was manna from heaven: William H. Young with Nancy K. Young, *The 1930s* (Westport, CT: Greenwood Press, 2002), p. 6.

43 "skill born of long practice": Karen Plunkett-Powell, *The Nancy Drew Scrapbook* (New York: St. Martin's Press, 1993), p. 17.

43 "The books were seventy-five cents each": Ford Notebooks, B37.

43 "crashed a Valhalla": Plunkett-Powell, *The Nancy Drew Scrapbook*, p. 24.

43 "Daddy's little girls": Kathleen Chamberlain, "The Secrets of Nancy Drew: Having Their Cake and Eating It Too," *The Lion and the Unicorn* 18, no. 1 (June 1964): 1.

44 "would be earning my own living": Ford Notebooks, F28.

Chapter 6: Young and Beautiful

45 "a smart little daughter": Carolyn Keene, *The Mystery at Lilac Inn* (New York: Grosset and Dunlap, 1930), p. 196.

45 went back to Great Neck: Great Neck High School is today the John L. Miller–Great Neck North High School.

45 "put on plays in the house": Interview with Eileen Ford, Oldwick, NJ, February 15, 2010.

45 "We set up a table": Ford Notebooks, B79 and D65.

45 "very, very strict about no gambling": Ibid., B78.

45 "chatting to a friend on the telephone": Ibid., A1.

46 "looked at every single present": Ibid., D4.

46 a high-quality East Coast education: Dr. King Odell, archivist at Moses Brown School, e-mail to Susan Camp, November 6, 2013.

46 "throw him down the stairs": Ford Notebooks, D6.

47 "they are called 'tough'": Ibid., F21.

47 "an only child": Ibid., F29.

47 "conditioned as a little girl": Eileen Ford, *Eileen Ford's Beauty Now and Forever: Secrets of Beauty After 35* (New York: Simon and Schuster, 1977), p. 167.

47 "all the world's problems": Ford Notebooks, F28.

48 "the feeling of the conqueror": Ernest Jones, *The Life and Work of Sigmund Freud*, Volume 1 (New York: Basic Books, 1957), p. 5.

48 redbrick high school: Great Neck High School North, Wikipedia, http://en.wikipedia.org/wiki/John_L._Miller_Great_Neck_North_High_School.

48 "I failed sewing twice": Ford Notebooks, F38.

48 "I loved Latin": Ibid., F34.

49 "He wasn't laughing": Ibid., F38.

49 "I ate pheasant so often": Ibid., F40.

49 "not far from Saratoga": Ibid., F31, January 18, 2011.

49 "I remember the first day I met Bo": Ibid., F31.

49 "most popular young men": *Arista*, Great Neck High School yearbook, 1938, pp. 38 and 46, Susan Camp Archive.

50 "I knew in my heart": Ford Notebooks, F31, B36, and F38.

50 a facetious "Class Will": *Arista*, p. 29.

50 "very good at organizing": Ford Notebooks, B36.

50 "Glenn Miller used to play": Ibid., A79 and D58.

50 "The call woke my mother": Ibid.

Chapter 7: Something Mellifluous

52 was of Ashkenazi Jewish descent: James Gleick, *Genius: The Life and Science of Richard Feynman* (New York: Pantheon Books, 1992), p. 49.

52 "Never admit more than five Jews": David M. Oshinsky, *Polio: An American Story* (New York: Oxford University Press, 2006), p. 98.

52 Yale accepted just five: Gerard Burrow, *A History of Yale's School of Medicine*, 2002, pp. 107 and 143–44, cited ibid., p. 98.

52 Asian students: Amy Chua and Jed Rubenfeld, "What Drives Success?" *New York Times*, Sunday Review, January 25, 2014. See also Richard D. Kahlenberg, "Elite, Separate, Unequal: New York City's Top Public Schools Need Diversity," *New York Times*, June 22, 2014.

52 "We limit the number of Jews": Barron H. Lerner, "In a Time of Quotas, a Quiet Pose in Defiance," *New York Times*, May 26, 2009.

53 applications by Jewish students: Valerie B. Kolko, *A History of Jews in American Higher Education* (Bloomington: Indiana University Press, 2003), p. 6.

53 questions about religious affiliation: Stephen Steinberg, *The Academic Melting Pot: Catholics and Jews in American Higher Learning* (New York: McGraw-Hill, 1974), p. 230.

53 "damned curve-raisers": Lerner, "In a Time of Quotas, a Quiet Pose in Defiance."

53 disdained religious and racial exclusivity: Rosalind Rosenberg, "Virginia Gildersleeve: Opening the Gates," *Columbia Magazine*, Summer 2001, http://www.columbia.edu/cu/alumni/Magazine/Summer2001/Gildersleeve.html.

53 in the interest of diversity: Ibid.

54 "Cup-and-Saucer": Interview with Eileen Ford, New York City, July 26, 2013.

54 "People have always encountered difficulty": Supreme Court of the State of New York, Nassau County, Name Change Petition, Ottensoser, September 16, 1938.

54 "been able to ward off the shocks": Ibid.

55 FDR's "Jew Deal": Robert Underhill, *First the Black Horse* (Pittsburgh, PA: Dorrance Publishing, 2011) p. 98.

56 "Rosenbergs became Rosses": Off-the-record interview, London, Rosh Hashana, 2013.

56 "This is Leonard Bernstein": Humphrey Burton, *Leonard Bernstein* (New York: Faber and Faber, 1994), pp. 85 and 212. I am grateful to Humphrey Burton for drawing this to my attention and for his help.

Chapter 8: Model Student

58 "It was a revelation to me": Telephone interview with Eileen Ford, January 18, 2014.

58 "Barnard made me work hard": Eileen Ford e-mail to author, January 17, 2014.

59 patronage of the Art in Trades Club: Ford Notebooks, A27.

59 "I met Jean Compo": Telephone interview with Eileen Ford, January 26, 2014.

59 Gerald Rudolph "Jerry" Ford, Jr: See *Look* magazine, March 12, 1940, pp. 25, 28, and 29, for examples of the future president's work as a Conover model.

60 she became a cover girl: Ford Notebooks, B2.

60 "The skates were the reason": Ibid., C21.

60 outfits for Saks–34th Street: *Mademoiselle*, August 1941, p. 10.

60 "To See Them Is to Want Them!": *Vogue*, August 1941, p. 17.

61 "Weekly for Everybody": *Liberty*, September 6, 1941, photographed by Mead Maddick Lownds.

61 "Conover never paid me a penny": Ford Notebooks, D56.

61 "I had a bet": Ibid., B62.

61 "Eleanor Roosevelt came to visit": Ibid., A21 and A25.

61 "The war started in December": Ibid., A22.

Chapter 9: *Le Meilleur Moment de l'Amour*

62 "*Le meilleur moment*": This often-cited saying is a paraphrase of words of a character in Clemenceaus's novel *Les Plus Forts* (The Strongest, 1919).

62 "coming out of the cinema": Ford Notebooks, A161.

62 "had read about the Japanese": Ibid., B59.

62 "doing a lot of washing up": Ibid., p. B58.

63 Eileen's particularly elegant advertisement: *Vogue*, August 1941, p. 9.

63 "just a kiss on the cheek": Ford Notebooks, A78. The French words seem to be her misquotation of Clemenceau.

63 "I had all these fiancés": Ford Notebooks, A79.

64 Shep Sheppard and the Swingers: Photo of "Shep Sheppard and the Swingers" band in background information from Stephen Sheppard, e-mail to Susan Camp, February 13, 2014.

64 "All Hail to Kerens!": "Kerens High School Band in Concert on Friday Evening," *Daily Sun* (Corsicana, TX), February 10, 1942.

64 Shep enlisted with the navy: U.S. Navy officer biography sheet for Charles P. Sheppard, May 16, 1972, p. 1.

64 "We met in Charleston": Telephone interview with Eileen Ford, January 26, 2014.

64 "just twelve days or so": Ibid.

65 "I wanted to end the marriage": Ibid.

65 "a very, very decent man": Jamie Craft, e-mail to author, December 31, 2013.

66 brave and distinguished wartime service: U.S. Navy officer biography sheet for Charles P. Sheppard, May 16, 1972, p. 1.

66 the strain of telling the lie: Annulment of Marriage, Mrs. Eileen Otte Shepherd, March 27, 1944, Nassau County Court House, State of New York.

66 "a bad idea that never happened": Jamie Craft, e-mail to author, December 31, 2013.

67 "if you pull that thing down": (Lawrence, KS) *Journal World*, February 1984.

67 "Ham was older" . . . "had been to Europe": Ford Notebooks, A87 and D59.

68 "a very short time in my life": Ibid., F41.

68 "But then, in July": Ibid.

Chapter 10: Jerry

69 "What a day!": Betty Comden and Adolph Green, "Lucky to Be Me," from *On the Town*, with music by Leonard Bernstein, 1944.

70 His end-around exploits: Robert Craft, e-mail to author, May 9, 2014.

70 the Gold Rail, a student hangout: Today it is the site of Mel's Burger Bar, on Broadway between 114th and 115th streets, with a style and layout that would seem to have changed very little in the last sixty years.

70 "When Jerry stood up": Ford Notebooks, D70–71.

70 "to go to the dance with Jerry Ford": Ibid.

70 "I was a baby-snatcher": Ibid., A185.

71 "Jerry dressed with great style": Ibid., A159.

71 an entertainment allowance of three hundred dollars: Interview with Allen Ford, October 29, 2011, Washington, DC.

71 "We knew times were hard": Ibid.

71 he never realized he was poor: Lacy Ford Williams, Ford Notebooks, C37.

71 "Jerry was a *haimish* guy": Michael Gross, Jeth Weinrich interview, n.d.

72 "When you think about elopement": Telephone interview with Eileen Ford, January 2014.

72 "I left a note": Ford Notebooks, A67.

73 Eileen wore them to City Hall: Ibid., A68.

73 "didn't know he wanted to get married": Ibid., D1.
74 "he married me": Ibid., D1, October 14, 2010.
74 "saying no to Eileen?": Ibid., A181.

Chapter 11: Stylist

75 as a "commercial photographer": The entry actually reads, "comm. photographer."
75 "had just finished a hot dog": Telephone interviews with Eileen Ford, March 20 and 21, 2014.
76 "the flowering of a half century": "Yes, My Darling Daughter," *Saturday Evening Post*, August 5, 1944, p. 24.
76 The photographs appeared early: Ibid.
76 "looking for a secretary/personal assistant": Ford Notebooks, D57.
76 "When it came to calculating": Ibid.
76 "a new kind of *young* magazine": *Seventeen*, September 1944, inside cover.
77 "Teen Departments of the best stores": Ibid.
77 could claim some small role: "Seventeen Is Five," *Newsweek*, August 29, 1949, pp. 47, 48.
77 "I was lonely of course": Ford Notebooks, B65.
78 "She impressed us": Allen Gregory Ford, e-mail to author, March 24, 2014.
78 "I don't know whether": Ford Notebooks, D56.
79 "hard work for long hours": Interview with Lorraine Davies Knopf, Los Angeles, January 13, 2011.
80 Eileen's job was to coordinate: Gross, *Model*, p. 92.
80 her first experience of serious negotiation: Roy P. Drachman, *This Is Not a Book, Just Memories* (Tucson, AZ: R. P. Drachman, 1979), chap. 12.
80 "Whadaya mean": Ford Notebooks, A37, B44, and D58.
80 "made Judge Judy sound like a lady": Ibid., A37.
80 "They were pages": Ibid., A3.
81 "It was my job" . . . "I made a terrible mistake": Ibid., A3 and A37.
81 "I was supposed to do *facts*": Ibid., A35 and B29.
82 "was just as well you quit": Ibid.

Chapter 12: Agency

83 "makes a great model": Paul Vitello, "Bert Stern, Elite Photographer Known for Images of Marilyn Monroe, Dies at 83," *New York Times*,

June 27, 2013, http://www.nytimes.com/2013/06/27/arts/bert-stern-elite-photographer-known-for-images-of-marilyn-monroe-dies-at-83.html?_r=1&.

83 "my supervisor took the credit": "Natalie Nickerson Paine," *New Mexican* (Santa Fe), March 28, 2003, p. B2. Also, Wingate Paine II telephone interview, March 7, 2013.

84 Natálie had some previous experience: Telephone interview with Wingate Paine II, March 7, 2013.

84 "used to sleep on a camp bed": Ford Notebooks, G29.

84 she was on the cover of *Vogue:* The Rawlings-Nickerson January 1946 U.S. *Vogue* jacket was repeated on British *Vogue* for March 1946.

85 After a false start: "The Glamor Co-Op," *Newsweek*, September 11, 1944, p. 77.

85 "His secretary whispered it": Gross, *Model*, p. 94.

85 take over her own billing: "Three L.A. Agencies Adopt Voucher System," *Hat Box Girl*, May 1947, p. 1.

85 her own numbered accounts book: Interview with Lorraine Davies Knopf, February 13, 2011.

85 "Models were treated": Wingate Paine II Family Papers.

86 "for any operation to be successful": Gross, *Model*, p. 94.

86 did not put all this money: Ford Notebooks, B30.

87 "nine months to the day": Interview with Jamie Ford Craft, July 23, 2010.

87 "to some marvelous parties": Ford Notebooks, A69.

87 "I wasn't so much of a booker": Ibid., A41.

87 "The thing about Eileen": Interview with Joan Pedersen, January 17, 2011.

88 Eileen might have been working: *Today's Woman*, May 1949, pp. 10, 11.

88 a green maternity suit: Ford Notebooks, A35, A37, and A39.

88 "I had so many calls": Ibid., B59.

88 "before I went into the hospital": Ibid.

88 "He would play good cop": Michael Gross, filmed interview with Jeff Weinrich.

Chapter 13: New Look

90 "We started when Dior started": Ford Notebooks, A157.

90 His rivals Balmain and Balenciaga: Worsley, *100 Ideas That Changed Fashion*, p. 110.

90 Dior had confided: Jonathan Walford, *Forties Fashion: From Siren Suits to the New Look* (London: Thames and Hudson, 2008), p. 192.

91 "that takes up an entire suitcase?": Jessica Kerwin, "Coco's Cinderella Story: Edmonde Charles-Roux's Biography of Chanel Reveals the History She Strove to Hide," *W*, June 1, 2005.

91 she used American fabrics: Rebecca Arnold, *The American Look: Fashion, Sportswear, and the Image of Women in 1930s and 1940s New York* (London: I. B. Tauris, 2009), p. 199.

92 "Milton Green, Art Kane, and [Irving] Penn": Interview with Bill Helburn, November 30, 2010; and telephone conversation, October 4, 2014.

92 "Lillian Bassman dropped in": Ibid.

93 "going to be a star": Interview with Carmen Dell'Orefice, April 11, 2014; and Ford Notebooks, A117–21.

93 "I had been earning seven-fifty": Interview with Carmen Dell'Orefice, April 11, 2014.

94 "It was deeply embarrassing": Ibid.

94 "I never knew my father": Interview with Barbara Mullen, Zurich, October 2, 2013.

94 "How she crept through": Ibid.

95 "they had lined up this model": Ibid.

95 "had become bigger than the magazines": Ibid.

95 "So you're the new model": Ibid.

Chapter 14: Goddesses and Masterpieces

97 "wary about the fashion game": Interview with Bill Helburn, November 30, 2010; Ford Notebooks, E46.

98 "switched from Conover to Hartford": Interview with Lorraine Davies Knopf, Los Angeles, January 12, 2010.

98 "For all that activity": Lisa Rebecca Gubernick, *Squandered Fortune: The Life and Times of Huntington Hartford* (New York: G. P. Putnam's Sons, 1991), p. 74.

98 "It was a religious thing": Ibid.

98 traced Hartford's priapic tendencies: Ibid., p. 28.

99 "A lot of very good models": Ibid., p. 74.

99 "He had no idea": Gross, *Model*, p. 100.

99 "It was right at the beginning": Ford Notebooks A99 and D72.

99 "an old brown 1941 Ford": Ibid., A97.

100 a young model called Jean Patchett: Gross, *Model*, p. 87.

100 "turned out to be none of that": Charles Castle, *Model Girl* (Secaucus, NJ: Chartwell Books, 1977), p. 91.

100 "I was just stunned by the look of Jean": Ford Notebooks, B29.

100 "Jean was just breathtaking": Ibid.

100 "big as a house!": Patchett family correspondence.

101 "He had five hundred girls": Ibid., p. 87.

101 "Each of those early models": Ford Notebooks, B29.

101 "no legal contract on earth": Ibid., B30.

101 "took out mortgage loans": Ibid., A31 and B52.

102 a 50 percent partner: Dissolution of Partnership Agreement Between Natálie Paine and Eileen Ford, March 24, 1953, Clause 5, p. 2.

102 "a business deal between friends": Interview with Jamie Ford Craft, July 23, 2010.

Chapter 15: Model Types

103 "make them into big girls": David Bailey and James Sherwood, *Models Close-Up* (London: Channel 4 Books, 1998), p. 26.

103 the weather had been atrocious: Interview with Roland Schucht, Oldwick, NJ, November 27, 2010.

104 "Successful models might ask": Ibid.

104 "introduced cancellation fees": Ibid.

104 "there was Jerry Ford": Ford Notebooks, B7; interview with Dick Richards, Quogue, June 18, 2010.

105 "send over for test shots": Interview with Dick and Hilke Richards, Quogue, June 18, 2010; Ford Notebooks, B10.

105 ferocious attention to detail: Interview with Rusty Zeddis, January 7, 2015.

105 three categories of model: Eileen Ford, "Do You Want to Be a Model?" *Seventeen*, March 1962, p. 111.

105 "There are two good reasons": Eileen Ford, "Modeling," *Seventeen*'s *Beauty Workshop* binder, 1967, p. 16.

105 "the super-sleek models": Ford, "Do You Want to Be a Model?," p. 111.

106 turned down the young Grace Kelly: Ford Notebooks, C27.

106 "Eileen Ford had the inside track": Gross, *Model*, p. 97.

106 "say the Wool Bureau called": Ibid., p. 95.

106 "not exactly honest": Ibid.

107 "not worthy" of their girls': "Family-Style Model Agency," *Life*, October 4, 1948, p. 69.

107 "her husband answers one telephone": Ibid., p. 63.

107 "popular with its models": Ibid.

108 "it all was staged": Telephone interview with Joan Pedersen Coleman, May 9, 2014.

108 "half the Fords' girls": "Family-Style Model Agency," p. 63.

108 "The other agencies had": Telephone interview with Joan Pedersen Coleman, May 9, 2014.

108 "Eileen was like a mother hen": Interview with Lorraine Davies Knopf, Los Angeles, January 13, 2011.

108 "just loved entertaining": Interview with Carmen Dell'Orefice, March 11, 2012.

109 "this new travel idea": *Life*, October 4, 1948, p. 3.

109 "bookings came rolling in": Telephone interview with Joan Pedersen Coleman, May 9, 2014.

109 Winchell swept Eileen and Jerry off: Ford Notebooks, A73 and A75.

110 "Just look at that waist!": Gross, *Model*, p. 133.

110 clicked his shutter a good thousand times: Ibid., p. 134.

111 "Dorian knows what you want": Interview with Grace Mirabella, New York, October 19, 2010; Ford Notebooks, D29.

111 "a neurotic lay": Gross, *Model*, p. 82.

111 "Dorian was wild": Ford Notebooks, G65.

111 "Oh, my God!": Ibid., F17.

112 "virtually every nook and cranny": Bosley Crowther, "Movie Review: Cover Girl (1944)," *New York Times*, March 31, 1944.

Chapter 16: Scouts and Bookers

114 "be silly enough to think": Thomas More, *The New Island of Utopia* (1516), p. 11.

115 "You'd make that call": Ford Notebooks, H34.

115 "A good booker puts in": Interview with Monique Pillard, New York, April 22, 2011.

115 "knew their models well": Joan Pedersen Coleman, interview with Susan Camp, May 21, 2014.

116 "As well as the model": Telephone interview with Dottie Franco Solomon, May 10, 2012.

116 In 1948 the business: Joint accounting summary 1948–1952, sheet 1, "Income from Fees."

116 the "family-style" modeling agency: "A Model Family," *Illustrated*, May 7, 1949, pp. 14–15.

116 "American millionaire agents": Ford Notebooks, A91.

116 "We tried the Hyde Park Hotel": Ibid., A93.

117 Kark's expansion plans included: Gross, *Model*, p. 176.

117 "all *looked* brilliantly classy": Interview with Polly Ferguson, New York, July 20, 2010.

118 "Her voice was so high": Ford Notebooks, F23.

118 "'If I'd known Egypt": Ibid.

118 according to Avedon: Gross, *Model*, p. 133.

119 "Someone had advised Jerry": Ford Notebooks, E17.

119 "When we were with Marvin": Ibid., B4 and B5.

119 according to the "Ford Stable" list: "The Ford Stable," *Photography Workshop*, Summer 1950.

120 apply for U.S. citizenship: "French Models Thrive in the U.S.," *Life*, July 24, 1950, p. 53.

120 "I never received more": Gross, *Model*, p. 131.

120 the neatly typed stacks of figures: Joint accounting summary 1948–1952, sheets 1–6, "Income from Fees."

121 "I felt cheated and betrayed": Gross, *Model*, p. 131.

121 "to be with them": Ibid.

121 "On behalf of my clients": Agreement between Eileen Ford and Natálie Paine of June 1, 1953, pp. 1, 2.

122 also agreed to surrender: Ibid., p. 3.

122 "couldn't think of a name": Gross, *Model*, p. 131.

122 To "sweeten the pot": Ibid.

123 "Natálie got too greedy": Ford Notebooks, E57.

123 Plaza Five would flourish: Jennifer Paine Welwood, e-mail to Susan Camp, June 14, 2014.

Chapter 17: Ideal for Entertaining

124 "certain women seem to emerge": Harold Koda and Kohle Yohannan, *The Model as Muse* (New Haven, CT: Yale University Press, 2009), p. 106.

124 The roll call of her "girls": Susan Camp Archive, Ford Models head sheets and rosters from July 1957; April 1, 1962; September 1, 1966; December 1, 1966; October 1974; January 1, 1975; February 1, 1976; February 1979; Summer/Fall 1983; 1984/1985; 1985/1986; 1988/1989; 1989/1990; Summer 1993, Ford Paris; 1994/1995 Runway; 1995.

124 "Bringing up my children": Ford Notebooks, A19.

125 "In those early years": Ibid.

125 "multiplies the numbers of governesses": Jamie Ford Craft, e-mail to author, June 2, 2014.

126 "Eileen's children were always": Interview with Kay Bourland, July 25, 2010.

126 "the most organized and dedicated parents": Interview with Centa Mayer, October 18, 2010.

126 "quite a pleasant place to live": Ford Notebooks, G63.

126 "It was a beautiful apartment": Ibid., G69.

127 "She slept in my bedroom": Jamie Ford Craft, e-mail to author, June 2, 2014.

127 One of the assignments: *Picture Post*, December 18, 1954.

127 "see a lot of Mary Jane Russell": Ford Notebooks, H44.

128 Then there was Barbara Mullen: Interview with Barbara Mullen, Zurich, October 2, 2013.

128 "They'd sit at a long table": Ibid.

128 "don't trust the hatcheck girl": Off-the-record interview.

129 "how Eileen talked to Jerry": Interview with Rusty Donovan Zeddis, January 15, 2012.

129 Dancing one night in 1954: Interview with Barbara Mullen, Zurich, October 2, 2013.

129 "thought no more about it": Ibid.

Chapter 18: Shoes Under the Bed

130 "What lips my lips have kissed": Edna St. Vincent Millay, "What Lips My Lips Have Kissed, and Where and Why (Sonnet XLIII)," *Collected Poems* (New York: Harper Brothers, 1956).

130 "just bought this marvelous house": Interview with Barbara Mullen, October 2, 2013.

132 "beautiful almond-shaped eyes": Interview with Carmen Dell'Orefice, October 23, 2010.

133 "I was quite frankly": Gross, *Model*, p. 127.

133 "I can spend most of my time": Ibid.

133 "whatever decision Jerry made": Ibid.

133 "her hands start to tremble": Ibid., p. 128.

133 "jump out of a window": Off-the-record interview.

133 "very old-fashioned": Interview with Jamie Ford Craft, July 23, 2010.

134 "'Never have a best friend'": Ford Notebooks, B45 and G70.

134 "quite a simple thing": Ibid., B65.

135 "If Jerry Ford left me": Judy Bachrach, "Eileen Ford," *People*, May 16, 1983.

135 startled by the violence: Telephone interview with Judy Bachrach, September 11, 2011.

135 The ever-attentive Jerry: Ibid.

135 "she was too bossy": Bachrach, "Eileen Ford."

135 Eileen smiled demurely: Telephone interview with Judy Bachrach, September 11, 2011.

Chapter 19: *Bonjour*, Paris!

136 "Beauty is a short-lived tyranny": Diogenes Laertius, *Lives of the Eminent Philosophers* (thought to be from the third century of the Christian era), attributed this saying to Socrates.

136 an impressive portfolio of lovers: "Dorian Leigh: Supermodel of the 1940s," *Independent*, July 14, 2008.

136 an aristocratic Spanish playboy: Dorian Leigh, *The Girl Who Had Everything* (Garden City, NY: Doubleday, 1980), p. 135.

137 with some Parisian friends: Gross, *Model*, p. 137.

137 "a *bureau de placement clandestine*": Ibid.

137 "I went by myself": Gross, *Model*, p. 138.

138 "one of the hardest working": Leigh, *The Girl Who Had Everything*, p. 67.

138 "Dorian *was* Paris": Gross, *Model*, p. 139.

138 "She's wearing no underwear!": Ford Notebooks, A171.

139 the first truly international model: Leigh, *The Girl Who Had Everything*, p. 87.

139 "the finishing school of modeling": Interview with Iris Minier, Paris, June 16, 2014.

139 "We became the only importer": Gross, *Model*, p. 139.

140 in the same month: Dolores Hawkins, e-mail to author, October 22, 2014.

140 "The underfed, indoor, super-sophisticated": Phyllis Lee Levin, "A Fashion Model's Face Is Still Her Fortune," *New York Times*, February 10, 1958.

141 "the world's most successful": Ibid.

141 "the Scandinavians were different": Ford Notebooks, B62.

142 "Anna Karin was the first": Ibid.

142 "a present for Billy": Telephone interview with Anna Karin Erne, June 6, 2012.

142 "really take care of our models": Interview with Sandra Fosse, Copenhagen, March 30, 2011.

142 As Norman Parkinson once: Ford Notebooks, E89.

Chapter 20: Celebrity Models

143 the first-ever fashion model: Laura Jacobs, "Everyone Fell for Suzy," *Vanity Fair*, May 2006.

144 all the Frenchmen in the restaurant: Ibid.

144 "I was completely calculating": Leigh, *The Girl Who Had Everything*, p. 165.

145 "Daddy raced trains": Jacobs, "Everyone Fell for Suzy."

145 "Mrs. Pierre de la Salle": Bérénice de la Salle, "Beautiful Riddle: The

Strange Case of Suzy Parker," unpublished manuscript, http://www .beautifulriddle.com/.

146 "Count de la Salle?": Off-the-record interview, July 5, 2014.

146 Pitou was a playboy: Gross, *Model*, p. 118.

146 "a fine old French family": Leigh, *The Girl Who Had Everything*, p. 156.

146 "We only share it": De la Salle, "Beautiful Riddle."

146 compelled to admit the truth: "Veil off 1955 Wedding," *Kansas City Star*, June 12, 1958, p. 12.

147 Jerry had rescued Suzy: Jacobs, "Everyone Fell for Suzy."

147 "that sweet angel": Gross, *Model*, p. 118.

147 "did most of the work": Ford Notebooks, D51.

147 "Being married to a Frenchman": *Daily Telegraph*, Suzy Parker obituary, May 6, 2003.

147 "She had no more use": Ford Notebooks, A49.

148 "Those playboys saw these two girls": Telephone interview with Carmen Dell'Orefice, July 5, 2014.

149 "didn't have my husband": Gross, *Model*, p. 134.

149 "We were all virgin princesses": Ibid., p. 199.

149 "There is no reason": Ford Notebooks, D21.

150 "Eileen was a good friend": Interview with Robert Evans, Los Angeles, September 10, 2010.

151 Miss Anne de Zogheb became: "Anka Will Wed Parisian Model," *Ottawa Citizen*, February 12, 1963, p. 1.

Chapter 21: In the Eye of the Beholder

152 "Every woman can be her own sort of beautiful": Eileen Ford, *Learn to Be Beautiful: A Complete Course in Beauty* (1961), LP.

152 "We were very tempted": Ford Notebooks, A45 and A47.

152 "An inspector called": Gubernick, *Squandered Fortune*, pp. 125, 126.

153 "he's not going to buy you": Ibid., p. 126.

153 "Hartford had the best": Ford Notebooks, A45 and A47.

153 "We put down the deposit": Ibid., A99 and D72.

153 "it was time we grew up": Ibid.

153 "The place was full of garbage": Ibid.

154 "very proud of his office systems": Interview with Allen Gregory Ford, Washington, DC, February 28, 2011.

154 "The computer lived": Terry Reno, e-mail to author, July 16, 2014.

155 One drawback of the system: Interview with Rusty Donovan Zeddis, July 15, 2014.

155 "Eileen insisted that everyone stop work": Ibid.

155 some stray dog: Joey Hunter, interview with Susan Camp, October 13, 2014.

156 developing new makeup lines: U.S. Patent Office registration numbers 530,890; 579,108; 653,181.

156 "never met an unattractive woman": John Robert Powers and Mary Sue Miller, *Secrets of Charm* (Philadelphia, PA: John C. Winstone, 1954), p. vii. See also *News Tribune* (Muscatine, IA), March 5, 1949, p. 1; and *Daily Mail* (Charleston, SC), March 12, 1952, p. 11.

156 "Are you a Suzy Parker?": *Mademoiselle*, August 1960, p. 368.

157 "He was a charming guy": Interview with Rusty Donovan Zeddis, December 5, 2013.

157 "Dressing, like beauty, starts": *This Week*, September 11, 1960.

157 a Sunday newspaper supplement: "This Week Magazine Ends Publication," *New York Times*, August 14, 1969.

157 "an exercise for drooping chins": *This Week*, September 11, 1960.

157 "*What can be done*": Ibid.

158 "if I want to look intellectual": Ibid.

158 "voice was pitched too low": Interview with Eileen Ford, Oldwick, NJ, March 26, 2012.

159 "She was the obvious person": Ford Notebooks, K43.

159 "She deepened my voice": Interview with Louis Licari, Fifth Avenue, New York, March 26, 2012.

159 "We all loved Betty": Ford Notebooks, K43.

160 Eileen Ford Make-Up for Models: Ford, *Learn to Be Beautiful*; and Woolf Brothers advertisement, *Kansas City Times*, March 25, 1962.

160 approaching a billion dollars: "Borden Forecast Record New Income," *New York Times*, March 10, 1961.

160 "But I knew": Interview with Rusty Donovan Zeddis, March 26, 2011.

160 Borden purchased Eileen Ford Make-Up: "Borden Purchases Cosmetic Concern," *New York Times*, November 21, 1964.

161 a straight million dollars: Ford Notebooks, E81.

161 "eliminate their main competition": Ibid.

Chapter 22: Youthquake 1965

163 "Sexual intercourse began": Philip Larkin, "Annus Mirabilis," completed June 16, 1967, published in 1974 in the collection *High Windows*. Larkin, born in 1922, had in fact been in a sexual relationship as early as 1945.

163 "warm and gay as a kitten": Diana Vreeland, "Youthquake: Who's on Next?" *Vogue*, January 1, 1965, p. 12.

165 "We were so lucky": Ford Notebooks on Bailey and Shrimpton, H23 and H24.

166 "model doesn't have to sleep": Gross, *Model*, p. 167.

166 "She's too posh for you": Author conversation with Brian Duffy, ca. 1972.

166 to be proved wrong: Gross, *Model*, p. 168.

166 "Of course, I was": Ibid., p. 171.

166 "Bailey had taken these": Ford Notebooks on Bailey and Shrimpton, H23 and H24.

167 "way ahead of their time": Ibid.

167 "That was the cover": Ibid.

168 "I met China in the late fifties": Ford Notebooks, A127 and B11.

168 "and I loved my cigarettes": Ibid., G65.

168 "with a circular drive and pillars": Interview with Dick Richards, Quogue, June 17, 2010.

168 "We called it 'Tara'": Ford Notebooks, A153.

169 "We'd go there on Memorial Day": Ibid.

169 "the envy of New York": Interview with Dick Richards, Quogue, June 17, 2010; and Dick Richards, e-mail to author, September 29, 2014.

169 "The sheets were given out": Ford Notebooks, D22.

169 "a wonderful wine punch": Ibid., C12.

169 "not to be ridiculous": Ibid., B47.

170 "Never wear shorts in front": Interview with Jamie Ford Craft, July 23, 2010.

170 "could hear every word": Ford Notebooks, B48.

170 "Nineteen sixty-five was the year that Jamie": Ibid., B46.

170 "Penelope looked downright weird": Ibid., D52.

171 "quite bonkers": Penelope Tree, e-mail to author, October 15, 2014.

171 "Sir Ronald was just seething": Ford Notebooks, H5.

171 "loved working with Bailey": Interview with Penelope Tree, London, March 2, 2012.

171 "I didn't want to be mothered": Ibid.

172 "a pair of tweezers". Grace Coddington, *Grace: A Memoir* (New York: Random House, 2012), p. 50.

172 "never make a model": Helena de Bertadano, "Marisa Berenson: The It-Girl Who Grew Up," *Telegraph*, October 3, 2011.

173 "be great for the States": Gross, *Model*, pp. 187, 188.

173 "All the money I brought": Ibid., p. 188.

173 "didn't want him to tell me!": Ibid.

173 "that week's list of girls to cut": Interview with Jane Hallaren, September 30, 2014, and e-mails of January 3, 4, 2015.

174 "Do you think your figure": Thomas Whiteside, "Reporter at Large: A Super New Thing," *The New Yorker*, November 4, 1967, p. 66.

174 "Justin tried to hold us to ransom": Ford Notebooks, A181.

174 "She scares me shitless": Gross, *Model*, p. 182.

Chapter 23: Rivalries

175 "You don't give people what they want": Quoted in *Diana Vreeland: The Eye Has to Travel*, documentary (Studiocanal), DVD.

175 "walking along the Champs-Elysées": Gross, *Model*, p. 198.

175 "want Eileen Ford to eat crow": Ibid., p. 196.

176 "Willy was so professional": Telephone interview with Rusty Donovan Zeddis, August 3, 2014.

176 the slimmed-down Wilhelmina won: Susan Camp Archive, Ford Agency head sheet, April 1, 1962.

176 "We had Willy booked solid": Ford Notebooks, A49.

176 "the 405 girls who work under contract": Gross, *Model*, p. 197.

176 Teaming up with Irving Penn: *Vogue*, December 1, 1965.

176 "Wilhelmina puts the Shrimp and Twiggy": Gross, *Model*, p. 199.

177 "Why should I try": Ford Notebooks, A47.

177 "It's a very familiar song": Gross, *Model*, p. 202.

177 a dark and controlling character: Ibid., p. 199.

177 "Bruce was absolutely dreadful": Interview with Carmen Dell'Orefice, August 6, 2014.

178 "Eileen had her own way": Interview with Rusty Donovan Zeddis, August 3, 2014.

178 "Only liars like competition": "Ugly Competition for Pretty Faces," *Fortune*, December 3, 1979.

178 "advice about becoming a model": Interview with Melissa Cooper Margolin, July 6, 2014.

178 They were creditable runners-up: Eleanor Lambert, "Model Mother: Ex-Mannequin Launches New Faces," *Mansfield* (OH) *News Journal*, November 15, 1970, p. 26.

179 Natálie Nickerson Paine had retired: Jennifer Paine Welwood, e-mail to Susan Camp, June 14, 2014.

179 "That was the key distinction": Interview with Carmen Dell'Orefice, August 2014.

179 "hugely inspirational women": Beverly Johnson interview, November 19, 2014. All subsequent Beverly Johnson quotations are from this interview.

180 "disciplined athletic mind-set": Ford Notebooks, E82.

181 "You've got it!": William Norwich, "Beverly Johnson: Face of Change," *Vogue*, September 2009.

181 "afford the magazine": Ibid.

182 also funded the legendary party: Leigh, *The Girl Who Had Everything*, p. 180.

182 "It was quite an event": Ibid.

182 "I found Dorian waiting for me": Ford Notebooks, A49 and G70.

182 Dorian's own version: Leigh, *The Girl Who Had Everything*, pp. 180, 181.

183 steal model check payments: Ibid., pp. 175, 176.

183 "He was a good guy": Ford Notebooks, G70.

183 the Fords filed suit against Dorian: Leigh, *The Girl Who Had Everything*, p. 181.

Chapter 24: Breakfast at Seventy-Eighth Street

185 recalls being met by a butler: Interview with Rene Russo, September 17, 2010.

185 "He was not a butler": Ford Notebooks, C67.

186 "Eileen was always telling": Interview with Rene Russo, September 17, 2010.

186 "perhaps I needed to be bored": Interview with Jerry Hall, January 2, 2011.

186 "When Mick Jagger started calling": Ford Notebooks, B2.

187 "Jerry Faye was just a delight": Ibid., C38 and C39.

187 "she'd turn to the next one": Ibid., E44; interview with Elizabeth Peabody, November 29, 2010.

187 "I was lucky": Interview with Patricia van Ryckeghem, Washington, DC, January 29, 2011.

187 "Unless you eat": "The Secret Is This Diet Plus . . ." *Glamour*, June 1956.

188 "I eat it myself": Ibid.

188 on the popular *Dick Cavett Show*: Catharine Brewster, "Who Hates Models?" (Hagerstown, MD) *Morning Herald*, March 29, 1971, p. 10.

188 "Advertising?": Ford Notebooks, A187.

188 "I never worry about fat people": Eric Wilson, "Eileen Ford, a Founder of the Top Modeling Agency, Dies at 92," *New York Times*, July 10, 2014.

188 Eileen Ford's *New York Times* obituary: Ibid.

189 "They put on their eyelashes": Interview with William Forsythe, Frankfurt, June 9, 2012. All comments by William Forsythe in this chapter are from this interview.

191 "Eileen Ford paid for my wedding": Interview with Iris Bianchi, April 24, 2010; and Iris Bianchi, e-mail to author, June 18, 2014.

191 "after our daughters were born": Jan McGuire, e-mail to author, August 10, 2014.

191 "grow hair under my arms": Interview with Renée Toft Simonsen, April 1, 2011.

191 "There was no reproach": Ibid.

192 "go in to see them": Ibid; and Renée Toft Simonsen, e-mail to author, August 25, 2014.

Chapter 25: The Panorama

193 "The problem is that God": Robin Williams, *Huffington Post*, August 13, 2014.

193 "opened my very first agency": Interview with John Casablancas, November 27, 2010.

193 "totally shaking in my boots": Ibid.

194 "other agents told me her game": Ibid.

194 "really did drink a hell of a lot": Ibid.

194 "were a great double act": Ibid.

195 "Being kind to the weak": Ibid.

195 "knew nothing about models": Ford Notebooks, A135.

195 "We lost our factories": Interview with John Casablancas, November 27, 2010.

195 "My fatal attraction for beautiful": Casablancas, *Vida Modelo*, p. 80.

195 "give food to the poor": Ibid., p. 155.

196 "an absolutely spectacular blonde": Ibid., p. 128.

196 "Nothing had destined me": Ibid., p. 205.

196 "Larsen was the first person": Ibid., p. 142.

197 "Johnny was effectively bankrupt": Interview with Tischka Nabi, August 13, 2014.

197 "Johnny had all the talk": Ford Notebooks, A135.

198 "opening a completely separate agency": Casablancas, *Vida Modelo*, p. 189.

198 "Fernando had lost his job": Interview with Tischka Nabi, August 13, 2014.

198 "Fun was my signature tune": Interview with John Casablancas, November 27, 2010.

198 "My philosophy was simple": Ibid.

198 "John introduced sex": Gross, *Model*, p. 280.

199 "John had very loose morals": Interview with Tischka Nabi, August 13, 2014.

199 "Fernando did not compare": Ibid.

199 wanted an eye-catching emblem: Interview with Peter Marlowe, March 21, 2014.

200 "John came down to the lobby": Ibid.

200 "Ford didn't compel their models": Ibid.

201 "I went to a business fair in Copenhagen": Interview with John Casablancas, November 27, 2010.

201 "we did not think you would survive": Ibid.

201 "I went there soon afterward": Ibid.

201 "I never made any secret": Ford Notebooks, A135.

Chapter 26: Model Wars

203 "Eileen Ford's game is crystal-clear": Salley Rayl, Harriet Shapiro, and Lee Wohlfert, "The Fashion World Is Rocked by Model Wars, Part Two: The Ford Empire Strikes Back," *People*, August 4, 1980.

203 "right across from the new office": Interview with John Casablancas, November 27, 2010.

203 "came out of her corner fighting": Interview with William Forsythe, Frankfurt, June 2012.

203 "We reacted emotionally": Ford Notebooks, A83.

204 "Casablancas was basically unthankful": Interview with Soni Ekvall; Ford Notebooks, F78.

204 "had a gorilla style of doing things": Interview with Melissa Cooper, July 17, 2014.

204 "fatter paychecks": Dickinson, *No Lifeguard on Duty*, p. 122.

205 "staring threateningly": Casablancas, *Vida Modelo*, p. 224.

205 "When I appeared in court": Ibid.

205 "With a name like mine": Interview with John Casablancas, November 27, 2010.

205 "It was a big mistake by Eileen": Ibid.

205 "The verdicts proved it": Ibid.

206 "the mistake of Eileen Ford's life": Gross, *Model*, p. 309.

206 "I wanted composite cards, posters": Interview with John Casablancas, November 27, 2010.

206 "ten tons of paper in that container": Interview with Peter Marlowe, March 21, 2014.

206 "People passed it around the office": Interview with Patty Sicular, April 19, 2012.

207 "wanted me to do the same": Interview with Peter Marlowe, March 21, 2014.

207 "was after lunch and over coffee": Interview with Gussy Marlowe, 208 21, 2014.

207 "came out to see me, full of apologies": Interview with John Casablancas, November 27, 2010.

208 "We were in a terrible dilemma": Interview with April Ducksbury Fawcett, July 16, 2014.

208 "It was excruciating": Ibid.

209 "We can't go on in this way": Interview with April Ducksbury Fawcett, August 1, 2014.

209 "We liked dealing with both": Ibid.

209 "really impressed by the Elite offices": Ibid.

209 "I was met by Susan": Ibid.

210 "Eileen had left us this ultimatum": Ibid.

Chapter 27: The Ford Empire Strikes Back

211 "A model today has": Quoted in Michael Demarest, "Living: Come with Me to Casablancas," *Time*, August 25, 1980.

211 "It was John who 'discovered' me": Interview with Christie Brinkley, July 24, 2014.

211 "I went to see John": Ibid.

212 "couldn't wait to meet Christie": Ford Notebooks, L78.

212 "wearing a bikini with a sarong": Interview with Christie Brinkley, July 24, 2014.

212 "had been lining things up": Ibid.

212 "In Paris it was so casual": Ibid.

213 "John really did the loyalty number": Ibid.

213 "I can't say we were best pleased": Ford Notebooks, L78.

213 "Christie came back to Ford": Ibid.

214 "that I could not ethically": Interview with Shelley Promisel, Los Angeles, January 11, 2011.

214 "the Model Wars were good": Ibid.

214 "Even the makeup artists": Interview with Grace Mirabella, New York, November 28, 2010.

214 "were like yin and yang": Interview with Felicia Milewicz, November 29, 2010.

214 "She would get out the Hoover": Ibid.

215 "the last days of the Roman Empire": Ford Notebooks, D14 and G72.

215 "I went there just twice": Interview with Rene Russo, September 18, 2010.

215 "They chose you at the door": Interview with Eva Voorhees, Los Angeles, September 15, 2010.

215 "The problem was going home": Interview with Renée Simonsen, May 19, 2012.

216 "whether she really did install it": Interview with Anne de Zogheb Anka, September 15, 2010.

216 "Christy would take her clothes": Ford Notebooks, K66.

216 "She had developed a cough": Interview with Melissa Cooper, July 16, 2014.

217 "couldn't believe Willy was dead": Dickinson, *No Lifeguard on Duty*, p. 151.

217 "God makes models": Kinkead, "The Price of Beauty Is Getting Beyond Compare."

217 "The true competitors aren't": Ibid.

217 "has transformed modeling": Ibid., p. 61.

218 "I took my sixteen-year-olds to Rome": Ibid., p. 66.

218 "still the world's dominant agency": Rayl, Shapiro, and Wohlfert, "The Fashion World Is Rocked by Model Wars."

Chapter 28: Cover Girls

219 "the summer of 1980": Interview with Christie Brinkley, July 24, 2014.

219 "never made a pass at me": Ibid.

219 "the models were getting special deals": Ibid.

220 "like being home again": Ibid.

220 "She had a funny eye": Ford Notebooks, G77.

220 "the Barnard College of the South": Ibid., A169.

221 "the dream and the drugstore": Maureen Orth, "The Prime of Lauren Hutton," *Vanity Fair*, May 1989.

221 "that I'd caught Eileen's attention": Interview with Lauren Hutton, September 23, 2014.

221 "After smiling at the camera": Ibid.

221 UNICEF has a special department: Tara Mulholland, "Fashion Models Start Getting Their Hands Dirty," *New York Times*, December 28, 2009.

221 "a model sniffed at me": Interview with Lauren Hutton, September 23, 2014.

222 "She's swinging from a vine": "Eileen Ford: Models Remember the Iconic Modeling Agency Founder," *People*, StyleWatch, July 10, 2014.

222 Cover Girl rose to number one: "Brief History," Cover Girl Newsroom, P&G website, http://news.covergirl.com/about/history.

223   consistently ahead of both Revlon and Maybelline: "Cosmetics," *Advertising Age*, September 15, 2003.

223   He would withdraw all: Off-the-record interview.

223   "In the early advertisements": Interview with F. Stone Roberts, August 8, 2014.

224   "knew both Eileen and Jerry": Interview with Cheryl Tiegs, September 14, 2010.

224   her famous Revlon "Fire and Ice" advertisements: Gross, *Model*, p. 109.

224   "He thought I should be working": Andrew Tobias, *Fire and Ice: The Story of Charles Revson—The Man Who Built the Revlon Empire* (New York: William Morrow, 1975), pp. 130–33.

224   "Jerry told Revlon they couldn't": Ford Notebooks, A171.

224   "Dick took the pictures": Interview with Lauren Hutton, September 23, 2014.

225   "It was Jerry who proposed": Ford Notebooks, A171.

225   "He told me to leave work": Interview with Rusty Donovan Zeddis, October 3, 2014.

225   the economics of the perfume: Barbara Thau, "Behind the Spritz: What Really Goes into a Bottle of $100 Perfume," *Daily Finance*, May 22, 2012. See also Ashley Pearson, "Perfumes on Trial: The Truth About Our Scent Industry," *Daily Mail*, March 30, 2008.

225   "behind the counter in Bloomingdales": Ford Notebooks, A171.

226   "I got paid fifty thousand dollars": Interview with Eva Voorhees, Los Angeles, September 15, 2010.

226   a five-year exclusive contract: Koda and Yohannan, *The Model as Muse*, p. 102.

226   "the deal was much less": Interview with F. Stone Roberts, August 8, 2014.

226   "for the model and also for the agency": Ibid.

226   "He was an absolute gentleman": Interview with George Feld, July 24, 2014.

227   New York's long-term makeup contracts: Interview with Stanley Sokolsky, April 10, 2011.

227   "a black Town Car idling outside": Interview with Ken Steckla, November 26, 2010.

227   "so diplomatic": Interview with Patty Sicular, June 23, 2013.

228   "one year we made it to the final": Interview with Jack Scalia, Los Angeles, January 14, 2010.

228   "tried to summon up a smile": Ibid.

229 "a million-dollar, four-day job": Interview with Roland Schucht, November 27, 2010.

Chapter 29: Sex and Drugs and Supermodels

230 "embarrassing when you meet": Quoted in Bob Colacello, "A League of Their Own," *Vanity Fair*, September 2008.

230 "When people buy a beauty product": Interview with F. Stone Roberts, November 29, 2010.

231 "to kill the pain": Karen G. Jackovich, "Stan Dragoti's Ordeal," *People*, July 30, 1979.

231 he divorced the following year: Michael Gross, "The Dawn of the Supermodel," *New York Magazine*, April 3, 1995, p. 43.

231 "getting to one photographer's studio": Interview with Shelley Promisel, Los Angeles, January 11, 2011.

231 "When you're in the changing rooms": Ibid.

232 "Gia was two hours late once": Ibid.

232 "that was very thoughtful of Dick": Ford Notebooks, F53.

232 "When you're a booker": Interview with Ken Steckla, November 26, 2010.

232 "why Eileen was so dictatorial": Interview with Shelley Promisel, Los Angeles, January 11, 2014.

233 "No one could have helped": Ford Notebooks, D14.

233 "I always felt protected": Interview with Renée Simonsen, Ford Notebooks, G62.

234 Cybill Shepherd was its discovery: *Seventeen* magazine cover story, December 1968.

235 "always a quiet, sweet girl": Ford Notebooks, B49.

235 three of their brightest new models: Ibid., A95.

235 "the only advertising deal that I ever made": Ibid., A41 and B58.

236 "she was always going to succeed—with us or without us": Ibid., A85 and D18.

236 There are glamour girls: Martin Amis, *London Fields* (London: Jonathan Cape, 1989), p. 131.

236 "we do not wish to represent Naomi Campbell": Gross, *Model*, p. 441.

236 "I guess he finally discovered": Ford Notebooks, A85 and D18.

238 "a 'Wow!' moment": "Supermodels Sing 'Freedom! '90' at Versace's Fall 1991 Show," AOL on Style, n.d., http://on.aol.com/video /supermodels-sing--freedom--90--at-versaces-fall-1991-show -518021536.

238 "We have this saying": Jonathan Van Meter, "Pretty Women," *Vogue*, October 1990.

Chapter 30: Hopping Like Bedbugs

239 "You're product, baby": Dickinson, *No Lifeguard on Duty*, p. 162.

239 "did not want to pay us any more": Ford Notebooks, B58.

239 reduced rate: Off-the-record interview with former Ford executive.

240 "hopping from agency to agency": Michael Gross, filmed interview with Jeth Weinrich, n.d.

240 "She was beside herself with rage": Interview with Felicia Milewicz, November 29, 2010.

240 "Jerry and I certainly won": Ford Notebooks, F40.

240 In cold money terms: Michael Gross, "Model Mogul," *New York Magazine*, June 14, 1993, p. 36.

241 "It was a brilliant idea": Interview with Roland Schucht, November 2010.

241 "Jerry and I were quite ready": Ford Notebooks, E29 and E30.

241 "sat down to negotiate seriously": Interview with Roland Schucht, November 2010. For a detailed article on Esch and his business career, see Gross, "Model Mogul," pp. 34–42.

242 "bought this wonderful plot of land": Interview with Roland Schucht, November 2010.

243 "as if she'd seen a ghost": Gross, *Model*, p. 469.

243 "I trusted Jean-Luc": Ford Notebooks, G50.

243 "I came back from Denmark": Interview with Renée Simonsen; Ford Notebooks G62.

243 "Much more healthy than tea": Ford Notebooks, E77.

243 "As she became tipsy": Off-the-record interview.

244 "Once it was a strict rule": David Schonauer, "Eileen Ford on Money, Sex, and Power," *American Photo*, May–June 1993, p. 77.

244 "Let's not call it sex": Ibid.

244 "no matter how much money": Interview with Patty Sicular, November 23, 2010.

244 "Ann did wonderfully for us": Ford Notebooks, G68.

244 "Older people don't want": Ford Notebooks, F55.

244 "I look at myself in the mirror": Bachrach, "Eileen Ford."

245 "Don't wait for success": Lloyd E. Shefsky, *Entrepreneurs Are Made, Not Born: Secrets from 200 Successful Entrepreneurs* (New York: McGraw-Hill, 1994), pp. 90, 92.

245 "The opposite of work": Ibid., p. 89.

Chapter 31: Full Circle

246 "And quiet sleep and a sweet dream": John Masefield, "Sea Fever," in *Sea-Water Ballads* (1902).

246 twenty fire companies battled the blaze: W. Speers, "Model-Agency Fords Lose N. Jersey Home to Fire," *Philadelphia Inquirer*, March 4, 1993.

246 "It was our third country house": Ford Notebooks, C12.

246 "Jerry was especially embarrassed": Interview with Roland Schucht, November 27, 2010.

246 losing all the family silver: Ford Notebooks, G78.

247 "one thing you need to know": Interview with Mark Stankus, November 22, 2010; Ford Notebooks, E24.

247 "it looked like strands of DNA": Jamie Ford Craft, e-mails to author, September 29 and November 30, 2014.

247 "It doesn't get much better": Ibid.

248 "He would dress in big checks": Inger Malmros and Torgny Vikbladh of Sweden Models, March 31, 2011, Malmö, Sweden; Ford Notebooks, G44.

248 "The whole family of the Fords": Interview with Felicia Milewicz, November 29, 2010.

249 "We never got married in church": Ford Notebooks, C15.

249 "a tender and very moving occasion": Jamie Ford Kraft, e-mail to author, November 30, 2014.

249 After two months in the hospital: Jamie Ford Craft, e-mail to author, September 16, 2014.

249 "He became like an old man": Interview with Roland Schucht, November 27, 2010.

249 decided on a last grand tour of Europe: Jamie Ford Craft, e-mail to author, September 16, 2014.

250 "He was just skin and bone": Ford Notebooks, G24.

250 "never seen vestments quite like that": Ibid., G23.

251 "Jerry was so proud of Katie": Ibid., D65.

251 "I'm very lucky": Ibid., D3.

252 "*Not* the Escada": Ibid., E11.

252 "a couple of procedures": Ibid., E81.

252 woe betide the driver: Ibid., A149.

253 "mind, body and soul": Erin O'Connor, e-mail to author, November 21, 2014.

253 "a jungle out there": Ford Notebooks, K47.

253 "And you went into *that*?": Telephone conversation with Katie Ford, July 28, 2014.

254 "Jerry was always her anchor": Interview with Roland Schucht, No-
     vember 27, 2010.

255 "laughing, and as Escada-ed as ever": Interview with Carmen Dell'-
     Orefice, July 29, 2014.

255 "It must be the steroids!": Off-the-record interview; interview with
     Carmen Dell'Orefice, July 29, 2014.

256 "She told me, as we said good-bye": Interview with Iris Bianchi, July
     29, 2014.

Epilogue: Beauty Business

257 "pursuit of physically attractive individuals": Boaz Levy, Dan Ariely,
     Nina Mazar, Won Chi, Scott Lukas, and Igor Elman, "Gender Differ-
     ences in the Motivational Processing of Facial Beauty," *Learning and
     Motivation* 39 (2008): 143.

258 $142 million: Natalie Robehmed, "Newcomers to the World's Highest
     Paid Models List: Jourdan, Anja, and Cara," *Forbes*, August 18, 2014.

259 "idiots and leeches": Guy Adams, "The Divas of Decadence," *Daily
     Mail*, July 23, 2013.

260 "Dragon Lady": Barbara Summers, *Skin Deep: Inside the World of Black
     Fashion Models* (New York: Amistad Press, 1998), p. 189.

260 "Strong loving industry pioneer!": Sierra Marquina, "Eileen Ford
     Dead," *US Weekly*, July 10, 2014.

260 "kittens, beautiful kittens": Matthew Schneier, "Eileen Ford's Legacy,"
     New York Times, July 18, 2014.

260 "She kept an eye out": Quoted in ibid.

260 "her very ambitious wish": Robert Craft, e-mail to author, September
     18, 2014.

261 the proper attire: Bill Cunningham, "Paying Respects," *New York Times*,
     On the Street, October 24, 2014, http://www.nytimes.com/2014/10/26/
     fashion/bill-cunningham-paying-respects.html.

262 chained shut: Jason Burke and Saad Hammadi, "Bangladesh Textile Fac-
     tory Fire Leaves More Than 100 Dead," *Guardian*, November 25, 2012.

262 many of them women: Jason Burke, "Rana Plaza: One Year on from
     the Bangladesh Factory Disaster," *Guardian*, April 19, 2014.

263 "greet her again": Order of service, *A Memorial Service in Thanksgiv-
     ing for the Life of Eileen Cecile Otte Ford*, October 24, 2014, St. Thomas
     Church, Fifth Avenue, New York, p. 7.

BIBLIOGRAPHY

Books

Agins, Teri. *The End of Fashion: How Marketing Changed the Clothing Business Forever.* New York: HarperCollins, 1999.

Arista 1939. Yearbook. Great Neck, NY: Graduating class of 1939, Great Neck High School.

Arnold, Rebecca. *Fashion, Desire and Anxiety: Image and Morality in the 20th Century.* New Brunswick, NJ: Rutgers University Press, 2001.

Avedon, Richard. *Hiro Photographs.* London: Jonathan Cape, 1994.

Baguret, Gabriel. *Alexey Brodovitch.* New York: Assouline Publishing, 2005.

Bailey, Beth, and David Farber, eds. *America in the Seventies.* Lawrence: University Press of Kansas, 2004.

Bailey, David. *Models Close-Up.* London: Macmillan, 1998.

Bassman, Lillian. *Lingerie.* New York: Abrams, 2012.

Beerbohm, Max. *Zuleika Dobson.* New York: Modern Library, 1926.

Berghoff, Hartmut, and Thomas Kühne. *Globalizing Beauty: Consumerism and Body Aesthetics in the Twentieth Century,* New York: Palgrave Macmillan, 2013.

Bowlby, Rachel. *Just Looking: Consumer Culture in Dreisser, Gissing and Zola.* London: Methuen, 1985.

Brandt, Erik. *Being Brandt: The Story of Erik and Margit Brandt.* Trans. Rachel Morgan. Copenhagen: Erik Brandt, 2006.

———. *Brandt.* Copenhagen: People's Press, 2005.

Brannum, Mary, et al. *When I Was 16.* New York: Platt and Munk, 1967.

Brown Gurley, Helen. *Sex and the Single Girl.* New York: Random House, 1962.

Burton, Humphrey. *Leonard Bernstein.* New York: Doubleday, 1994.

Bushman, Richard L. *The Refinement of America: Persons, Houses, Cities.* New York: Alfred A. Knopf, 1991.

Buttolph, Angela and 11 Others. *The Fashion Book.* London: Phaidon Press, 1998.

Cantor, Eddie, with David Freedman and Jane Kesner Ardmore. *My Life Is in Your Hands and Take My Life: The Autobiographies of Eddie Can-*

tor. 1928 and 1958; repr., New York: Rowman and Littlefield Publishing Group, 2000.

Casablancas, John, and Ana Maria Baiana. *Vida Modelo.* Rio de Janeiro: Editora Agir, 2008.

Cashman, Betty. *Betty Cashman and You in Personality, Acting, Public Speaking.* New York: Pama Press, 1949.

Castle, Charles. *Model Girl.* Secaucus, NJ: Chartwell Books, 1977.

Castronovo, David. *The American Gentleman: Social Prestige and the Modern Literary Mind.* New York: Continuum, 1991.

Clark, Gregory. *The Son Also Rises: Surnames and the History of Social Mobility.* Princeton, NJ: Princeton University Press, 2014.

Coddington, Grace. *Grace: A Memoir.* London: Chatto and Windus, 2012.

Davis, Gwen. *The Pretenders.* New York: Warner Books, 1987.

Dawnay, Jean. *How I Became a Fashion Model.* London: Thomas Nelson and Sons, 1958.

Derrick, Robin, and Robin Muir. *Vogue Model: The Faces of Fashion.* London: Little, Brown, 2013.

Dickinson, Janice. *Check, Please!* New York: HarperCollins, 2006.

———. *Everything About Me Is Fake . . . and I'm Perfect.* New York: HarperCollins, 2004.

———. *No Lifeguard on Duty.* New York: HarperCollins, 2002.

Drachman, Roy P. *This Is Not a Book, Just Memories.* Tucson, AZ: R. P. Drachman, 1979.

Drake, Alicia. *The Beautiful Fall.* London: Bloomsbury Publishing, 2006.

Dwight, Eleanor. *Diana Vreeland.* New York: HarperCollins, 2002.

Edmonson, Patricia K. "The Tension Between Art and Industry: The Art-in-Trades Club of New York, 1906–1935." Unpublished thesis. Newark: University of Delaware, 2008.

Elgort, Arthur. *Models Manual.* New York: Grand Street Press, 1993.

Ellis, Brett Easton. *Glamorama.* New York: Alfred A. Knopf, 1998.

———. *The Rules of Attraction.* New York: Simon and Schuster, 1987.

English, Bonnie. *A Cultural History of Fashion in the 20th Century.* New York: Berg, 2007.

Etcoff, Nancy. *Survival of the Prettiest.* London: Abacus, 1999.

Ewen, Stuart. *All Consuming Images: The Politics of Style in Contemporary Culture.* New York: Basic Books, 1988.

———. *Captains of Consciousness: Advertising and the Social Roots of the Consumer Culture.* New York: McGraw-Hill, 1976.

Ewing, Elizabeth. Revised by Alice Mackrell. *History of 20th Century Fashion.* London: Batsford, 2005.

Fedorko, Susan. *Cricket: Secret Child of a Sixties Supermodel*. Parker, CO: Outskirts Press, 2013.

Fitzgerald, F. Scott. *The Great Gatsby*. 1925. Repr. London: Wordsworth Classics, 1992.

Ford, Eileen. *Eileen Ford's Beauty Now and Forever: Secrets of Beauty After 35*. New York: Simon and Schuster, 1977.

———. *Eileen Ford's Book of Model Beauty*. New York: Trident, 1968.

———. *A More Beautiful You in 21 Days*. New York: Simon and Schuster, 1972.

———. *Secrets of the Model's World*. New York: Trident, 1970.

Ford, Eileen, and Joan Hellman. *The Ford Model's Crash Course in Looking Great*. New York: Simon and Schuster, 1985.

Fraser, Antonia. *Dolls*. London: Weidenfeld and Nicolson, 1963.

Fried, Stephen. *Thing of Beauty: The Tragedy of Supermodel Gia*. New York: Simon and Schuster, 1993.

Garner, Philippe. *John Cowan: Through the Light Barrier*. London: Schirmer/ Mosel Publications, 1999.

Gleick, James. *Genius: Richard Feynman and Modern Physics*. London: Little, Brown, 1992.

Goldstein, Judith S. *Inventing Great Neck: Jewish Identity and the American Dream*. New Brunswick, NJ: Rutgers University Press, 2006.

Gross, Michael. *Model: The Ugly Business of Beautiful Women*. New York: It Books, repr. ed., 2011.

Gubernick, Lisa Rebecca. *Squandered Fortune: The Life and Times of Huntington Hartford*. New York: G. P. Putnam's Sons, 1991.

Haden-Guest, Anthony. *Bad Dreams*. New York: Macmillan, 1981.

———. *The Last Party: Studio 54, Disco, and the Culture of the Night*. New York: William Morrow and Company, 1997.

Hakin, Catherine. *Honey Money: Why Attractiveness Is the Key to Success*. London: Allen Lane, 2011.

Halberstam, David. *The Fifties*: New York: Ballantine, 1994.

Hammermesh, Daniel S. *Beauty Pays*. Princeton, NJ: Princeton University Press, 2011.

Harrison, Martin. *Appearances: Fashion Photography Since 1945*. London: Jonathan Cape, 1991.

Helvin, Marie. *The Autobiography*. London: Weidenfeld and Nicolson, 2007.

Hemphill, Christopher. *Allure: Diana Vreeland*. New York: Chronicle Books, 2010.

———. *Jerry Hall's Tall Tales*. London: Elm Tree Books/Hamish Hamilton, 1985.

Herschdorfer, Nathalie. *Coming into Fashion: A Century of Photography at Condé Nast.* London: Thames and Hudson, 2012.

Hill, Rodney, and Gene D. Phillips. *The Encyclopedia of Stanley Kubrick.* New York: Facts on File, 2002.

Hope, Laura Lee. *The Bobbsey Twins.* London: Amazon e-book, undated.

Howard, Sandra. *Tell the Girl.* London: Simon and Schuster, 2014.

Javna, John, and Gordon Javna. *60s! A Catalogue of Memories and Artefacts.* New York: St. Martin's Press, 1982.

Johnston, Patricia. *Real Fantasies: Edward Steichen's Advertising Photography.* Oakland: University of California Press, 1997.

Jones, Geoffrey. *Beauty Imagined: A History of the Global Beauty Industry.* New York: Oxford University Press, 2010.

Kammen, Michael. *American Culture, American Tastes: Social Change and the Twentieth Century.* New York: Basic Books, 1999.

Kazanjian, Dodie, and Calvin Tomkins. *Alex: The Life of Alexander Liberman.* New York: Alfred A. Knopf, 1993.

Keenan, Brigid. *The Women We Wanted to Look Like.* London: Macmillan, 1997.

Keene, Carolyn. *The Best of Nancy Drew.* New York: Simon and Schuster, 1930.

Kelsey, Rayner Wickersham. *Centennial History of Moses Brown School, 1819–1919.* Providence, RI: Moses Brown School, 1919.

Koda, Harold, and Kohle Yohannan. *The Model as Muse: Embodying Fashion.* New Haven, CT: Yale University Press, 2009.

Koszarski, Richard. *Hollywood on the Hudson.* Washington, DC: Library of Congress, 2010.

Leigh, Dorian. *The Girl Who Had Everything.* Garden City, NY: Doubleday, 1980.

Mansel, Philip. *Dressed to Rule: Royal and Court Costume from Louis XIV to Elizabeth II.* New Haven, CT: Yale University Press, 2005.

Masset, Claire. *Department Stores.* Oxford: Shire Publications, 2010.

McQueen, Alexander. *Savage Beauty.* New York: Metropolitan Museum of Art, 2011.

Mears, Ashley. *Pricing Beauty: The Making of a Fashion Model.* Oakland: University of California Press, 2012.

Menkes, Suzy. *How to Be a Model.* London: Spear Books, 1969.

Mills, Nicolaus. *Culture in an Age of Money.* Chicago: Ivan R. Dee, 1990.

Mirzoeff, Nicholas. *An Introduction to Visual Culture.* London: Routledge, 1999.

Moran, Caitlin. *How to Be a Woman.* London: Ebury Press, 2012.

National Industrial Conference Board. *The Cost of Living in New York City, 1926*. University of Michigan digital reprint.

Ogilvy, David. *Ogilvy on Advertising*. London: Prion, 1983.

Oppenheimer, Jerry. *Front Row: Anna Wintour—The Cool Life and Hot Times of Vogue's Editor in Chief*. New York: St. Martin's Press, 2005.

Orvell, Miles. *American Photography*. New York: Oxford University Press, 2003.

Oshinsky, David M. *Polio: An American Story*. New York: Oxford University Press, 2005.

Otis, Carré, with Hugo Schwyzer. *Beauty Disrupted*. New York: Harper-Collins, 2011.

Perrett, David. *In Your Face*. New York: Palgrave Macmillan, 2010.

Petit, Jeanne D. *The Men and Women We Want: Gender, Race, and the Progressive Era Literacy Test Debate (Gender and Race in American History)*. Rochester, NY: University of Rochester Press, 2010.

Phang, Jonathan. *Jerry Hall: My Life in Pictures*. London: Quadrille Press, 2010.

Picardie, Justine. *Coco Chanel: The Legend and the Life*. London: Harper-Collins, 2010.

Plunkett-Powell, Karen. *The Nancy Drew Scrapbook: 60 Years of America's Favorite Teenage Sleuth*. New York: Simon and Schuster, 1993.

Potok, Chaim. *The Chosen*. Evanston, IL: McDougal Littell, 1998.

Powers, John Robert, and Mary Sue Miller. *Secrets of Charm*. Philadelphia: John C. Winstone, 1954.

Purcell, Kerry William. *Alexey Brodovitch*. London: Phaidon, 2011.

Quant, Mary. *Autobiography*. London: Headline Publishing Group, 2012.

Ravitch, Diana. *The Troubled Crusade: American Education, 1945–1980*. New York: Basic Books, 1985.

Reich, Charles A. *The Greening of America*. New York: Random House, 1970.

Rhode, Deborah L. *The Beauty Bias: The Injustice of Appearance*. New York: Oxford University Press, 2010.

Roberts, Michael. *Fashion Victims*. New York: HarperCollins, 2008.

Schopenhauer, Arthur. *Essays and Aphorisms*. London: Penguin Classics, 2004.

Schulman, Bruce J. *The Seventies: The Great Shift in American Culture, Society, and Politics*. New York: First Da Capo Press, 2002.

Seventeen's Beauty Workshop. New York: Triangle Press, 1967.

Seymour, Stephanie. *Beauty Secrets for Dummies*. Foster City, CA: IDG Books Worldwide, 1998.

Shields, Brooke. *Down Came the Rain*. London: Penguin Books, 2007.

———. *On Your Own*. New York: Villard Books, 1985.

Shrimpton, Jean, with Unity Hall. *Jean Shrimpton: An Autobiography*. London: Ebury Press, 1990.

Solomon, Deborah. *Lillian Bassman: Women*. New York: Abrams, 2009.

Squiers, Carol, and Vince Aletti. *Avedon Fashion: 1994–2000*. New York: Abrams, 2009.

Stuart, Amanda Mackenzie. *Empress of Fashion: A Life of Diana Vreeland*. London: Thames and Hudson, 2013.

Summers, Barbara. *Skin Deep: Inside the World of Black Fashion Models*. New York: Amistad Press, 1998.

Thomas, Dana. *Deluxe: How Luxury Lost Its Luster*. New York: Penguin, 2007.

Tiffany, John. *Eleanor Lambert: Still Here*. New York: Pointed Leaf Press, 2011.

Tobias, Andrew. *Fire and Ice: The Story of Charles Revson—The Man Who Built the Revlon Empire*. New York: William Morrow, 1975.

Train, Susan, with Eugène Clarence Braun-Munk, eds. *Théâtre de la Mode: Fashion Dolls—The Survival of Haute Couture. Essays*. Portland, OR: Palmer/Pletsch, 2002.

Tyler, Gus. *Look for the Union Label: A History of the International Ladies Garment Workers' Union*. New York: M.E. Sharpe, 1995.

Twitchell, James B. *Living It Up: America's Love Affair with Luxury*. New York: Simon and Schuster, 2002.

Walford, Jonathan. *Forties Fashion*. New York: Thames and Hudson, 2008.

Wallop, Harry. *Consumed: How We Buy Class in Modern Britain*. London: William Collins, 2014.

Walter, Natasha. *Living Dolls: The Return of Sexism*. London: Virago, 2010.

Webb, Veronica. *Veronica Webb-Sight: Adventures in the Big City*. New York: Hyperion, 1998.

Wenger, Beth S. *History Lessons: The Creation of American Jewish Heritage*. Princeton, NJ: Princeton University Press, 2010.

Wharton, Edith. *The Age of Innocence*. 1920; repr., Hertfordshire: Wordsworth Classics, 1999.

Whykes, Maggie, and Barrie Gunter. *The Media and Body Image*. London: Sage Publications, 2005.

Wilson, Eliza. *Adorned in Dreams: Fashion and Modernity*. London: Virago, 1985.

Winchester, Jim. *The World's Worst Aircraft*. London: Barnes and Noble, 2005.

Wolfe, Naomi. *The Beauty Myth*. London: Vintage, 1991.

Woodhead, Lindy. *Shopping, Seduction and Mr. Selfridge*. London: Profile Books, 2012.

Wren, Crystal. *Hungry*. New York: Simon and Schuster, 2009.

Wright, Robert. *The Moral Animal*. New York: Pantheon, 1994.

Yohannan, Kohle, and Nancy Nolf. *Claire McCardell: Redefining Modernism*. New York: Harry N. Abrams, 1998.

York, Peter. *Style Wars*. London: Sidgwick and Jackson, 1980.

Zola, Émile. *The Ladies' Paradise*. 1883; repr., New York: Oxford University Press, 2012.

Newspaper Articles

Brewster, Catharine. "Who Hates Models?" *Morning Herald*, March 29, 1971, p. 10.

Larkin, Kathy. "A Powerhouse in the Modeling Biz." *Journal-World*, February 8, 1984.

Schneier, Matthew. "Eileen Ford's Legacy." *New York Times*, July 18, 2014, http://www.nytimes.com/2014/07/20/fashion/eileen-ford-legacy-ford-models.html.

Wilson, Eric. "Eileen Ford, Grande Dame of the Modeling Industry, Dies at 92." *New York Times*, July 10, 2014, http://www.nytimes.com/2014/07/11/business/eileen-ford-a-founder-of-top-modeling-agency-dies-at-92.html.

Magazine Articles

Bachrach, Judy. "Eileen Ford." *People*, May 16, 1983, http://www.people.com/people/archive/article/0,,20085008,00.html.

Demarest, Michael. "Come with Me to Casablancas." *Time*, August 25, 1980, pp. 48, 50.

"Family-Style Model Agency." *Life*, October 4, 1948, p. 69.

Ford, Eileen. "Do You Want to Be a Model?" *Seventeen*, March 1962, p. 111.

———. "The Secret Is This Diet Plus . . ." *Glamour*, June 1956, p. 54.

"The Ford Girls." *Photography Workshop* (Summer 1950): p. 24.

Haden-Guest, Anthony. "Model Wars." *New York*, July 25, 1977, pp. 29–35.

Hargrove, Marion. "Beauty and Bedlam." *McCall's*, April 1955, pp. 60, 62, 64, 66, 68, 70.

Kinkead, Gwen. "The Price of Beauty Is Getting Beyond Compare." *Fortune*, December 3, 1979, pp. 60–66.

Mills, James. "The Godmother." *Life*, November 13, 1970, p. 63.

Rayl, Salley, Harriet Shapiro, and Lee Wohlfert. "The Fashion World Is Rocked by Model Wars, Part Two." *People*, August 4, 1980, http://www.people.com/people/article/0,20077110,00.html.

Spears, W. "Model-Agency Fords Lose N. Jersey Home to Fire." *Philadelphia Inquirer*, March 4, 1993.

Wohlfert, Lee. "It's High Noon in the N.Y. World of Models, and John Casablancas Says He's the Guy in the White Hat." *People*, June 13, 1977, pp. 84–85.

LPs

Ford, Eileen. *Learn to Be Beautiful: A Complete Course in Beauty*. Ford Modeling Agency Record 4091, circa 1961, 33⅓ rpm.

Documentaries

About Face: Supermodels Then and Now. Documentary by Timothy Greenfield-Sanders. HBO Documentary Films, 2012. DVD.

Diana Vreeland: The Eye Has to Travel. Documentary codirected and edited by Bent-Jorgen Perlmutt and Frédéric Tchen. Mago Media Ltd. Distributed by Studiocanal, 2012. DVD.

Picture Me: A Model's Diary. Codirected by Ole Schell and Sara Ziff. Strand Releasing and Digital Bazooka, 2009. DVD.

The Powder and the Glory. Documentary by Ann Carol Grossman and Arnie Reisman. PBS Home Video, 2007. DVD.

Scratch the Surface. Documentary directed by Tara Fitzpatrick. Vanguard, 1997. DVD.

The September Issue: Anna Wintour and the Making of Vogue. Documentary directed by R. J. Cutler. A&E IndieFilms in Association with Actual Reality Pictures, 2009. DVD.

Versailles '73: American Runway Revolution. Documentary by Deborah Riley Draper. Coffee Bluff Pictures, 2012, DVD.

INDEX

ABOUT THE AUTHOR

ROBERT LACEY is the *New York Times* bestselling author of twenty books, including *The Queen: A Life in Brief, Ford: The Men and the Machine, Great Tales from English History, The Year 1000,* and *Inside the Kingdom.* He lives in London.

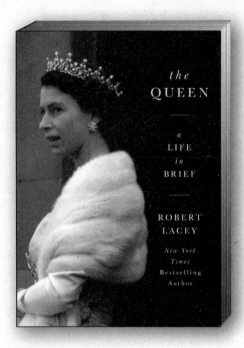

THE QUEEN
A Life in Brief

Elizabeth II was not born to be queen. She came into the world on April 21, 1926, the equivalent of the modern Princess Beatrice, first-born daughter of the Duke of York, destined to flutter on the royal fringe. So while Lilibet was brought up with almost religious respect for the crown, there seemed no chance of her inheriting it. Her head was never turned by the personal prospect of grandeur—which is why she would prove so very good at her job. Elizabeth II's lack of ego was to prove the paradoxical secret of her greatness.

For more than thirty years, acclaimed author and royal biographer Robert Lacey has been gathering material from members of the Queen's inner circle—her friends, relatives, private secretaries, and prime ministers. Now, in *The Queen*, Lacey offers a life of the celebrated monarch, told in six succinct chapters, accentuated by elegant color and black-and-white photographs that capture the distinctive flavor of passing eras and reveal how Elizabeth II adapted—or, on occasions, regally declined to adapt—to changing times.